MARKETING 2.0

Bridging the Gap between Seller and
Buyer through Social Media Marketing

Bernie Borges

Marketing 2.0: Bridging the Gap between Seller and Buyer through Social Media Marketing

Published by Wheatmark®
610 East Delano Street, Suite 104
Tucson, Arizona 85705 U.S.A.
www.wheatmark.com

International Standard Book Number: 978-1-60494-288-0
Library of Congress Control Number: 2009926134

To contact the author, select from the links below.

Blog: http://www.findandconvert.com/blog
Twitter: http://twitter.com/berniebay
LinkedIn: http://linkedin.com/in/bernieborges
Facebook: http://profile.to/bernieborges
Facebook Fan Page: http://companies.to/findandconvert/
Video Summary: http://www.findandconvert.com/video/

ACKNOWLEDGEMENTS

This book is a result of encouragement and inspiration received from friends, colleagues, and clients who have seen me speak either in public or private events on various marketing topics, mostly about the Internet. Some of these special people have provided inspiration to me in the recent past and some in many years past. I wish to acknowledge those who have directly inspired me in this book.

To Debra Curtiss for telling me (as opposed to merely suggesting) to write this book after hearing me speak on social media marketing.

To Ed Yourdon for being my first employer and for being a fine example of a man of intellect, innovation, and of family character.

To Murry Shohat for being a special part of my extended family and for his invaluable wisdom, counsel, and loyal friendship.

To the late Dr. Richard Gerson for being generous with his time and talents and giving me inspiration to be both an author and a speaker.

Acknowledgements

To Steve Tingiris for showing me how to be a passionate entrepreneur unafraid to take calculated risks, and for being a loyal friend.

To Ray Rodriguez for being like a brother to me my entire life and for his kick-in-the-pants advice many years ago to become an entrepreneur.

To Chuck Palm for being my podcasting partner, friend, and humorist.

To Tom Voiland for being an example of loyalty, character, and faith.

Each of these special people has provided me inspiration, motivation, and accountability. Watching them do life in their unique way has been invaluable to me.

There are three people who provided extremely valuable contributions to this book. I'm very grateful to Mike Volpe,[1] V.P. Inbound Marketing at HubSpot, for so willingly writing the foreword. I truly enjoy his marketing insights. Thanks to Joe Pulizzi,[2] CEO of Junta42, for his advice and praise on the back cover. Thanks to Gary Katz,[3] CEO of Marketing Operations Partners, for his praise on the back cover. Gary also authored the chapter on *Marketing Operations*, offering you great insights into an emerging aspect of marketing, which seeks to make Marketing Operations a profit center, not a cost center.

Other people I want to thank include Newt Barrett of SucceedingToday. com for his early endorsement of this book on his blog. Many thanks go to Shaun Pope for his contribution to the chapter on video. Also, many thanks to Lola McIntyre, a successful realtor in Indianapolis; Victoria Edwards of Linkshare, and author and marketing consultant Becky Cortino, whose online friendships and encouragement have meant more to

---

1   Mike Volpe: http://www.mikevolpe.com/
2   Joe Pulizzi: http://blog.junta42.com/about.html
3   Gary Katz: http://www.google.com/profiles/mopartnersceo

me than they know. Many offline relationships have contributed too with special thanks to my loyal friends and colleagues Ron Licata and Clint Babcock.

I also want to thank my loyal team at Find and Convert for their patience with me while I wrote this book, not to mention their valuable ideas and tireless commitment to making my web marketing agency a trusted resource to our clients. Thanks to Michelle Berdeal, Charles Eidschun, Billie Ginther, Dianna Kersey, and Jackie Weber.

When I conducted research to showcase people and companies succeeding in social media marketing strategies, I found some terrific examples. I specifically wanted to showcase nontraditional businesses whose brands are not household names. I'm very grateful for the availability and cooperation of the following people to tell me their stories so I can share them with you. Thanks to Mike Volpe of HubSpot; Brent Britton, attorney extraordinaire; Rick Short, marketing communications director at Indium Corp.; George Wright of Blendtec; Marc Mandt and Linda Olson, cofounders of WOMbeat!; Kim Albee, CEO of Genoo LLC; Chris Griffith, Keller Williams Realtor; Michelle Riggen-Ransom of BatchBlue Software; Christopher Penn of the Financial Aid Podcast; Wendell Brock, founder and CEO of De Novo Strategy; Stacey Monk, CEO of Epic Change; Justin Levy of Camino Argentinean Steakhouse; and Carrie Young of Socialcast for referring me to the NASAsphere pilot.

Special thanks go to Jay Winchester, president of the Winchester Group,[4] for doing the first round of edits and helping me to restructure it, making it a better book for you. Thanks to Hayley Love from Wheatmark Publishing for the detailed final editing and excellent suggestions that completed this book.

---

4   Jay Winchester: http://www.winchestergrouponline.com/

Acknowledgements

My biggest thanks go to my loving family. I thank my wife, Jean, and my kids, Amanda and Derek, for their moral support while I wrote this book and balanced it with running a business and being a husband and a father. Their patience with me during this time is very special. To say thank you to my loving parents seems so inadequate. They taught me the meaning of life, love, hard work, and character.

Ultimately, I attribute all gifts and inspiration to God. My faith is strengthened daily through his word as illustrated by my favorite scripture in Galatians 2:20.[5]

---

5   Galatians 2:20: http://www.biblegateway.com/passage/?search=galatians%20
     2:20&version=31

CONTENTS

Contents

FOREWORD

by Mike Volpe, V.P. Inbound Marketing, HubSpot

New technologies often drastically change society. What people sometimes don't realize is that often it takes a long time for society to figure out what the new technology can enable. When a technology is first introduced, it is often seen as something different or novel, not something that will have a large and useful effect on mainstream society.

Telephone technology was first developed in the 1840s and perfected in the 1870s, but at that time, telephones were leased as a point-to-point connection between just two parties, not as part of a shared network connecting everyone. Only in the early 1900s did the telephone really start to resemble the devices and networks we know today. It took about two decades of experimentation for this new technology to reach its full potential.

The Internet has changed the way we live our lives, consume information, and purchase products. But again, it took time for society to understand how the technologies—specifically the experiments of trailblazers and entrepreneurs—could be used to society's best advantage. And it took time for marketers to understand how this technology could change marketing.

Starting in the mid-1990s through about 2001, there was a huge boom for the commercial Internet, mostly related to the ability of people to consume online information, as well as to buy consumer products through ecommerce. During this time, marketers started to look at the Internet as a new lower-cost and more targeted method of selling products. However, marketing professionals started to apply their old marketing models and mind-sets to the Internet. Online ads were like print ads. Direct mail and cold-calls became email blasts. Sure, there were some changes—online campaigns are easier to track and analyze—but the mind-set and basic marketing assumptions did not change. My job as a marketer was still to spend money on ad space next to something people wanted to read, try my best to distract them from that media with my advertisement, and then get them to take the action I wanted. The media had changed, but the marketing really had not. The crash of the stock market bubble and the September 11 terrorist attacks in 2001 sent the economy into a decline and dampened marketers' enthusiasm for how the Internet might positively affect business and society.

But the Internet did not fade away. In the shadows of a burst bubble, people started to use the Internet in a new way. WordPress blogging software first appeared in 2003, Facebook was founded in 2004, and YouTube was founded in 2005. Normal, everyday people were starting to use the Internet to not just consume information, but also to produce, publish, share, and discuss information among each other. Along with this new use of the Internet came other technologies—accelerated growth of caller ID, spam and ad-blocking software, TiVo and the digital video recorder (DVR)—giving consumers increasingly more control over the information they chose to consume and how and when they consumed it. As of April 2009 Facebook has more than 200 million members, YouTube delivers more than 5 billion video views a month, and Technorati has indexed more than 130 million blogs.

People use the Internet much differently today than they did ten years ago. But, most marketers are still plodding along, trying to apply their old mental and business models to the new medium. Many marketers have an *outbound marketing* (interruption-based marketing) mind-set to the Internet, and it is not working. The harder they try to apply outbound marketing principles on the Internet, the worse the results. Many marketers therefore are frustrated with the Internet as a marketing platform.

People have become accustomed to controlling how and when they consume information. Why watch ads on TV when I can fast-forward through them using my DVR? Why watch something I don't enjoy on one of my two hundred cable TV stations if there are more than one hundred thousand videos uploaded to YouTube each day? Why read the mainstream news from the *New York Times* when I can subscribe to the exact topics I want to read using Really Simple Syndication (RSS) on my computer and mobile device? Why get interrupted by telemarketers when I can use caller ID and let it go to voicemail? Why get distracted by email blasts when I can interact with the people I trust on Facebook and Twitter? Why read white papers and industry reports when I can download them to my iPod as podcasts and listen to them in the car while driving to and from work?

Many marketers today are still trying to apply their old way of outbound marketing to the new media, and they are failing. Successful marketers have changed the way they think. They are using *inbound marketing* strategies to attract customers to their business without distracting or interrupting them. These inbound marketers are getting higher return on investment (ROI) than most would dream of. This new paradigm of inbound marketing is what *Marketing 2.0* is all about.

My relationship with Bernie Borges is a product of this new marketing paradigm. I first met Bernie online. In fact, my friendship and professional relationship with Bernie is one of many new relationships I have made in the past few years using tools such as Facebook, LinkedIn, my web log (blog), and Twitter. Bernie and I had discussed lots of topics— brand-building online, search engine optimization, blogging, and online videos—and built a relationship without ever meeting each other.

When I met Bernie in person for the first time at the inaugural Inbound Marketing Summit in 2008, where he was a speaker, I remember shaking his hand and already feeling a deep connection. This wasn't the normal conference meet-and-greet; Bernie and I already knew each other. I didn't really know what he looked like, save for some online profile pictures, and I didn't know what his voice sounded like. But I had a deeper understanding of who he was because we had shared information about ourselves and discussed numerous topics online. In essence, our relationship began before we ever met in person.

Bernie is one of a new breed of marketing professionals who is blazing the path for how the Internet is powering this new paradigm in marketing. Even before this book is published, a Google search for *Bernie Borges* returns results for Bernie's blog, his LinkedIn profile, his Facebook profile, his Twitter profile, his podcasts, an interview he did with another blogger, a video of Bernie's presentation at the Inbound Marketing Summit, and presentations that Bernie has posted on Slideshare. Thousands of people listen to what Bernie has to say through Facebook, Twitter, LinkedIn, his blog, and his podcasts. Thousands of links on the Internet point to his website. Bernie doesn't pay for Yellow Pages ads or direct mail to build his Internet marketing business. Bernie builds his presence online and lets his customers come to him. Bernie is just one man, but through inbound marketing strategies, he has built a larger presence for himself than has ever been possible before. Turn the page and read *Marketing 2.0* to learn how Bernie and others like him have changed the way they think about marketing and get results no longer possible through outdated marketing principles. *Marketing 2.0* is a book about getting results by embracing these inbound marketing strategies and principles. The technologies mentioned are enablers, not the answer. The answer starts with an understanding of the possibilities and guidelines to use them to achieve great results.

Introduction: Why Traditional Marketing Doesn't Work Anymore

There is a gap out there in the market. The gap exists between sellers and buyers. Sellers are using shouting tactics in attempt to reach buyers, and it just doesn't work well anymore. The outbound marketing tactics that worked in the 1980s and 1990s just don't work anymore in the late first decade of the new millennium. Buyers have too many filters available to them. Buyers can limit the content they consume through RSS subscriptions, use caller ID to filter out unwanted phone calls, record television programs and skip through the commercials, and sift through unwanted mail. Marketers play a numbers game, celebrating 0.5 percent response rates to shouting style marketing campaigns. This form of marketing is not just ineffective from an ROI perspective; it's plain ineffective.

What buyers want is a relationship. They want to know you and your people. They want to know that you're listening to them, and they actually want to engage you, the seller, in conversations. Why? Because they can, and because you can, and because you should. If you don't … well, you just may lose your buyer.

The initial inspiration for this book came primarily from speaking engagements, where my audiences typically comprised small and medium-size business (SMB) executives. The purpose of these presentations was to discuss the evolution of Web 2.0 and the effect of social media marketing on business. Each presentation provided a brief high-level overview of the history of the Internet from a technology perspective, as well as the conventional Internet marketing strategies currently in use, such as search engine optimization, pay-per-click advertising, permission email marketing, and banner advertising. The presentation then transitioned to a discussion of marketing opportunities made possible through the evolution of tools and technologies on the social web. These tools include blogs, wikis, podcasts, social networking sites, bookmarking sites, video, and photo sharing sites. I also discussed the technological, demographic, and cultural evolutions that have made these tools so popular.

Each presentation usually begins with my asking the audience for a show of hands in response to a few basic questions in order to gauge the makeup of the audience. The audience size for most of my presentations ranges from 25 to 125. The questions I usually ask (along with the answers I receive) are:

- "How many of you are with a company the size of (less than 100, 100 to 250, 250 to 500, more than 500)?" The vast majority of attendees are with firms with less than 500 employees, many with less than 100 employees.

- "How many of you actively read a blog?" Usually about one-third raise their hands.

- "How many of you actively maintain your own personal or company blog?" Usually two to five people raise their hands.

- "How many of you have a profile in a social network such as LinkedIn, Facebook, or MySpace?" More than half usually raise their hands—most are on LinkedIn.

- "Of those who have a profile in a social network, how many of you actively participate in the social network at least once per week and consider this time well-spent?" Unfortunately, very few hands usually go up to this question. In other words, many people have completed a profile in a social network but they don't do much with it.

- "How many of you feel that social networking or blogging or any type of social media marketing has the potential to be a valuable aspect of your marketing strategy?"

I usually get an interesting response to this last question. Usually a few hands are raised, maybe in the 10 percent to 20 percent range of the audience. But, judging by the body language and blank stares in the audience, I can see that most in the audience don't have good answers to this question. Perhaps they don't know how to answer it, or maybe they haven't given it much thought. Or, maybe they don't know much about it. Initially, I was greatly puzzled by this response and it started me thinking … that's how this book came into being.

My goal is to help you—the business owner or marketing executive in a small or medium-size business—understand what marketing on the social web is, what it means within a business context, and how it can be a valuable component of your marketing strategies. As you read, consider the marketing mind-set: how do successful marketers on the web think? What assumptions do they make? What principles do they use? How do they engage with their target market? How do they produce results? How do they measure results? While this book is written primarily for the SMB executive, nonprofits can benefit as well. Any reference to business goals should be replaced by your specific goals. Since I am a blogger, I wrote this book in plain English in a somewhat conversational tone. I wrote a book I would want to read. I tried to connect dots for you. My hope is that you will take away from this book sensible and actionable ideas and strategies that will have a valuable impact on your business. If you are in a larger company, I believe the principles in this book apply to you as well, depending on where your company is in the adoption of social media strategies.

Another part of the inspiration for this book comes from my own active participation in social media marketing. I run an Internet marketing agency, so it should come as no surprise that I have an interest in all things marketing on the web. That said, I spent more than twenty years in corporate jobs in technology sales and marketing, and I don't consider myself a web geek. I am more of a business–marketing strategist who happens to be in the Internet marketing business. I do admit that I am very encouraged by how many businesses around the world are actively using social media to engage their customers in community and conversations on the web. However, I also am discouraged by how few SMBs have yet to embrace the social web at the time of this writing. There are many case studies regarding the effective use of social media by larger, well-recognized brands such as Apple, Best Buy, Cisco, Comcast, IBM, and Oracle. I encourage SMB CEOs and their marketing and sales managers to embrace the social web as three things: a *culture*, a *mind-set*, and a *platform*. Marketing on the social web is not a technology strategy, although technology plays an important role. The social web allows any business of any size in any location to reach the people they desire to reach and build solid relationships with them. Often, these relationships evolve offline into traditional and productive relationships. The social web is a place to relate to others, not a place to launch shouting-style campaigns, although campaigns are possible using the social web. The social web is a place to listen because people are talking—and they may be talking about you, your products, your team, your competitors, and ideas that could someday become your future products. The social web is a *mind-set*. And any business that doesn't understand the mind-set is at risk of being left behind or using it inappropriately, producing negative results. Understand that effective marketing on the social web requires a revisit to your organization chart. The people you need to implement your social media strategy may or may not be the people in your current org chart. Your current boss may not embrace the social web, in which case you may need to assess whether your career is at risk.

This book is for people who don't mind admitting they are just getting started in social media marketing, and who want to learn how to develop a strategy and learn what mistakes to avoid. You don't need an advanced degree to understand Marketing 2.0 concepts. However, you do need to be willing to let go of old paradigms. You may need to stretch yourself and your organization in ways that may be uncomfortable at first. The examples I have provided of companies that range from individuals, small start-ups, to midsize companies that use the social web successfully in their marketing strategies will help you realize its potential. This book was written during the height of our most recent global economic decline. Headlines are currently dominated by credit financial crises, federal bailouts of huge banks, and massive company layoffs. Yet the SMB marketers who have successfully implemented social media marketing strategies have survived if not thrived.

I've also provided a resources section that points you to excellent books and web logs (blogs) to help you gain other valuable perspectives and insights regarding social media marketing from other thought leaders. I strongly urge you to use these valuable resources.

I don't mind telling you that I struggled on a title for this book. Throughout most of my writing, I was planning to title it *Social Media Marketing for the Rest of Us* because it's not written for the Fortune 1000 brands, but rather for SMBs and nonprofits. I changed the title to *Marketing 2.0* primarily because *social media* is still an evolving term for many in the SMB world. I really want you to grasp that this book is about a marketing mind-set that involves producing meaningful content and building relationships *on the web*. It just so happens that the web has become a social gathering place where relationships and authenticity win out over shouting and deals of the month. The web has also gone from being a flat, one-dimensional platform to a multidimensional, multisensory experience.

I really want to stress the importance of having a mind-set for marketing on the web that requires and facilitates changes in the way you think. As Mike Volpe described in the foreword, most marketers have a history of pushing out a message (outbound marketing) aimed at disrupting the target audience. For decades we got away with that. Sorry, but that just doesn't work anymore. The sooner you accept that, the sooner you can enjoy the results available in *Marketing 2.0*. The consumer (your buyer) is now in control. She knows where to go to find the products and services she needs and is willing to talk to people who have something to say about your products, your business, your people, and your competition. What she hears from them is going to influence her buying decision, and you cannot and will not control that—unless you are engaging the consumer in authentic relationships on and off the web. Only then can you have a positive influence on how she thinks about you.

At some point in this book, I may offend you a little, not with offensive language but rather with strong and blunt sentiment. I don't sugarcoat my sentiments, and I offer no apology for that. My goal is to shake you up and get you thinking differently so your competitors don't eat your lunch. You'll see examples in the case studies of companies that are competing effectively against competitors many times their size by building relationships with customers online, giving them great content, and listening to and engaging them through the social web.

There is one truth you simply can't deny: social media is growing at an amazing rate. *The Universal McCann Report: Power to the People, Social Media Tracker: Wave 3*[1] offers some amazing statistics worth noting. This report, completed in March 2008, was compiled through interviews of 17,000 Internet users across twenty-nine countries. Here are a few summary statistics:

- 57 percent of Internet users have joined a social network

- 73 percent have read a blog

- 34 percent post opinions about products and brands on blogs/social media

---

[1] Universal McCann Report: Power to the People, Social Media Tracker: Wave 3: http://www.universalmccann.com/Assets/2413%20-%20Wave%203%20 complete%20document%20AW%203_20080418124523.pdf

- 36 percent think positively about companies that have blogs

- 83 percent have viewed video on the social web

- 184 million people worldwide actively maintain a blog

In the *2008 Technorati Report: State of the Blogosphere*,[2] Technorati surveyed 1.2 million bloggers around the world who had registered with its service. Here are some summary statistics:

- 133 million blogs are registered with Technorati

- These blogs are from sixty-six countries in eighty-one languages

- Blogs have representation in top 10 website lists in all key categories

- Blogs are now a part of mainstream media

- Bloggers are savvy and sophisticated in driving traffic to their blog

- Bloggers are meticulous about tracking statistics about their blog

- Bloggers are successful—they are achieving career enhancement opportunities including speaking engagements

- The majority of bloggers are advertising on their blog, producing an income stream for themselves

- 90 percent of bloggers say they write about the products and services they love or hate (take note of this!)

---

2   Technorati: The State of the Blogosphere: http://technorati.com/blogging/state-of-the-blogosphere/

BusinessWeek

In May 2005, *BusinessWeek* featured a cover story titled, "Blogs Will Change Your Business."[3] The article focused on how blogs had transitioned from the Internet fringe to the business mainstream. Blogs were no longer just a tool for individuals to rant about their favorite recipes, movie stars, or political viewpoints. Businesses were deploying blogs, and people were visiting them, reading them, and participating in the blog conversations. Brands awakened to the fact that bloggers working within a corporate setting had become influential. Prospects were visiting corporate blogs to read what they couldn't read on websites and gaining insights from bloggers who had something provocative or insightful to say about vendors, their products, and their employees. The voice of the blog was being heard loud in the business arena. *BusinessWeek's* cover story included a subtitle: "Your customers and rivals are figuring blogs out. Our advice: catch up ... or catch you later."

In May 2008, *BusinessWeek* did something they had never done before. They wrote a cover story as a follow-up to a previous cover story (May 2005). This story, titled, "Beyond Blogs,"[4] opened with this sentence: "Three years ago our cover story showcased the phenomenon (blogs). A lot has changed since then." Is that ever an understatement! The May 2008 story discussed the evolution of the social web to include platforms such as YouTube, Facebook, MySpace, Twitter, and sites such as Digg, StumbleUpon, and Flickr. The article pointed out the risks of employees wasting time hanging out with friends on the Internet or leaking secrets on social networking sites. And it also highlighted the power of the social web to facilitate connections with resources in order to "assemble global teams for collaborative projects, and connecting with people capable of opening doors for new deals and strategic opportunities." It also pointed out that "the resume is 140 characters," referring to the explosive popularity of

3   BusinessWeek: Blogs Will Change Your Business: http://www.businessweek.com/magazine/content/05_18/b3931001_mz001.htm
4   BusinessWeek: Beyond Blogs: http://www.businessweek.com/magazine/content/08_22/b4086044617865.htm

Twitter. *Business Week* admits this story's appropriate headline is, "Social Media Will Change Your Business."

Marketing on the social web is not appropriate for all businesses, but probably is for most. If you're in an industry where your customers don't use the web, or you sell to a very small, finite customer base, the social web is not necessarily a viable place to market. However, using the social web for your research and education is strongly recommended.

In the end, I will judge the success of this book primarily not by how it sells but by feedback from the community. The social web will allow me to hear readers' reactions to and opinions about what I've written, and I will engage them in conversations online. What will matter most to me is the feedback regarding this book's effect on your willingness to embrace the social web as part of your marketing strategy. I invite your feedback at my blog, http://www.findandconvert.com/blog/.

The tools and technologies I discuss in this book evolve. Some may cease to exist or be made obsolete by others. This book isn't about Facebook, LinkedIn, Twitter, or YouTube, though I cover them extensively. This book is about how to embrace the most viable tools and platforms to bridge the gap between you (the seller) and your buyers.

I truly hope *Marketing 2.0* has a positive impact on the way you think about reaching your customers, the employees you hire, and your future products and services. Most of all, I hope you embrace the two core concepts—the pillars—of Marketing 2.0: a content marketing strategy and a focus on building relationships through social media. The tools and technologies discussed are not the answers but the enablers. If Marketing 2.0 becomes a mind-set in your organization, you will bridge the buyer-seller gap, compete effectively, win market share, grow, thrive, prosper, and possibly reinvent your business along the way, if that's what it takes. Marketing 2.0 offers you endless possibilities if you allow yourself the opportunity to engage, listen, and take action on the social web.

Closing the Loop between Marketing and Sales

I always find it interesting to observe the wide spectrum of attitudes toward marketing among businesses. On one extreme, some businesses don't believe in marketing at all. These businesses are usually sales-driven, using old-style sales organizations that make cold-calls, attempting to fill their pipeline, and living by the numbers that say for every ten prospects in the pipeline, two will close (or whatever the ratio is).

Other businesses believe in marketing, measuring their marketing budget as a percentage of total revenue. The key difference is these businesses believe that their marketing efforts contribute to filling their sales pipeline, and therefore they continue to invest in marketing activities, even in hard economic times.

Before getting into marketing on the social web, I will discuss strategies for closing the loop between marketing and sales, whether you use offline or online marketing strategies. Throughout my career, I've had to measure the relationship between marketing and sales. You might say it's in my blood.

The Purpose of Marketing

Many will argue with me when I say that the sole purpose of marketing is to set up the sales department to do their job as efficiently as possible. In other words, *marketing's role is to tee up sales for success*. If you cringe when reading this, give me a chance to make my case.

Fundamentally, there are two basic types of marketing: online marketing and offline marketing. When we speak of online marketing, we refer to activities that include your website, marketing your website through organic search engine optimization, and paid search marketing such as pay-per-click advertising (also called SEM), directory listings, and banner campaigns. Online marketing also includes email marketing and electronic newsletters. And, of course, online marketing includes everything discussed in this book characterized as social media marketing.

Offline marketing includes telemarketing/cold-calling, direct mail, and advertising in various media channels such as print, radio, television, and billboards. Offline marketing also includes trade shows and use of promotional products such as pens, cups, and other trinkets that help brand and promote your business and may also include contests and premium giveaways.

Where does public relations fit into these two categories? In short, while it straddles the line between offline and online marketing, in my opinion, it leans more toward online marketing. Historically, PR has been a function in many marketing departments that has been staffed separately from the main marketing department. The primary reason for this separation is PR's editorial nature. The PR department's primary role in most businesses used to be to *get ink*. David Meerman Scott's book,[1] *The New Rules of Marketing and PR*, does an excellent job of explaining how the world of marketing and PR has shifted from communicating to a select few who control the communication channel—media journalists and industry analysts—to marketing directly to your target audience and building relationships with them through social media. Scott also points

---

1   The New Rules of Marketing and PR: http://www.davidmeermanscott.com/
    books.htm

out some of the difficulties in measuring social media when old style metrics are applied.

So let's agree on two points as this chapter unfolds. First, most businesses continue to use a combination of online and offline marketing strategies. There are always exceptions to this, and some businesses use more of one over the other. However, it can be argued that shifting the mix between online and offline marketing is always worth considering. In fact, that is what this chapter is about.

The other point is that, in most businesses, a shift toward more online marketing benefits them in the long run. I admit that I am a little uneasy making this statement across the board because online marketing can benefit some businesses more than others depending on their respective industries. If you operate a chain of funeral homes, your online marketing strategies may not be as important as if you run a software company. In the former, there probably isn't a large community of people talking about it. That said, the power of online word-of-mouth marketing can positively affect even the most obscure industries. See examples in the case study section including an example of a midsize manufacturer of kitchen blenders. No matter how strongly you agree or disagree with this point, I contend that if a business is doing little or no online marketing, it is missing an opportunity. If such a business has many competitors, and those competitors are using effective online marketing strategies, that business will eventually be damaged in some way by those competitors.

Closing the loop between marketing and sales is essentially a combination of justifying the role and expense of marketing and measuring the results. There are four key principles involved in this process.

The Four Pillars of Closing the Loop

In any business, there are essentially four pillars that must be considered and used when building a bridge between marketing and sales. These four pillars are: *relational, strategy, best practices,* and *measurement.* Let's look at each one.

Relational. I put this one at the top of the list because too many marketing departments, whether they employ one or one hundred, either miss this altogether or minimize its importance. An intellectual understanding of the relational factor, rather than a casual intuitive understanding of it, can dramatically improve marketing and sales results.

In any business, there are core functional executives. In most businesses there is a chief executive officer (CEO), a chief financial officer (CFO), a chief information officer (CIO), a marketing executive, a sales executive, and at least one other executive responsible for running the delivery functions of the operations. Regardless of the titles in your business, here is a basic lesson in organizational structure. If this lesson seems remedial to you, that's not my point. My point is that our role in marketing must be aligned with the vision and goals of the key executives in the business. In some businesses, however, alignment with the CIO is not needed, while in others, not being aligned with the CIO is the kiss of death. So replace these titles as needed to fit your business; these are the people in your company who are critical for alignment.

I'll single out one title to illustrate this pillar further. However, be sure to consider the roles of the executives in your business and how these principles apply. Let's single out the top sales executive. If your role is the top marketing executive, being aligned with the top sales executive is mission critical. In fact, if you're not aligned with sales, you won't survive. Let's look at two examples.

In the first example, the marketing executive and sales executive are very well-aligned. The sales objectives are clearly stated at all levels. The main objective is not just growing revenue, but is also clearly defined as growing market share for a specific product line that enjoys market leadership. The opportunity to dominate in this category is readily apparent, so the sales infrastructure is aligned organizationally to attack this market segment full force. The sales team needs strong brand-building and door-opening marketing strategies with clear messaging that helps position the business as the market leader. The sales and marketing executives collaborate to design strategies addressing this goal. All resources are marching to the same sheet of music. The marketing and sales executives meet often. Their offices are near each other, and they frequently eat lunch together. Even when one of them is on the road, they are in constant contact with each other using a variety of communications methods. Their attitudes toward each other are more than just courteous and respectful; there is a humble recognition that they each require the other's contributions in order to succeed. So they work very closely together to achieve their common goals.

Unfortunately, real life sometimes creates scenarios where there may be alignment between sales and marketing, but the respective executives responsible for these functions don't get along or ever see eye to eye. If they are both competent and mature adults, they can and should agree to disagree on certain details, but they must march together toward achieving the company's objectives. The realities of company politics can sometimes even determine if that company is driven by marketing or sales. If the company is sales-driven, marketing's role may become subservient to sales. Or the situation might be reversed, with marketing exerting control over sales. Even in such disparate political realities, the marketing team can still produce stellar results—but only when healthy executive alignment exists. Often, alignment issues are not limited to just one executive. Typically, the CEO is the critical executive with whom others seek to align themselves. In any environment, a clear understanding of the CEO's mission and goals is crucial to closing the loop between marketing and sales.

A common mistake made by many marketing executives is being too closely aligned with their immediate superior, whether it is a middle manager or a top executive. At the same time, they don't align with other key executives whose influence and decision-making matter to the success of the business. For simplicity's sake, I'll use the sales role to illustrate this point. If a marketing executive is aligned with the immediate boss, but not aligned with the sales executive, it creates a potentially dangerous and highly political situation. Even if the immediate boss is the CEO, not being aligned with the top sales executive is still very risky. If the marketing executive is rolling out new strategies including new social media plans and he or she has support from the boss (CEO or otherwise), but the top sales executive doesn't understand either what's being done or why, that marketing executive is taking a dangerous risk. Don't ever assume that all is well just because your immediate superior is on board with your marketing plans. The truth is that if you are not aligned with the top sales executive, your actions—no matter how correct or effective—may be helping you write your own pink slip. Eventually, a situation may arise where it's obvious to the sales executive—and probably other influencers in the organization—that there is a substantial disconnect between your efforts and his requirements. If that sales executive ever needs to provide a justification for not making his numbers, you could be creating a convenient excuse. Even if you are not at fault and such an accusation is made, the lack of proper organizational alignment becomes a smoking gun.

In both of the above examples, I've provided mostly political factors for alignment. The point is that few factors are more essential to being able to close the loop between marketing and sales than ensuring the proper relational alignment in your business. Since a Marketing 2.0 strategy requires such a paradigm shift for most businesses, alignment with key executives is not an option.

Strategies. The strategies you define should start with a clear understanding of the behavior of your target market. In Marketing 1.0, you were taught to define and understand your target market. In Marketing 2.0, it's not enough to understand who that is. You must know much more about that market. To know and understand its behavior means you know where the people in that market spend time, with whom they spend it, and what their interests are. The way you learn these things about your target is not through surveys of data that are at least twelve months old when you read them. Instead, you learn what you are required to know by engaging them in online relationships where you can learn about them every day in real time. Getting instant feedback from your target audience on a daily or hourly basis dwarfs any value inherent in the antiquated survey model. Sure, some surveys may have value, but the best way to understand the behavior of your target is to engage it daily, taking its temperature throughout the day by using social marketing strategies online.

Your strategies must include very clear messaging. Sometimes the most broken aspect of a business's marketing is its message. And it starts internally. If you ask twenty people in your business to describe your company and products, and you get fifteen different answers, you know you have a message problem. Get your message straight internally, and then put strategies in place to communicate that message to your markets on a consistent basis. And if your market tells you unequivocally it doesn't understand your message, go back to the drawing board. If your CEO dictates the marketing message, and it doesn't work, do your best to craft a new message based on the resultant market input. The easiest way to sell your CEO on the new message is to remind her that the people buying your products are sending a clear signal: it's your message, not your product, that's broken.

Understand your company's strengths and weaknesses. Don't develop marketing plans that play right into your competitor's strength if you have an inferior product or an inability to compete. Leverage your strengths while minimizing your weaknesses. This is yet another example of how proper alignment is so important. For example, if your sales executive isn't on board with your marketing strategy, step back and reassess your plans. Don't continue rolling out plans that set him up to fail. You'll look like a fool in the process.

Understand the difference between "A" opportunities and "B" opportunities. As you put your marketing plans together, make sure you're developing plans that produce truly meaningful sales opportunities. In social media marketing, you could produce interest in a part of the business that is not as profitable or as meaningful to other parts of the business. Again, this issue comes full circle to being properly aligned.

The strategies you develop should be defined in writing. Strategies are similar to objectives; they are not tactics. A strategy may read something like this: "Positioning our company in the market as innovators and thought leaders in _(fill in the blank)_ so that our sales team will be well-received when making appointments." That's a clear statement of strategy.

Defining the tactics that will achieve this strategy is extremely important. A clear tactical example aimed at achieving the above strategy statement may read something like this: "We will achieve this strategy by participating in online communities where our customers and prospective customers participate, listening to their main issues, and developing white papers that address their needs. We will market these white papers through banner ads and select social websites, as well as on our website. We will optimize organically for keywords based on extensive research. We will distribute news releases on our initiatives around these topics and set up blogs using internal subject matter experts. When we exhibit at industry trade shows, we will blog about it three months in advance, and tell our Twitter community that it can expect to meet us there to discuss certain topics and engage us in workshops and other venues." All of these tactics are written in support of the strategy. Remember—both the strategy and the tactics must be properly aligned with the key stakeholders to ensure a successful execution.

As you roll out your strategies, make sure you have the resources to pull them off. If you are diving into social media marketing for the first time, start slowly—especially if you are the only one in your company who is blogging or Twittering or whatever. Get buy-in for the resources you need to roll out the next phase of your social media plan. Social media marketing takes time to develop and measure. Without the proper resources (and alignment), you can fail.

Consider marketing strategies correlating to your long-tail markets. The long tail pertains to very specific market segments usually defined by three or more words. If you sell to specific market segments, clearly define them in your messaging strategy. Don't use broad terms like "software" when you can more specifically define it as "project accounting software for office furniture dealers." Long-tail marketing can be very effective because of the economies afforded to us on the web, coupled with the behaviors of your buyers who are looking for products according to their long-tail needs. Make sure you are in alignment with stakeholders on your long-tail strategies.

Best Practices. The reason best practices exist in any industry is because someone figured out how to do something well and they wrote it down. Best practices usually emerge after considerable collaboration and trial and error. Here are some best practices in social media marketing for you to consider. Your industry may offer others.

- *Eat lunch with your stakeholders.* While some may not consider this a best practice, I do. I've stressed the importance of alignment throughout this chapter. Find the equivalent of eating lunch with your most important stakeholders in your business such as a standing weekly one-on-one phone call to review progress and issues.

- *Content is king, queen, prime minister, and president!* Produce a lot of content. Don't limit the content format to the written word. Produce photos, video, podcasts, wikis, blog posts, newsletters, white papers, blue papers, purple papers, et cetera. Okay, so I got a little carried away. I'm stressing the point that producing a lot of good content is one of the most effective ways to market in Marketing 2.0. Let your content *be* your marketing!

- *Understand your competitors.* Know everything about them. Know their executives, how they think, where they go, what they do, what they talk about, and how they compete. Sun Tsu wrote the famous book *The Art of War.*[2] This book was written around 600 BC. It was translated to many other languages and to this day is used as a model for military and business strategy. At its core, the book stresses the importance of understanding your competition and developing plans to defeat your competitor's plans. Sun stresses that your best-laid plans may not succeed if you don't react to the reaction of your enemy. The same thinking applies in

---

2   The Art of War: http://en.wikipedia.org/wiki/The_Art_of_War

business: know your competition, understand how they operate, and develop strategies to defeat their strategies.

• *Test, measure, and revise often.* I am a huge fan of characterizing a marketing plan as a *test*. When you test something, it is implied that you will be measuring results to determine its success, as well as determining next steps you should take, if any. When you start your new social media plans, test them, measure results, and make revisions according to what you learn. If you get buy-in from your stakeholders to test something such as a Twitter strategy, you gain their agreement to try it. I recommend you clearly discuss the risks and rewards you may experience from your test. When you test new plans, you must be prepared to measure and report the results, and be prepared to revise or possibly abort the plan. Be careful to get buy-in for a reasonable testing period, which is usually measured in months, not days or weeks.

• *Don't be afraid to fail.* If this sounds bizarre, move to Silicon Valley, where many entrepreneurs feature their failures on their resumes as if they were badges of honor. This might seem a little extreme for most of us, but the point is that if you test new marketing plans and you fail, you will learn something from that experience. Assuming you were wise enough to test a marketing plan that didn't risk the future of the company, you can probably leverage what you learned. For example, you could test a new blog strategy where you have four blog hosts, each one with different topics according to their subject matter expertise. You might go into it expecting two of the four to be very popular and you turn out to be half right. The surprise is that the two you didn't expect to garner much of a following turned out to be much more popular than the other two. Now, based on the failure of the two unpopular blog topics, you should examine your existing alternatives: discontinue all four blogs; replace the blog hosts with other writers; or spin off a new blog focused on the two popular topics. The key here is that whenever you fail—and you will—learn from it and take decisive action. Meet with your stakeholders to discuss openly what you learned from your failure. If the plan was positioned properly as a test with buy-in from your stakeholders, the postmortem discussion should be well-received and agreement on your next steps should also be relatively easy to determine. By the way, be sure you position the next steps as another test. If it also fails, you'll be glad you did.

Measurement. Now we come to a subject marked by struggle and controversy for many in marketing: how do we measure the results of our social media marketing efforts? As marketers embarking on social media strategies, we want to measure as much as we possibly can. Ultimately, our desire as marketers is to close the loop between our marketing activities and sales results. In other words, the best possible scenario is to be able to associate each sale with one or more marketing activities in order to justify the marketing activities and their associated budgets. The extent to which we can measure is determined at least in part on the size of our budget and the resources we have at our disposal. In most cases, success means we get to keep our jobs in marketing in order to keep the process going. If we are able to clearly demonstrate a solid connection between marketing activities and sales, we may also get to increase our budget and/or staff.

You should seek to measure the following factors: *traffic, buzz, leads,* and *sales.* I'm sure there are other elements of the plan you can measure in your business. Take these ideas and apply them to your business to help measure the things you must in order to achieve your objectives.

- *Traffic.* Hopefully, measuring website traffic is something already familiar to you. If you use website analytics or stats-tracking programs, you should be accustomed to measuring and analyzing the traffic visiting your website. You should already be studying the keywords that drive that traffic, the average bounce rate from your website, and the bounce rate of your keywords. *Bounce rate* refers to the rate at which visitors leave your website without visiting any other pages besides the initial page they visited. You should also be tracking which search engines and other referring sites drive traffic to your website. When you implement a social media strategy, you can measure referring sites from social media properties such as social networks, Twitter and blog posts. As you see traffic increasing to your website from social media sites, you are starting to measure results. Measuring the keywords that drive traffic to your website is another key metric to follow. If previously your company name was the most popular keyword search resulting in traffic to your website, or there have been few other keywords responsible for driving traffic, your social media strategy can result in an increase in traffic from other desirable keywords. By producing content with your most important keywords, you can drive traffic from those keywords and see the increased visitors in your website analytics. If you experience an increase in sales activity correlating to your social media strategy, that's a clear indicator of success.

- *Buzz.* Some say it's difficult to measure buzz. The truth is that it all depends on your budget. When measuring buzz, I like to balance qualitative elements with quantitative ones. You can certainly measure how many times your name or company name is mentioned online through various tools ranging from (free) Google Alerts to (fee-based) tools such as Radian6. However, one of my favorite ways to measure is through conversations. When you get unsolicited feedback from your community about what you're doing, that's buzz. When people compliment you or give you word-of-mouth advertising based on your content and social marketing activities, that's buzz. What's that worth? Who knows? All I know is that I'd rather have buzz than not have it, especially when it's manifesting for the right reasons. If your sales team has an easier time getting appointments or finds that its sales cycle is shortened, and you can trace these things back to the buzz you've created, that's tangible ROI.

- *Leads.* Leads are one of the most desired outcomes of any marketing activity. In social media marketing, producing leads is an attainable outcome. If you're producing great content in your community and you're driving more traffic either to your website or to a landing page, you can produce more leads. If you're producing good buzz and you're sending out emails with a call to action to your community, you can produce leads. If your blog is growing in popularity and more people are moving from your blog directly to your website, you can produce more leads. If you produce webinars that feature good content in social media, you can produce more leads. The point is that social media marketing combined with lead-producing marketing tactics is very measurable.

- *Sales.* Finally, we come to the holy grail, the object of all your efforts. Admittedly, measuring sales by tying them back to social media marketing is not always an easy thing to measure. There are many dependencies for accurate measurement of the sales tied back to social media marketing. They include company size and budget, how long the company has been implementing social media marketing strategies, and frankly, the quality of the company's content. Another factor is how good you are at getting engaged in online communities. Using tools such as HubSpot and Eloqua, you can measure sales tied to social media marketing plans. Another less scientific approach, but nonetheless a viable one, is to measure the growth rate of sales before you implemented your social media plans and compare it to the growth rate after the implementation. Additionally, consider that Marketing 1.0 strategies are becoming increasingly ineffective. So if you measure how you were producing sales using Marketing 1.0 strategies compared to Marketing 2.0 strategies, you should be able to discern a measurable difference. Also, you can ask your customers in both online and in offline conversations to delineate the factors influencing their buying decisions. You are likely to learn that some of the factors include your content, as well as your activities in social media communities.

Closing the loop between marketing and sales is the ultimate objective of any marketing executive. Sometimes our raises, bonuses, and even our jobs depend on our ability to accurately measure the results of our marketing efforts. For decades, businesses have conducted marketing activities with little to no ability to measure either their effectiveness or ROI. In this chapter, I have attempted to provide both qualitative and quantitative guidelines that can be applied in your business to close that loop, measure online marketing success or failure, and give you guidelines for action steps based on what you measure.

Marketing 2.0

The 2.0 concept is worth discussing. The existence of 2.0 implies there was once, and might still be, a 1.0. The leap from 1.0 to 2.0 is an order of magnitude or more. It is far more significant than going from 2.0 to 3.0 or from 3.0 to 4.0. A 1.0 to 2.0 leap is metaphorically monumental. Here are some examples of leaps from 1.0 to 2.0:

World 1.0 was once believed to be flat.
World 2.0 pushed that belief into obsolescence when it was proven that the world was actually round.

Software 1.0 was installed from a disk or tape.
Software 2.0 isn't installed at all. You access it and run it from the web.

Encyclopedia 1.0 was purchased as a fifteen-volume set of textbooks (with some obsolete content the moment it arrived).
Encyclopedia 2.0 is accessed on the web and is always current because it's constantly updated.

Music 1.0 was purchased on vinyl, then on tapes, and then on CDs.
Music 2.0 is downloaded from iTunes and other music-sharing sites.

Video production 1.0 was strictly the domain of Hollywood.

Video production 2.0 is now the domain of anyone with a digital camcorder and access to YouTube.

Worldwide sales 1.0 was only achievable by large companies with worldwide manufacturing and distribution infrastructures.

Worldwide sales 2.0 is achievable by companies of any size—and even individuals—that understand the value of online marketing and outsourced relationships, facilitating worldwide manufacturing and distribution.

These few examples set the stage for discussing how Marketing 2.0 represents a fundamental shift from Marketing 1.0. Let's see how.

If we characterize Marketing 1.0 as being intrusive, interruptive, and a style of one-way shouting at our customers (outbound marketing), we can characterize Marketing 2.0 as being about conversations, collaboration, communities, and word of mouth (inbound marketing).

I like to boil down Marketing 2.0 to two pillars: content marketing and relationship-building (on the web).

But Marketing 1.0 is still prevalent worldwide. One of the most blatant examples of traditional Marketing 1.0 is the television commercial. The painful truth is that commercials are intrusive. To rub salt in the wound, television commercials are even louder than the regular telecast because marketers know that their viewing audience usually leaves the room for a bathroom or kitchen run during most commercials, so they amplify the volume of their ads. This example—and there are many others; if you don't believe me, just go to your mailbox to see more—makes the point that conventional Marketing 1.0 is not only intrusive, but also it is strictly one-way communication.

With the advent of social media where communities are formed, opinions are shaped, and marketers who understand this phenomenon are effectively participating in creative ways, the old style of marketing is rapidly becoming a dinosaur. For proof, just look at the state of the mainstream newspaper industry. They are on the decline industrywide while their online content counterparts are on the rise. According to the Audit Bureau of Circulation[1] among more than 500 newspaper's weekday circulation was down 4.6% and Sunday circulation fell 4.8 percent. Each of the large mainstream news media—CNN, the *Wall Street Journal*, *Forbes*, and *BusinessWeek*—have thriving businesses online. They each have invested significantly in infrastructure and marketing in their online properties. And with the green movement, it's only a matter of time before the print versions of each of these publications become relics of a distant past. Even if you live in a metropolitan area such as New York City and ride the subway with your favorite newspaper, you'll someday read it on an electronic device similar to Amazon.com's Kindle. The Kindle is the first digital reading device. Our grandchildren will learn about newspapers in history class while consuming all their content on digital devices. This transition has already begun in our lifetime. Do you remember the typewriter? If you do, then you get my point.

Marketing 1.0 is characterized as a marketer's attempt to interrupt our lives with their message, hoping that a small percentage of us will respond. Let's review some of the most common methods of Marketing 1.0 and how we can consider repurposing these strategies using a 2.0 mindset:

- *Trade shows.* At these events, we set up elaborate displays of our wares and strive to tell prospective buyers about our products. We often engage in creative, loud, and bizarre antics to rise above the noise surrounding us (that we helped create) and to get noticed by the crowd in hope that a subset of the people we encounter will become interested in our products. Some of the most meaningful conversations that take place at a trade show are those that occur off the exhibit floor over coffee or in a private suite where smaller groups come together. Bucking the trend, many marketers purposely choose *not* to exhibit at industry trade shows, instead opting to rent private suites to set up private conversations. This can

---

1   Audit Bureau of Circulation Report: http://www.nytimes.com/2008/10/28/
     business/media/28circ.html

be a very effective, alternative approach to traditional trade show marketing. These private conversations are far more productive than the shouting that takes place on the floor. Through the use of social media, a 2.0 mind-set can engage people before, during, and after the trade show. Prior to the event, communicate to your online communities the interesting and value-laden topics you'll be discussing at the trade show. Be sure to invite them to engage with you. Offer them content that improves their lives or work in some meaningful way, then invite them to learn more about it at the trade show. Use a medium such as Twitter to provide real-time streams of your content directly from the show floor. Today, many marketers with a 2.0 mind-set exhibit at fewer trade shows now due to the effectiveness of other marketing channels including virtual trade shows held online. There are still trade shows in each industry that are very worthwhile. Your trade show ROI will be more effective, however, when you engage the online community before, during, and after the event.

- *Advertising.* In Marketing 1.0, we deliver a one-way message through various advertising channels: television, radio, print, and even the Internet. I'm not against advertising. Advertising will live on. However, the contemporary marketer understands that the role of advertising is different today. Depending on your industry, advertising is meant to create two things: awareness and differentiation. Frequently, the person who responds favorably to your advertisement uses the Internet to learn more about you, either by visiting your website, conducting research, contacting his online community to ask about you, or all of the above. This being the case, the role of advertising has shifted from a medium often credited with driving buying decisions to a medium limited to creating an impression of your brand. Essentially, advertising has been relegated to brand development with the balance of the buying process being influenced by communities and word of mouth, both of which can occur online and offline. Today's consumer or buyer has access to so many online tools and communities that effective advertising actually serves to help the buyer conduct his due diligence. Advertising that tries to close the deal usually fails. Another way to look at the role of advertising is to acknowledge that buyers are evaluating you, so your advertising should encourage them to complete what will hopefully be a favorable evaluation of your company, your products, or your services.

- *Telemarketing/Telesales.* We intrude on our prospective customers with an unwelcomed phone call, frequently interrupting their dinner, or the middle of their work day, and we deliver our pitch. We may even try to disguise it as a survey or some other seemingly friendly dialogue. Even worse, we sometimes start the call with a pre-recorded message and then force the recipient to wait for a live agent. Countless business-to-business sales organizations still employ people to make phone calls all day long. They have targets or quotas specifying the number of calls they must make each day, such as one hundred calls in a day, targeting ten *connects* and developing two leads. Their calls are frequently monitored and timed and usually measured strictly by the numbers. It can be a high-pressure environment. As a means of protection from unwanted calls, most businesses have phone systems with caller ID, ensuring that calls are screened either by a gatekeeper or the phone system. Making cold-calls to generate sales opportunities is a dying breed of marketing because the mathematical odds of cold-calling success are so stacked against the caller. It is hard to justify it any longer. Still, thousands of businesses continue to use it. That said, the phone can be an effective tool when used wisely in combination with other marketing activities. Ideally, the phone calls should come into your sales team based on effective inbound marketing strategies. If that sounds like a pipe dream (and in some industries, it's hard to imagine that ever happening), please be sure to read the case studies in this book. Engaging your target audience with content of interest dramatically increases the chance of getting a return call when you leave a message. Marketing's purpose is *always* to create sales opportunities. When prospective buyers respond to an offer, or request information or content through some online activity, they are inviting the phone call. However, the tone of the call should be conversational, not sales-oriented. So make sure the caller is well-qualified to engage in intelligent conversation. Your prospect is typically well-informed and generally further along in the evaluation process than someone who has not done her homework. The two most important considerations in using the phone are the way in which you use it: 1) set up a warm call, and 2) employ qualified staff that is focused on engaging potential customers in conversations. Develop processes that track the behavior of your buyers by helping them move further along their path of evaluation and decision.

- *Direct mail.* We clutter the mail slots of our prospective customers with colorful (and not-so-colorful) postcards, letters, and even more creative, three-dimensional mailers with outdated calls to action, all in hopes of getting a 1 percent response rate. That's right, 1 percent! Now I'm not against direct mail. In fact, integrating personalized direct mail with personalized web landing pages can be very effective. If you send a direct mail piece to me with my photo on the cover, uniquely personalized with my name in the piece, and invite me to download content that is uniquely meaningful to me, you can increase your response rates into the 20 percent and 30 percent range (this is not a typo). Marketers who can pull off highly targeted and personalized direct mail campaigns combined with measurable online marketing activities can get great results. Direct mail should be a component of your content strategy, not the sole medium. A content focused mind-set in your direct mail strategy will not only change how you use direct mail, but also it will also change the way you measure results.

Marketing 2.0 is a *mind-set*. Its two pillars are content and relationship-building. It is not a set of tactics. The metrics you use to measure results or ROI are not the same as those used in years past. The mindset of Marketing 2.0 is to determine where your customers and their surrounding constituents spend time on the web. Once you determine that, go there to share great content and build relationships with them. By the way, your target customer shouldn't be limited to just those who buy your products. There are surrounding people who influence the buying patterns of your target customers. They are just as important to your marketing efforts as your target customer. If you can effectively engage these influential people in meaningful ways, you can earn their trust. The contemporary buyer is smarter than in years past. She doesn't have to put up with your shouting anymore. She simply won't listen to it. Engage her. Inform her. Be a friend to her. Win her trust, and you have your best chance at winning her business.

Next, let's examine how we evolved to this thing we call the social web.

What Is Web 2.0 and
Social Media?

T he following story of my early career serves as an analogy to explain how we got to Web 2.0 and the social media revolution ... I began my career in 1979 in New York, working for Yourdon, Inc., where I learned about the art of software development. The founder and CEO of Yourdon, Inc. is Ed Yourdon, a man who literally wrote the book on how to design software using a then-new methodology called Structured Systems Development (SSD). Yourdon is now in the computer hall of fame and has authored twenty-seven computer-related books.[1]

In the 1960s and '70s, software systems were mostly run by midsize to large corporations on mainframe computers. Software systems development was very labor-intensive and, consequently, very expensive. Therefore, software systems were mostly limited to mission-critical applications such as financial systems. In simple terms, the idea behind his SSD methodology was for business analysts to spend a considerable amount of time defining the business requirements of a software application. This was typically accomplished through extensive interviews with the business users of a new software system (the stakeholders), writing

---

1   Ed Yourdon's website: http://www.yourdon.com/.

down everything they said was needed in the software application. In Yourdon's SSD method, diagrams known as *data flow diagrams* were used by the business analysts to literally illustrate how the software would function when it was completed. This "picture" allowed the users (who were mostly non-programmer types) to understand how the interpretation of their requirements had led to the system-to-be. Eventually, the user group and the data processing group arrived at a consensus on the specifications of the new software application, using the data flow diagrams as the blueprint. Upon user sign-off, the analysis phase was completed. The end result of the analysis phase was a definition of *what* the system was intended to accomplish.

Next came the design phase. In this phase, the analysts and engineers would lay out the structure of the application, defining *how* it was going to programmatically accomplish the overall system requirements. Once all stakeholders signed off on the design blueprint, the design phase was completed. The design of the system defined how the system was going to be developed. Up until this point, no programming code had yet been written, which is a stark contrast to the previous method of software systems development.

In the final phase, the programming code was applied. In this coding phase, programmers used the design blueprint to write the code that would actually build the software application that addressed the business requirements defined in the earlier system analysis.

Back in those days of mainframe and minicomputer software development, these new structured systems development techniques were considered revolutionary and a paradigm shift. For the people involved in the SSD methods, it was a major mind shift. They were accustomed to doing very limited analysis and a lot of programming. The three phases described above became known as structure analysis, structured design, and structured programming. Prior to these new techniques, approximately 70 percent of a software development project time went to programming (coding). The remaining 30 percent went to analysis and design. Yourdon's new SSD model turned this paradigm upside down. Under the SSD model, roughly 70 percent of the time and effort went into analysis and design, with the balance going to programming.

The logic inherent in SSD certainly made sense. At the simplest level, SSD was all about taking the necessary time to clearly define the business problem (*what* the system is intended to do) and clearly design the solution (*how* the system would be built), then writing the code (implementation of the design blueprint) to develop the software. From this new software development model flowed many case studies of more efficient software development, mostly characterized by systems that did a better job of what the users actually wanted. Most telling was the dramatic reduction in costs for software development, largely due to the lower cost associated with discovering errors early in the project (analysis or design), as compared with finding errors later in the programming or testing phases, or once the systems were in use. Most SSD-based software applications were delivered closer to budget and timeline projections, and that resulted in more satisfied user communities.

So what does any of this have to do with Web 2.0 and social media? Two things. First, SSD was in actuality Software Development 2.0. Until SSD became widely adopted, thanks largely to Yourdon and his trained disciples who taught the SSD methodology worldwide, Software Development 1.0 was very inefficient and wildly expensive for businesses everywhere. Yourdon and his SSD methodology turned this upside down!

Second, whenever software applications are developed and rolled out, they are always labeled by a version number. This holds true for software applications developed by businesses for internal use, as well as commercial software products developed for sale. Open any software application today, whether it's a corporate application, one you installed on your personal computer, or one you accessed over the web, and it will have a version number.

Version 1.0 of any software application has always been characterized as being just good enough to launch, far less than perfect. Often, version 1.0 is buggy, bloated, slow, and lacking in needed features. In short, version 1.0 is often not much more than a beta or early release.

However, when we speak of Web 2.0, we are *not* referring to another version of the web. So what is Web 1.0 and what is Web 2.0?

When I think of Web 1.0, the first thing that comes to my mind is a dial-up connection. Do you remember when you connected to the web using a modem and a phone line? Argh! It's laughable now, but those of us who used dial-up connections to the Internet suffered through very slow connection and download speeds.

Web 1.0

To understand this concept of Web 1.0, let's take a quick history lesson on the formation of the Internet. While Al Gore would like to take credit for its invention, the Internet's actual invention dates back to the 1960s. Two men—Levi Finch and Robert Taylor—developed a movement among computer professionals to connect computers around the globe. Concurrently, several research efforts exploring ways to network computers residing on physically separate computers sprung up, which led to the development of packet switching. This all happened at a time when computers were typically stand-alone islands of information.

The first recognized example of a connected network of computers using packet switching was the Advanced Research Projects Agency Network (ARPANET),[2] used by the U.S. Department of Defense. This system was the world's first operational packet-switching network, widely recognized as the predecessor to the global Internet we know today. In 1989, Sir Timothy John Berners-Lee, a computer scientist in the European Organization for Nuclear Research in Geneva, Switzerland, coined the term *World Wide Web*. He has played an active role in developing many of the web standards still in place such as markup languages and the World Wide Web Consortium, which oversees the web's continued development.

In order for the World Wide Web to be available to the general public,

---

2   For a full chronology of ARPANET and the history of the Internet visit http://en.wikipedia.org/wiki/ARPANET.

an interface was required. In 1992, Mosaic was developed by the National Center for Supercomputing Applications (NCSA) and released as the world's first commercial browser in 1993. Mosaic was officially discontinued in 1997, though it can still be downloaded from NCSA.[3]

The Mosaic browser was the catalyst that accelerated the evolution of the web and related technologies such as TCP, IP, ftp | nntp | gopher | http, URL, and HTML. The next person to come on the scene and accelerate the availability of the web through browser technology was Marc Andreessen and his Netscape Navigator. Today, the two most popular web browsers in the world, Firefox and Microsoft's Internet Explorer, still maintain many of the characteristics of the original Mosaic graphical user interface (GUI).

The World Was Once Flat

Most websites are still Web 1.0 sites. That is to say that site visitors cannot interact with the website. The purpose of a Web 1.0 website is to offer information about a company, organization, or person, typically the website's owner. Web 1.0 sites are by nature static, read-only websites. All we can do on these websites is read the content. We cannot become engaged. Sure, we can often fill out a form to request information or download something. But, the primary purpose of these websites is to provide content to be read and prompt site visitors to take some desired action based on that content.

What about Ecommerce Websites?

Visiting Web 1.0 sites with online catalogs where you can view products, add them to a shopping cart, and make a purchase is, in essence, a hybrid experience. It's mostly a Web 1.0 experience because these websites still limit our interaction to viewing, reading, and adding comments about a

---

3   Source: http://www.ncsa.uiuc.edu/

product we purchased. The ability to comment on products we've purchased is where the hybrid aspect comes into play.

The World Really is Round!

Once our civilization discovered that the world was actually round, it forever changed the way we looked at our planet. More importantly, the discovery made the flat world theory obsolete. At this writing, most websites are still Web 1.0; most sites are limited in their ability to allow visitors to interact with each other or with the site's owner.

Here is an example: let's say your company is a manufacturer of industrial equipment with annual sales of $10 million. Your Web 1.0 site has about fifty pages. You have the standard pages: Home, About Us, Products (with many subpages), Partners, How to Buy, and Contact Us. The site contains a nicely designed color catalog. Altogether you've invested about $25,000 in website development fees. You also run pay-per-click (PPC) search marketing campaigns to generate sales leads, with an average monthly click spend of about $3,000. In a year's time, you've invested $61,000 in your site. In year two, you don't have the expense of developing the website other than some updates costing about $5,000. Assuming a flat PPC marketing spend, your annual spend is $36,000. However, in year two, you also invested in the services of a search engine optimization (SEO) firm with a monthly spend of $2,000. In year two, your total investment in search marketing (paid and SEO) and website maintenance was $65,000. How do you measure your return on investment (ROI)?

In a Web 1.0 scenario, the only way you can measure ROI is based on sales generated from your website—period! There is no other way to measure ROI. The people who visit your website are handcuffed. You don't allow them to interact with you unless they contact you. But you say, *I want them to contact us! I want sales leads!* Really? I've got news for you: Most visitors to your Web 1.0 site are not ready to contact you. Why? Because most visitors want to check you out for some period of time before they call you or fill out your annoying form where you ask for an email address. To illustrate my point, I ask you: how quickly are you willing to hand over your email address when you visit a website for the first time?

Here's the point: unless your website sells a low price point product, visitors to your website are mostly there to visit, study, and evaluate you. They are not there to buy ... at least not yet.

But remember—the only way we can measure ROI for Web 1.0 sites is based on sales attributed directly to the website. So in a Web 2.0 world, how do we measure ROI?

Web 2.0

If Web 1.0 is characterized as a *flat* world, then Web 2.0 is characterized as a *round* world. If Web 1.0 is *read-only*, then Web 2.0 is *read-write*! A Web 2.0 site has these characteristics:

- Visitors can *contribute* content or comments.

- Visitors can *subscribe* to your content.

- Visitors can share your content easily with others.

- Visitors can rate your content.

- Visitors can form *communities* and *collaborate* with each other.

- Visitors can *influence* the opinions of others positively or negatively.

- Visitors can get engaged in productive ways before they are ready to buy your widget.

- Visitors are not limited to your company website but can also link to other destinations on the web that interest them.

Web 2.0 is an expression coined by Bill O'Reilly at a conference in 2004. He referred to the next generation of websites where destinations on the web are interactive, communities are formed online, and relationships occur. The communities formed online are influential. Content is created and shared among the community.

Web 2.0 has become synonymous with social media because in a Web 2.0 scenario, the interaction that occurs is social. In fact, the evolution of web technology into what is known as Web 2.0 is as much a social phenomenon as a technological one. Consider that we are social creatures. We took social studies class in school. We attend social functions. We work in social settings, unless you work from home, in which case much of your social contact is on the web. We eat in restaurants, go to malls, ride buses, subways, and airplanes, drive on freeways, and, whether we want to or not, like it or not, we interact socially with other people. These examples are things we often do with little or no choice or thought. However, when we do participate in a social activity by choice—a cooking class, a martial arts class, a wedding or a business networking event—we interact with others. And when we interact in these social settings, we look to interact with people with whom we have something in common. Sometimes in these social settings, we have interesting conversations. Sometimes we make recommendations about restaurants, movies, activities, or products we like (or dislike). Sometimes we receive similar recommendations from others. And when these recommendations and opinions are expressed in social settings among people with whom we have something in common, a social phenomenon occurs. People very often listen to these recommendations. In other words, ideas, opinions, and recommendations made in a social setting among communities of people with similar interests carry weight—a lot of weight.

What does this have to do with Web 2.0? Everything! While there are technological advances that have facilitated the rapid adoption of Web 2.0 and social media, the single largest contributing factor to its rapid growth is the inherent social phenomenon. But wait—what is so phenomenal about that? What's so surprising about that? Nothing, really. We are social creatures, remember?

It's worth noting that not all Web 2.0 applications fall into the category of social media. The Web 2.0 applications that are available to the public are indeed social. However, there is a growing list of private applications developed by organizations around the world that are also considered vital parts of Web 2.0. Business applications running as *software as a service* (SaaS) are Web 2.0 applications, but they are used only by authorized personnel with a login ID. Some newly developed corporate websites are Web 2.0 by virtue of their use of Web 2.0 technologies.

Let's look at how Web 2.0 has created a social media revolution and its effect on marketing strategies.

Types of Web 2.0 and Social Media

You're probably reading this book because you've had some exposure to Web 2.0 or social media terminology. You've probably read about it in mainstream publications such as *BusinessWeek, USA Today,* or even your local newspaper or evening television news. Perhaps you have visited blogs, created a profile in a social network, or attended a local seminar or a webinar on the topic. In short, you've heard about social media without searching for it. You may be wondering, *Is it hype or is it really worthwhile? It seems like a waste of time. Can my business (or career) really benefit from it? I don't have time for social media, should I?*

In this chapter, let's identify the primary attributes of Web 2.0 so we can be grounded in the proper terminology and concepts explored here and in later chapters.

Web 2.0 comprises destinations (websites) on the web that fall into one of three categories:

- Shared content

- Published content

- Social networking

Below are basic definitions of each of these terms, as provided by Wikipedia,[1] which is itself one of the most exciting examples of a Web 2.0 software application.

Shared content destination sites are those where people share content with others. One of the most dramatic attributes of social media is that anyone can share content with anyone else. Indeed, sharing is often what popularizes content and creates the so-called *viral effect.*

The viral effect is often mentioned as one of the most desirable benefits of social media marketing. When you consider the total amount of content available in social media, very little actually ever reaches viral status. However, the viral effect of content in niche markets can be very effective. When content goes viral it means that certain members of an online community have embraced that specific content—whether it's a blog post, a group, a video—and they tell other community members about it. The people within that community who see the content then share it with more people. Through this domino effect, the content receives a considerable amount of attention and continues to spread across the Internet, much like the common cold or flu does through society. Hence the term viral effect.

However, content doesn't have to go viral for it to be valuable to the owner of the content. Over time, producing content that is shared in your community and attributed back to the author (a person or a company), contributes to brand reputation (and sales leads).

Examples of public shared content sites include the following:

- Reddit: http://www.reddit.com/

- Digg: http://digg.com/

- Delicious: http://del.icio.us/

- StumbleUpon: http://www.stumbleupon.com/

---

1   Source: http://en.wikipedia.org/wiki/Main_Page

These aren't the only shared content sites on the social web, but they are certainly some of the most popular ones at the time of this writing. Let's briefly review each one.

Reddit is a social news website on which users can post links to content on the web. Other users may then vote the posted links up or down a list, causing them to appear more or less prominently on the Reddit home page, depending on the voting.

The site also features discussion areas in which users may discuss the posted links and vote for or against others' comments. When there are enough votes against a given comment, it will not be displayed even by default, although a reader can display it through a link or preference. Users who submit articles that others like and subsequently vote up receive karma points as a reward for submitting interesting articles.[2]

Digg is a website intended as a destination where people discover and share content from anywhere on the Internet. They do this by submitting links and stories and voting or commenting on others' submitted links and stories. Digg is a true display of both the social and democratic spirit in action. The ability to vote stories up or down is the site's cornerstone function, respectively called either *digging* or *burying*, depending again on the voting. Stories are submitted daily, but only the most *dugg* stories appear on the front page. Digg's popularity has prompted the creation of other social networking sites with a story submission and voting system.[3]

A website or social destination site that allows you to submit content to Digg contains a graphical button labeled *Digg*. The Digg button displays a number indicating how many people have previously *dugg* the content. If no one has dugg the content, the number is zero. Visiting Digg allows you to see the most popular content, as voted by the masses, at any moment in time on their home page. You can also see popular content in

---

2   Source: http://en.wikipedia.org/wiki/Reddit
3   Source: http://en.wikipedia.org/wiki/Digg

other categories such as world and business news, science, gaming, life-style, entertainment, and sports. You can even search for content by topic using the site's search function.

Del.icio.us uses a nonhierarchical keyword categorization system in which users can tag each of their bookmarks with a number of freely chosen keywords (see folksonomy).[4] A combined view of everyone's bookmarks with a given tag is available; for instance, the URL http://del.icio.us/tag/wiki displays all of the most recent links tagged wiki. Its collective nature makes it possible to view bookmarks added by similar-minded users. Del.icio.us has a *hotlist* on its home page and *popular* and *recent* pages, which help to make the website a purveyor of Internet themes and trends. Many features have contributed to making Del.icio.us one of the most popular social bookmarking services. These include the website's simple interface, human-readable URL scheme, a novel domain name, a simple REST API, and RSS feeds for web syndication.

All bookmarks posted to Del.icio.us are publicly viewable by default, although users can mark specific bookmarks as private, and imported bookmarks are private by default. The public aspect is emphasized; the site is not focused on storing private (not shared) bookmark collections. Del.icio.us linkrolls, tagrolls, network badges, RSS feeds, and the site's daily blog posting feature can be used to display bookmarks on web logs.[5]

StumbleUpon is a web browser plug-in and Internet community that allow its users to discover and rate web pages, photos, and videos. web pages are presented when the user clicks the *Stumble!* button on the browser's toolbar. StumbleUpon chooses which new web page to display based on the user's ratings of previous pages, ratings by his or her friends, and ratings by users with similar interests. It is a recommendation system using peer and social networking principles. The site also features built-in, one-click

---

4   http://en.wikipedia.org/wiki/Folksonomy: also known as collaborative tagging or social indexing.

5   Source: http://en.wikipedia.org/wiki/Del.icio.us

blogging as well. Users can rate, or choose not to rate, any web page with a thumbs-up or thumbs-down, and clicking the Stumble button resembles channel surfing the web. Toolbar versions exist for Firefox, the Mozilla Application Suite, and Internet Explorer, but it also works with some independent Mozilla-based browsers.[6]

Published content sites are those social media sites where anyone can publish content. The harshest critics of the Web 2.0 platforms are those who complain that *anyone* can publish content. The effect on the newspaper industry is apparent as the creation and consumption of news on the web is widely available for free.

Below are a few of the most popular types of publishing sites, starting with the oldest and arguably, the most popular—blogs.

A *blog* (a contraction of the term *web log*) is a website, usually maintained by an individual, with regular entries of commentary, descriptions of events, or other material such as graphics or video. Entries are commonly displayed in reverse chronological order. *Blog* can also be used as a verb, meaning *to maintain or add content to a blog.*

Many blogs provide commentary or news on a particular subject; others function more as personal online diaries. A typical blog combines text, images, and links to other blogs, web pages, and other media related to its topic. The ability for readers to leave comments in an interactive format is an important part of many blogs. Most blogs are primarily textual, although some focus on art (artlog), photographs (photoblog), sketches (sketchblog), videos (vlog), music (MP3 blog), or audio (podcasting), and are considered part of a wider network of social media. With the advent of video blogging, the word *blog* has taken on an even looser meaning, now referring to any bit of media wherein the subject expresses his opinion or simply talks about something.[7] According to the December 2008

---

6   Source: http://en.wikipedia.org/wiki/Stumbleupon
7   Source: http://en.wikipedia.org/wiki/Blog

State of the Blogosphere report,[8] the U.S. audience for blogs is estimated at 88.9 million and 346 million worldwide.

Microblogging is a form of blogging that allows users to write brief text updates (usually 140 characters) and publish them, either to be viewed by anyone or by a restricted group that can be chosen by the user. These messages can be submitted by a variety of means, including text messaging, instant messaging, email, MP3, or the web.

The most popular microblogging service is Twitter, which was launched in July 2006 and won the Web Award in the blog category at the 2007 South by Southwest Conference in Austin, Texas. The popular social networking websites Facebook, MySpace, and LinkedIn also have a microblogging feature, called *status update.*[9]

Microblogging, and especially the popularity of Twitter, is an ongoing source of debate as to its usefulness in social media marketing. More on this topic is discussed in the Twitter chapter.

YouTube is a video-sharing website where users can upload, view, and share video clips. Three former PayPal employees created YouTube in mid-February 2005. The San Bruno, California-based service uses Adobe Flash technology to display a wide variety of user-generated video content, including movie clips, TV clips, and music videos, as well as amateur content such as video blogs and short original videos. In October 2006, Google Inc. announced that it had reached a deal to acquire the company for $1.65 billion in Google stock. The deal closed on November 13, 2006.

Unregistered users can watch most videos on the site, while registered users are permitted to upload an unlimited number of videos. Some videos are available only to users of age eighteen or older (e.g., videos containing potentially offensive content). The uploading of videos containing pornography, nudity, defamation, harassment, commercial advertise-

---

8   State of the Blogosphere: http://technorati.com/blogging/state-of-the-blogosphere/

9   Source: http://en.wikipedia.org/wiki/Micro-blogging

ments, and material encouraging criminal conduct is prohibited. Related videos, determined by title and tags, appear onscreen to the right of a given video. In YouTube's second year, functions were added to enhance user ability to post video "responses" and subscribe to content feeds.

Few statistics are publicly available regarding the number of videos on YouTube. However, in July 2006, the company revealed that more than 100 million videos were being watched every day, and 2.5 billion videos were watched in June 2006. In May 2006, the company disclosed that 50,000 videos were being added per day, and this increased to 65,000 by July of that same year. In January 2008 alone, nearly 79 million users had made more than 3 billion video views.

In August 2006, the *Wall Street Journal* published an article revealing that YouTube was hosting about 6.1 million videos (requiring about 45 terabytes of storage space), and had about 500,000 user accounts. As of April 9, 2008, a YouTube search returns about 83.4 million videos and 3.75 million user channels.

As of the first quarter of 2008, YouTube is not profitable, with Google referring to its revenues in a regulatory filing as being *immaterial*. Its bandwidth costs are estimated at approximately $1 million a day. It is estimated that in 2007, YouTube consumed as much bandwidth as the entire Internet in 2000, and that around ten hours of video are uploaded every minute.[10]

Flickr is an image- and video-hosting website, web services suite, and online community platform. It was one of the earliest Web 2.0 applications. In addition to being a popular website for users to share personal photographs, the service is widely used by bloggers as a photo repository. Its popularity has been fueled by its organization tools, which allow photos to be tagged and browsed by *folksonomic* means. As of November 2007, it claims to host more than 2 billion images.[11]

---

10 Source: http://en.wikipedia.org/wiki/YouTube
11 Source: http://en.wikipedia.org/wiki/Flikr

Social networking sites are destinations on the web where people interact with each other in very social ways by *friending* each other, connecting across common interests and generally forming communities.

A *social network service* focuses on building online communities of people who share interests and activities, or who are interested in exploring the interests and activities of others. Most social network services are web-based and provide a variety of ways for users to interact, such as email and instant messaging services. Social networking has created powerful new ways to communicate and share information. Social networking websites are being used regularly by millions of people, and it now seems that social networking will be an enduring part of everyday life. The main types of social networking services are those that contain directories of categories (such as former classmates), as a means to connect with friends (usually with self-description pages), and recommender systems linked to trust. Popular methods now combine many of these, with MySpace and Facebook being the most widely used in North America; Bebo, MySpace, Skyrock Blog, StudiVZ, Youmeo, Facebook, and Hi5 in parts of Europe; Orkut and Hi5 in South America and Central America; and Friendster, Orkut, and Cyworld in Asia and the Pacific Islands. CouchSurfing is a new type of social network called *hospitality exchange networks.*[12]

These Web 2.0 destination sites represent the landscape of social media. Now let's examine how marketers use these as platforms and tools to market in our contemporary economy.

---

12   Source: http://en.wikipedia.org/wiki/Social_networking

Technology and Social Drivers of Web 2.0 Applications

n the previous chapter, we summarized the types of Web 2.0. Now, let's review the technology and social developments that have allowed Web 2.0 to evolve, grow, and flourish at an impressive pace. Social media applications are made possible in large part by the technology enablers discussed here. For simplicity I've broken the list into two general categories: *technology enablers* and *social enablers.*

Technology Enablers

Really Simple Syndication (RSS) is the technology enabler allowing you to subscribe to any content which is RSS enabled. Anytime you see the universal orange RSS symbol, you can subscribe to that content. Once you are subscribed, your *RSS aggregator* will automatically display the most current content from the source(s) to which you have subscribed. RSS aggregators are also known as newsreaders, feed aggregators, or feed readers. They all do the same thing—channel (aggregate) syndicated web content to you, allowing for easy access.

An RSS aggregator is like a newspaper. Each time you open your favorite newspaper, the current news is brought to you in sections: world news, regional news, local news, business news, sports news, political news, et cetera. You have the choice of reading the sections that interest you most within the current news brought to you for these sections. The web medium eliminates the need for you to go searching for news in those categories. You may subscribe to more than one newspaper, but each one serves the same purpose of *feeding* you news according to your preference. An RSS aggregator does the same thing, the only difference being that sometimes the content arrives more frequently than daily.

The most common use of RSS aggregators is to efficiently organize and deliver the headlines of the content to which you have subscribed. For example, if you have subscribed to ten different blogs, each time you visit your favorite RSS aggregator, the most current content for these ten blogs will be displayed. This allows you to peruse your ten blogs to see their *headlines* that comprise the most recent posts. You can then selectively visit the blogs of your choice from one central point of *news*. Sample RSS aggregators include the following:

- *Feedreader*. A default aggregator that comes with Windows. It's pretty basic, but it does the job. The icon is the universal orange RSS icon.

- *Google Reader*. A simple aggregator with good labeling functions. It has some limitations, but it's easy to configure and very flexible.

- *Bloglines*. A popular aggregator with many of the same characteristics as Google Reader.

- *Yahoo! News*. Also very popular, it offers dozens of RSS feeds you can read in My Yahoo! or using third-party RSS newsreader software.

There are many other RSS aggregators. You can easily find them on the Internet searching for *RSS feed readers* or other similar keywords. The readers listed above are all free, and most others you'll find are also free.

XML. When examining the technology enablers of Web 2.0, XML cannot be ignored. While this book is not intended to get very technical, we can digress momentarily just to connect some dots.

XML stands for *extensible markup language.* It is part of the evolution of languages that uses the *markup* method of programming in which instructions are provided using markup codes that determine the way the text on a web page is displayed. The most common of these languages is HTML, used on the Internet in websites and in emails to make them more graphically appealing.

XML is more of a general-purpose specification that allows content (text and graphics) to be distributed across different platforms Internetwide. The most compelling example of this is RSS. RSS, considered the killer application in Web 2.0, is made possible solely by XML. The XML standard also helps make possible the distribution and delivery of software as a service (SaaS) all across the Internet. As a business user of social media, you only need to understand that XML is a key technology enabler. This is similar to not having to understand how microprocessors work, but knowing that they are a key technology enabler in the production of PCs and laptops.

AJAX. No, this isn't laundry detergent. It is an acronym for *Asynchronous JavaScript and XML.* Since we covered XML above, and again, it's not my intent to convert you to a developer, I will explain this technology in the simplest terms possible. First, to understand what AJAX means to us as users of websites and web applications, consider the non-Web 2.0 or traditional method of displaying results on a web page that doesn't use AJAX (most websites at the time of this writing).

When you are on a web page and you click on anything clickable that requests data, the entire web page refreshes. The website is requesting an updated version of the page. This eats up bandwidth and also takes a few seconds to load because the entire page is loading. A few seconds doesn't sound like a lot, but multiply that by a lot of clicks and a lot of requests, and it adds up both for the user and for the server on the back end of the website you're visiting.

Enter AJAX, offering a more advanced way to serve up data when we request it. Using the *asynchronous* attributes of this technology enabler, when you make a request for something on a web page—say, a map update on Google Maps—the only part of the web page that gets updated is the part you requested. The web application is able to carve out the specific request you made and only process that request in the background, leaving the rest of the page unchanged. This allows us to get the results quicker, because the only part of the web page that is being changed or refreshed is the part we just clicked. Look at it this way. A web application or website such as Google Maps, Gmail, or Flickr is chopped up into various components. On the web page, the human eye sees a pleasant display of everything working cohesively. But, behind the scenes in the code, the AJAX technology has carved out several pieces of the logic to allow us to request information through clicks, and each request is treated on its own. The advantages are obvious. We get faster results.

There are some disadvantages to AJAX, most of which are being addressed by developers. One disadvantage is that the history of a web page is not stored the same as a non-AJAX page. This means that if you click the Back button in your browser, the page it will return to is not the previous state before your Back click, but rather the last page you visited.

Again, as a user of social media, you don't need to understand the bits and bytes of how AJAX works. My intent is to help you understand that AJAX is another key technology enabler that allows more sophisticated web applications to be developed, offering us more enjoyable and productive experiences on the social web. The forms of social media described in the following sections are made possible, in large part, by the technology enablers discussed here.

Availability of High-Speed Internet

If Web 2.0 applications had been introduced when the most common way to connect to the Internet was based on dial-up connection, it would have been way ahead of its time. However, in the past ten years, the availability of high-speed Internet access has exploded. The ease of connecting to the Internet at home through cable modem and the digital subscriber line (DSL) is greater than ever and available at reasonable cost. The vast majority of businesses provide their employees with high-speed Internet access. And the wide availability of wireless Internet access also is a huge factor in providing Internet access to the public. Starbucks and Panera Bread are two examples of coffee or restaurant chains providing free Wi-Fi Internet access to their patrons. Such Wi-Fi access points are known as *hot spots.* Indeed, members of the hospitality industry, including hotels, restaurants, and railway and other transportation companies are quickly concluding that offering free Wi-Fi access is a necessary amenity. Many U.S. airports provide free Wi-Fi public access.

Starting in late 2005, a national movement started with a goal of setting up citywide Wi-Fi access using a method known as *mesh networks* which chains together Wi-Fi antennas in succession with each group leading back to an Internet router. This configuration results in providing *hot zones* across a city at a reasonable cost to each city. However, this effort has been moving slowly, with little advancement to show at the time of this writing. The higher-than-expected costs of building the network combined with the limited profit opportunity for network providers have slowed progress.

Cities have three primary motivations for deployment of Wi-Fi access to the public. The first driving force is providing Internet access for low-income users. Most of us take for granted our daily access to the Internet, but there are thousands of people who are part of the *digital divide,* meaning they exist without Internet access and are separated from those of us with it. Providing such access contributes to educational and economic opportunities for the low-income population. A second driving force is the city's security interests. Internet access for the public helps improve communication in the event of acts of civil unrest or terrorism (assuming the network isn't taken out in the process). The third driver is purely economical. As the economic model of Wi-Fi access continues to evolve, don't be surprised if cities want a piece of the action whenever we download music or anything else we pay for on the Internet. Yes, I mean an Internet sales tax.

Outside the United States, the availability of Wi-Fi Internet access is even more prevalent. European cities offering free Wi-Fi access include Athens, Berlin, Bern, Brussels, Helsinki, Luxembourg, Madrid, Paris, and Rome.

The bottom line is that, on a global scale, our access to the Internet through high-speed connections is more available than ever before. This high-speed *information superhighway* lays the infrastructure track for the widespread adoption of social media applications.

Mobile Devices

People around the globe have developed an addiction to mobile devices. This started with the widespread adoption of laptop computers, most now featuring Wi-Fi access. This love affair for mobile connectivity spans all demographics and geographic boundaries, short of the jungles and forests of underdeveloped countries, though that is slowly changing, too. Blackberrys, iPhones, and other cell phones with text messaging and Internet access features are now the norm. As a global society, we have developed an addiction to the Internet.

The media certainly recognizes this addiction, as evidenced by the convergence of television- and Internet-based news. Just turn on your favorite television news channel and you'll hear reference to their online content. We're regularly invited to visit their website and blog site, download their podcasts, and subscribe to their web-based content as each media outlet competes for our loyalty across the blurred lines of the new media. This new media includes an Internet that is becoming so pervasive that accessing it is almost second nature. There are times when accessing the Internet is so expected that if the connection is not available—or worse yet, if the content is not available—we become frustrated. I regularly check news and sports updates on my cell phone, without feeling the need to turn on a television or radio. I get all my email on my phone. I do instant messaging with my IM list on my cell phone. And I even check and create some of my Twitter updates on my cell phone. If at any time, my cell phone connection is not available, I get very frustrated. I've come to not only expect it, but also rely on it.

Mobile devices play an important role in social media because, as a society, we have become so dependent on them. The innovators of social media applications are finding new and interesting ways for us to connect with each other. Location-based technology, as well as other interesting and useful mobile technologies, will continue to evolve, and social media applications will ride that wave with increasing momentum.

Social Enablers

A hurricane occurs when a tropical storm brews over the ocean. When it makes contact with warm ocean waters—if the temperature of the water is above eighty degrees Fahrenheit—the storm's heat and energy intensify. Winds rotate counterclockwise around a calm center called the eye of the storm. When the sustained speed of the winds reaches seventy-four miles per hour, the storm is officially classified as a hurricane.[13] Because I live in Florida, I'm exposed to tropical storms, which are tracked by meteorologists during the hurricane season, which runs from June through November. These weather professionals fill us with more facts and details than we really care about or, frankly, can comprehend. However, there is one fact we've heard on the evening news over and over again when following these tropical storms. Combining seventy-four-mph winds with water temperature reaching eighty degrees Fahrenheit produces a hurricane.

The social web, much like the hurricane, owes its explosive growth to a similar combination of twin factors that, when combined, result in the right climate for social media to become a hurricane.

---

13   Source: http://www.answers.com/topic/hurricane

The combination of the technology enablers, along with the social and demographic attributes of the world, has given rise to an explosion of social media that spans all ages and nationalities.

The youth of today only know high-speed Internet access. Anyone under age twenty-five never lived in a world without personal computers. And most young adults under the age of eighteen are accustomed to using devices and electronic gadgets, not all of which are connected to the Internet, but are nonetheless used in social ways.

The popularity of games such as Xbox 360, PlayStation, Nintendo DS, and the Wii is explosive, lending itself to a worldwide culture of people whose entertainment is supplied through technology at their literal fingertips. While kids and young adolescents are the primary consumers for these devices, there are many adults who enjoy them too.

The relationship of electronic gaming and entertainment to social media in business becomes more obvious with a second glance. First of all, the youth who consume these gadgets at lightning speed are the same youth who are now in the workforce. Business executives must understand the cultural and intellectual stimulus of this generation in order to harness its potential. The members of this generation are accustomed to using their fingertips and their minds to access information and process it very rapidly. If you have ever played an electronic game on any of the aforementioned devices, you may have had two experiences similar to my own. The pace of activity in most electronic games is incredibly fast. It requires a mind-boggling processing of stimuli coupled with highly coordinated activity with the fingertips. A kid who may not have much athletic skill can conceivably hold the highest score in FIFA 08 on a PlayStation game. The athletic skills of soccer on the field have absolutely no relationship to the skills needed to play electronic soccer. My own experience with most electronic games has been very humbling. I've always been pretty athletic and I stay in pretty good shape—but none of these attributes help me when playing electronic games.

Now, let's bring this discussion back to Web 2.0 and social media marketing in business. The point is that the shifting culture and demographics, combined with the availability of current technologies, have given rise to a worldwide population of people who are embracing social media more rapidly than we embraced the Internet. In other words, the environment is right for the social media hurricane to explode around the globe!

The shifting tide of how we spend our free time also factors into this. Today, people spend less time watching television and more time socializing on their computers. Television ratings for hit shows are down, as are ratings for traditional mainstream big television events such as the Super Bowl, World Series, and the Olympics. Many of us watching television often do so with a laptop on our laps, keeping tabs on real-time comments of the content we see on television. I watched President Obama's inauguration streamed live on the Internet through CNN on Facebook while sitting in my office. Look, Mom, no television!

The younger demographics of today's workforce, specifically those under thirty-five, are accustomed to using electronic tools for both work and entertainment. Workers who achieved their college educations within the past ten years had a laptop at their disposal during their school years, whether they owned one or accessed a PC at the school's library. Conducting research to write papers has been made infinitely simpler by *Googling* a topic to find vast amounts of information. Staying connected with friends through social media sites such as MySpace, Facebook, Bebo, and Xing is almost an everyday occurrence. Every one of these social and technological phenomena has appeared in the past ten to fifteen years. And like Moore's Law[14]—which states that the processing power of the computer doubles approximately every two years—the rapid pace of social media adoption has exploded, even blindsiding some people who now feel left behind.

Which demographic group was most affected, you ask? Mostly, it's people over the age of thirty-five. At the risk of offending some who fit this description—get over it. I fit this description, and even though I have embraced social media wholeheartedly, there is admittedly much going on in it that I can't relate to, no matter how hard I try. It has helped me

---

14   Source: http://en.wikipedia.org/wiki/Moore%27s_law

with my two teenagers at home who use most of the gadgets mentioned previously, and who also use MySpace and Facebook, as well as instant messaging. In fact, one of the most common struggles for parents of pre-teens and teenagers is monitoring the amount of time they spend on their computers, as well as what they do online. Can you relate to that?

In the workforce, businesses with executives over age thirty-five who have buried their collective head in the sand when it comes to the topic of social media find themselves facing a major risk. Social media has the potential to level the playing field for smart, enterprising marketers who embrace it as an effective mechanism for reaching a target market. Employees whose bosses don't embrace the social web are waiting for them to retire. In a strong economy, those employees won't hang around long before jumping ship.

When it comes to social media, the main point for businesses to understand is that the communities formed online comprising people who embrace social media are very influential. The myopic attitude of business executives who simply don't get the power of social media communities cannot only be blindsided—it can put them out of business. I know these are strong words. However, just keep watching—you may read about an example one day soon in your local paper or the *Wall Street Journal*. It's already happening in some industries, such as the print newspaper industry.

Just for a moment, let's get back to those kids who have the skills to use their fingers and their brains in a medium that so many business executives don't understand. These are the people who have already entered the workforce (eighteen-to-thirty-five-year olds). One such example is Mark Zuckerburg, CEO of Facebook, who was born in 1984. Yet by 2007, Zuckerburg was CEO of a company valued at $15 billion. Sure, there isn't an army of Mark Zuckerburgs out in the workforce, certainly not with his level of achievement. However, I argue that, in today's workforce and very likely within your own company, there are people very much like Zuckerburg. These are people whose creative juices and passion for ideas and innovation are fueled by the potent combination of the technological and social enablers discussed here. And they refuse to play by the old rules.

The rules I mean are the old way of doing things taught to many of us over thirty-five. Today's professionals make up their own rules. They don't run wild without regard for business protocol or business ethics. They innovate and go to market to reach target audiences with solutions that don't solve an existing problem and they make a market for it.

Zuckerburg started a social networking site at Harvard University for its students. He took this concept to the university student body en masse. When the popularity of his social networking site grew, he broadened the reach to *old people* over the age of twenty-five (his words, not mine). Along his journey to success, Zuckerburg has had a lot of help from friends who fit the same demographics. At the time of this writing, Facebook's fastest-growing demographic is people over thirty-five. It is considered one of the top five business social networking sites in the United States with huge global popularity.

While this story is just one in (pick your number), it is symbolic of the new generation of workers understanding both the power of the technology and the power of communities socializing online. This power is now so pervasive that businesses of all sizes must at least be aware of it, understand something about it, and actively search for ways of embracing it. Truth be told, there are some businesses that will never embrace it, and they are likely to fade away. Again, I know these are strong words, but that doesn't make them any less true, especially when it comes to business-to-consumer companies.

The most vulnerable businesses, those who should be racing to embrace social media, are companies manufacturing consumer products. This is especially true for those companies whose products are purchased by younger demographics. The younger demographics do not respond as favorably to many of the traditional shout-oriented marketing tactics. Television, print, and radio advertising has its place, but consumer products companies must consider shifting a portion of their marketing budgets online, because this is where their potential customers are, participating in communities, spending time friending each other, and helping shape opinions. Similarly, business-to-business companies that are capable of identifying a narrow niche market segment and can determine where this segment spends time online should also embrace social media. First-movers in social media marketing in specific market segments have a great opportunity to create brand awareness, strengthen a brand, or even reshape perceptions of a brand. However, at this point, the first-movers in most niches have only been there for a couple of years. Still, being absent from online communities (social media abstinence) is very risky.

FOSTERING COMMUNITY AND CONVERSATIONS

W henever I explain social media to business people, I use the following analogy. Think about a social event you attend with some regularity. Some common examples of regular events may include the chamber of commerce, industry or trade associations, conferences, Rotary, alumni clubs, community events, church gatherings, business clubs, and your health club or country club events. No matter the reason or the venue for the event, there are certain social do's and don'ts you have learned over the years. Perhaps you received some coaching on how to work the crowd or how to build relationships in these social gatherings. Most often, you've used common sense. One well-understood approach to successful social networking in the offline world is to be sincere and generous with your time and talents. This can take the shape of serving on a committee or offering your time and talents to a group or association. Volunteer work in social settings is often a very effective way to build relationships.

However, those who have years of experience serving in some volunteer capacity in any social setting understand that sincerity is paramount. People can smell insincerity a mile away. If you serve on a board or committee for the sole purpose of networking, relationship-building, or any other self-serving reason, your insincerity will eventually be recognized. The backlash can range from being cut off from meaningful relationships to a negative reputation, to even being kicked out of the community. In short, if you are a social member of a community, you have an obligation to be an upstanding citizen and contribute to it. It's really no different than the bigger picture of our social responsibilities in the world in which we live. When we disrespect our planet and its environment, bad things, like pollution, happen. When we show respect through contemporary green efforts, the effects on the environment are positive. And the effect on our reputation is also positive based purely on the sincere motive.

Perhaps you are one of those people who do not feel comfortable in these social gatherings, but you attend because you feel you have to. We have been trained and conditioned to behave a certain way at these social functions. In general, we should behave ourselves in a decent, professional, friendly, and cordial manner. Most of us could not even fathom doing or saying something at any of these events that has potential to tarnish our name or reputation. In fact, our goal is usually the exact opposite. Generally, we want to be contributing members of the communities to which we belong. We want to be well-respected—even liked—for being upstanding members of a community. Whether we admit it or not, there are certain protocols we follow to achieve that status of being liked, respected, and highly regarded in our communities.

A community can take many shapes and forms. At the simplest level, a community is a group of people who have something in common. The examples of the types of social events listed previously are based on some common interests ranging from local business, industry or market segment, religion, residential location, and fitness to the most narrow of reasons (e.g., a community of pit bull owners). In any community, there are two factions: the leadership and the membership. Leaders are a subset of the membership, but enjoy special privileges and powers, usually at the discretion of the membership. There are written and unwritten rules and protocols. Each community has a purpose and seeks to prosper. The prosperity of a community is often measured not in monetary ways but rather in altruistic ways. The growth and prosperity of a community is always the result of the community members' contributions and interactions with each other and certain actions they take (or don't take) in support of that community.

In my local community, the Tampa Bay Technology Forum (TBTF) organizes an annual fund-raising event called Tech Jam. It's known as "a party with a purpose" because 100 percent of the funds raised go to building and supporting local computer labs for kids living in economically stressed areas who don't have access to computers at home. Obviously, this is a great cause. Serving on the Tech Jam committee is a worthwhile volunteer activity. The sole purpose of anyone serving on this committee is to help this community achieve the annual fund-raising goal of the TBTF Foundation.[1]

Social media is all about communities. The only difference is these communities form online—on the web, in social networking sites, blogs and *groups* formed on the social web. The same protocols that apply to socializing in the offline world also apply online. The examples of communities discussed in the preceding paragraphs are nearly identical to the types of communities that are formed online. However, online social media breaks down the barriers of place, time, and physical size. Anyone can belong to a community that is open to others, regardless of their geographic location.

There are many online communities that are in fact purely social. However, these communities still operate under a common theme or purpose of some sort. Just visit Facebook to search for groups and you'll find communities focused on topics ranging from pets to real estate and just about any other topic. There are groups formed by people who are former employees of a company, which provides a great way to reconnect with former colleagues. There are communities formed around professional topics such as software development, financial accounting, sales professionalism, public speaking, and sports teams. And there are numerous communities built around hobbies and interests of all kinds, such as horse racing, dog breeding, mountain climbing, and yes, even basket-weaving.

---

1   Tampa Bay Technology Forum: http://www.tbtf.org/

When you join a group online, you are joining a community. The people in this community expect its members to behave according to the social morals and values we've grown accustomed to in the offline world. You are expected to be transparent, forthcoming, honest, sincere, and also to contribute something of worth. Admittedly, in the online world, you can easily hide in a community. You can just observe what goes on without contributing anything. You can't get away with that too easily in the offline world. But in online social media, you can hang out in a community and simply observe the conversations and interactions taking place. However, there is one thing you can't do in a community, whether in the offline world or online. You cannot be shamelessly self-serving. The community polices itself continually, and bad apples are rooted out rapidly. In the social media world, if you violate this protocol, you'll quickly be blocked from participation.

Another thing you should never do in social media is misrepresent your identity. John Mackey, CEO of Whole Foods, got in hot water for pretending to be someone else. He made comments about a competitor while disguised under another identity. When Whole Foods later acquired that competitor, he received much negative backlash for it.

In the communities that form online, people interact with each other. In social media, such interaction is known as *conversations*. Just like real-life conversations, conversations in the online community are very valuable and influential. Our modern media pundits have altered the definition of marketing to now mean *engaging in conversations with your target customers*. It is said that the marketing of yesteryear consisted of shouting at customers. Today, contemporary marketing revolves around engaging in conversations with customers and anyone else who is involved in the circle of life of your business.

If social media marketing is all about conversations and communities, then we're really talking about forging relationships on the web. This is a concept I've noticed some marketers struggle to grasp and embrace. To understand this, let's look at the types of relationships we form.

We generally have three types of relationships:

1. *Personal.* These are people with whom we have deep bonds, usually developed over the course of many years or for very personal reasons. These people include family, schoolmates, lifelong friends, neighbors, and fellow members of communities or clubs such as church, country club, or Little League. Any activity in which your child participates over time might result in close friendships. Generally, any social setting where the main characteristic of the relationship is a bond developed by getting to know someone personally without regard for socioeconomic attributes can be considered fertile ground for developing a personal relationship, especially if the age of the relationship spans many years. These relationships are with people you invite to dinner, take vacations with, and would drop almost anything to come to their aid, knowing they would do the same for you.

2. *Specialized.* These relationships most commonly involve people that we work with or have worked with. They come into our lives most often because we share a common profession. Another example involves clubs or associations we join where we meet and befriend people with common interests. These relationships can be very healthy and enjoyable, but they are usually more casual. These are people who don't typically get invited to our homes for dinner. However, while these relationships can become personal over time, the majority of them are casual, yet meaningful.

3. *Virtual.* These are people we meet online and we often never meet in person. In fact, many online relationships don't even result in a phone conversation. Most virtual relationships are just that—virtual. The nature of these relationships is usually far less personal. Unlike personal—and to some extent specialized—relationships, we are not limited by geography. The quantity of virtual relationships can become quite big, depending on your choice of online activities. When virtual relationships are carried offline, they have potential to transition into personal or specialized relationships. A common practice for virtual relationships is

to have a *meet-up* where people connect at an event or someplace with a common geography, and they carry their conversations into the physical realm.

In social media marketing, we are forging mostly virtual relationships. As marketers, there are at least two important attributes to understand about virtual relationships. First, virtual relationships do not require us to be as selective as specialized or personal relationships. We don't make big commitments in virtual relationships. These online relationships are casual, and it is generally understood that as a member of an online community, our role is to engage with each other when we have something meaningful to say or to contribute. Communities of people in online relationships are in a position to contribute opinions, content, and introductions to other relationships. These contributions offer great potential to marketers through the collective intelligence and collective influence of a community. Access to valuable opinions, content, and other relationships puts power at your fingertips (or mouse—depending on how you look at it) that was not available in years past. As marketers, it is vital we understand the power of these online relationships, as well as how to create them, how to leverage them, and what mistakes we must avoid in order not to damage them. As an example, in my business social networking, I have connected with Lola McIntyre, a successful real estate agent in Indianapolis. Lola listens to my podcasts and has been generous in her reviews and comments about them. I've had several productive contacts with Lola on LinkedIn and Twitter. We have a healthy virtual relationship. I've never met Lola or spoken with her by phone. Perhaps I may someday meet her or speak with her—and perhaps not.

The second attribute of virtual relationships is influence. Online communities are very influential. Their opinions and referrals are heard and often taken as gospel. What amazes me about the collective power of online communities is that it's not new. It is as old as civilization. Humans have always been influenced by word of mouth. The only thing new is the platform and the tools we use for global reach. Some who are more active than others in social media can influence more than others, but that's not new either. There have always been opinion leaders in social communities. It's the power of the medium that has propelled a centuries-old societal attribute into a modern-day phenomenon known as social media marketing.

DEVELOPING A SOCIAL MEDIA STRATEGY

With a discussion in previous chapters about the history of the Internet, the technology, and the social enablers as well as the role of communities and conversations providing foundational insights, let's get down to why you bought this book—*how to develop a social media strategy.* The very best place to begin is with your current organization chart. Each member of the leadership team should come to the table with his or her copy in hand and be ready to ask—and answer—some tough questions:

- Why do we think we need a social media strategy?

- What is our objective?

- What will the costs be?

- What are the staffing requirements?

- How will we measure results?

- What are the risks?

- What are the opportunities?

- What are our competitors doing in social media?

In this chapter, I will outline the most common components of a social media strategy. It's not my intent to suggest that every organization should use all of them. Instead, my intent is to explain them clearly enough so that you understand what they are and what may be the potential risks and benefits of each. You should decide which of these components fit your strategy and your organization.

Old School Meets New School

While Marketing 2.0 is a new-school marketing paradigm, there is no substitute for old-school research to gain valuable insights before you develop your social media strategy. Begin with research about your customers, target customers, online resources, competitors, and influencers. Take no less than a few days (at a minimum) and as much as a few months (depending on your industry, company size, and resources) to study the social web landscape in your industry. Conduct searches in Google, LinkedIn, and Facebook for the names of the CEOs of any company in your industry that is relevant. Include your competitors, your suppliers, and any other relevant company, including analysts and publications. Don't limit your name search to CEOs. Include any key people you know in your industry. Don't limit your search to these mentioned social networking sites. Include Twitter and YouTube as well as any industry-specific social web destinations. The objective of this research is to learn. If you are limited in staff, contract an eager MBA student intern who may just do a better job at this research than your internal resources anyway. Regardless of how you do it, this is a mandatory step that should not be cut short. If you don't do an adequate job at this research, you may develop a social media plan that is doomed from the beginning. This research should provide valuable insight into where your customers and relevant community are spending time on the social web. You'll learn what they're talking about and what *groups* exist by topic or by company. You'll learn what your competition is doing or not doing. Eventually, you will gain valuable insight that will drive your social media strategy.

Why Do We Think We Need a Social Media Strategy?

While I am a believer that most businesses can benefit from a social media strategy, if planned and executed according to their circumstances and staffing, this is still a very healthy question to ask. The research you conducted should answer this question very clearly. But let's explore this question anyway because it's a healthy exercise. This question is somewhat akin to asking, *What business are we in?* We've all heard stories of legendary executives who asked this question and shaped their business much differently than others would have. Walt Disney said, "We're in business to make people happy." The Disney empire started out producing films. If Disney had defined his business as film production, the company would not have ventured into many other forms of entertainment, ranging from movies and theme parks and other products, all of which exist to make people happy.

When you consider why you need a social media strategy, you should take some time and revisit this question about your core business. Why? Because if you have a good grasp on the answer to this question, it will be much easier to answer the question of why you may or may not need a social media strategy. A social media strategy serves one simple purpose: *it enables your company to engage in conversations with your community so you can improve your ability to attract and serve your customers.*

As I stated earlier, I do believe that most businesses should have a social media strategy. The reason I feel strongly about this is because, at a minimum, most businesses should be *listening to their customers' and potential customers' online conversations.* I am not suggesting that all businesses should be actively rolling out an aggressive social media campaign strategy. As this chapter unfolds, we'll discuss other factors to help you make that decision. The bare minimum, no-brainer decision is to find out where people have formed communities in your market and spend time listening to those conversations. Warning: being a no-show in those conversations may be harmful to your business.

What if there are no online communities in your market segment? If that is truly the case for you and your research proves it, you should watch carefully for the day when your community goes online. Don't assume it will never happen. Even blue-collar industries have vibrant online communities. Just do keyword searches in LinkedIn and Facebook, and you'll find groups worth monitoring. Consider starting your own group and building the first community in your market segment.

Ask yourself, *Which trade journals do I consider a must-read?* Which industry events do you consider must-attends? Most companies have developed a list of these must-attend and must-read events and news sources. I submit that most of them already have adapted to using Web 2.0 technologies. Do any of your must-read media deliver content that you can subscribe to through RSS? Can you download podcasts or videos from any of them? Can you post comments to articles you read in your industry? I'm sure the answer to at least some of these questions is yes. If you have already become active in consuming industry content through any of these aforementioned means, then you have already taken steps toward formulating your social media strategy.

My point is that these social media platforms allow us to be both content consumers and content producers. At a minimum, all of us should be consumers of social media-based content. So even if you never become a producer of content in social media, you should at least be an active consumer.

All I am suggesting is that—at a minimum—you should be actively consuming content on the social web, not just by email or from static websites. There are several ways to accomplish this. First, start by looking at mass media news outlets such as CNN, the *Wall Street Journal*, Fox, ABC, CBS, and NBC (or MSNBC). Visit their websites and you'll find content that you can subscribe to, download, and interact with. Do you want to be quoted in *BusinessWeek*? Visit *BusinessWeek* online and post comments to their articles. The same opportunity is available from many trade journals in your industry.

No matter what your industry may be, there exists online content that meets the Web 2.0 mantra.

So Begin Your Social Media Strategy by Listening!

You may be thinking, *This is no different than reading the content, which I've done for years.* That's exactly right! This isn't much different. However, the difference is that the content delivered to us on the social web is available to an abundant community on a technology platform (Web 2.0) that allows for engagement and interaction among all the consumers of the content. Unlike the read-only characteristics of News 1.0, the Web 2.0 platforms allow us to subscribe to content, and if we choose to participate, we can give our thoughts, opinions, and reactions to the news being reported.

So it's clear that the first answer to the question, *Why do we think we need a social media strategy?* is: because we owe it to our business to be actively listening to the conversations taking place online, and in most cases, we should be engaging in these conversations. Let's examine this further.

On one hand, it's obvious why we should be listening. It's the same reason we should be reading industry news—to stay informed. But remember that News 1.0 came at you from only one direction. The people whose job it was to deliver the news wrote it, and you read it. That's where it ended. In News 2.0, we are empowered to participate in the story. When you listen to the comments made by people who react to a news story, you are listening to your market in real time. Visit these stories online, make note of the dates on which the comments were made, and you'll often find people leaving comments on stories the same day along with a chronological history of people's comments from previous days or weeks. How valuable is that? I say it's hugely valuable! This is the very reason I feel strongly that all businesses should, at a minimum, be actively listening to conversations online.

Let's turn our attention back to the question of *why.* Now we're grounded in the principle that all businesses should be listening to online conversations, meaning we should all be consumers of social media. Still, should this mean that we also must become *producers* of online content?

Finding the right answer to this question means asking other questions first. Are your top competitors producing content? What do you risk if you become a producer? What do you risk if you don't become a producer? What commitment is required to becoming a producer? There are other questions to ask pertaining to staffing and budget, but these give you a great place to start.

If your top competitors are actively producing content in social media, your risk may be greater if you choose not to. It depends on your market position, but in general, your competitors might be capturing community and mindshare that eludes you. Your absence from online conversations may damage your brand. In short, competitive pressures may influence your decision to become a content producer.

If none of your competitors is actively producing content in social media, you may have an opportunity to be the first in your market segment, capturing both community and mindshare in the process. This alone is not reason enough to become a producer, but it is a factor worth considering. Being the first—or one of the first—to produce content using social media platforms enables you to accomplish two objectives. First, you strengthen your value to existing customers; second, you help build awareness within other communities who may be influential to future sales.

Remember, though, that using social media is not about direct sales. Social media communities are based on transparent, honest communication that informs, educates, inspires, and entertains. The point here is to let the content do the selling through its value to the community.

In summary, the most common answer to the *why* question is to gain access to online communities in order to build relationships that can ultimately leverage collective influence. Next, we'll examine how we should do this.

What is Our Objective?

You've done your research, and you've identified why you need a social media strategy. Now, it's time to clearly define your objectives. Your objectives should fall into one of these categories:

- Competitive differentiation

- Market share growth

- Your brand expansion

Let's consider ways to achieve each of these objectives.

Competitive Differentiation

A social media plan aimed at competitive differentiation is a wise strategy and often is a good place to start. The longer you wait to employ it though, the more difficult it may be, especially as your competitors begin engaging their own social media strategies. Achieving competitive differentiation through social media will, in the long run, eventually become a growth or brand strategy. Starting as a differentiation strategy in social media may initially require a lower budget and may be a lower risk approach. It can also be easier to get management buy-in as a first step. In many cases, it can be accomplished in one year or less if executed properly.

A competitive differentiation strategy requires you to increase your visibility on the social web in your market segment through online content commenting and new content creation. Identify the best sources of web-based content in your industry, including vertical industry media and associations. Task a member of your staff to monitor the content and the conversations in these online communities. Identify the subject matter experts in your organization who can get engaged in the conversations in these online communities or contribute new content. Consider a blog strategy if you have the staff to devote to it. Find a voice for your organization that can become a consistent voice in your market, delivering a consistent message on specific topics. Allow this voice to be active and free with ideas and valuable insights into the things about which the people in your industry care. Remember, this is not a direct sales strategy, though your management team may view it this way. Your differentiation goal is to allow the market to see how you think, how you serve, how you listen, how you respond, and generally how you add value to your market. Talking about your products in ways that interest your community is advisable. Shouting to them about features is not. Your goal is to make it easy for others to learn how your organization is different from your competitors. Encourage this voice to become well-known so that your organization achieves differentiation. One of the best differentiation outcomes you might achieve is for the person or people who execute your differentiation strategy to develop strong online personal brands.

When buyers in your market evaluate their choices, your organization's voice of differentiation on the social web can play a key role in making the short list of suppliers to consider even before they allow a live conversation to occur with your frontline sales team. Buyers turn to the web to do their research to identify suppliers of goods and services. By giving evaluators access to your voice of subject matter expertise, you set yourself apart from competitors who may still rely on their website and advertising to communicate their message.

In the case studies section, you'll read examples of competitive differentiation strategies, including BatchBlue Software and De Novo Strategy. BatchBlue Software competes in a very technical market and sets itself apart through blogging and video content. De Novo Strategy is a consultancy firm in a niche industry that differentiates itself by having a strong presence through a blog.

Market Share Growth

When we set out to grow our market share, we strive to increase revenue in our current or other market segment through our social media strategy. This is an admission that social media marketing is strategic to our business. This objective will require a strong strategy with an ongoing commitment to producing content. It requires you to revisit how you currently allocate your staff and your budget to ensure you can pull off a social media plan that will deliver measurable results. Presumably, you've established some differentiation in your social media plan through your content and platform strategy.

In setting out to grow your market share, you must be committed to staffing and producing diversified content on the social web. You must do more planning and be willing to experiment more often, even if it means taking more risk and failing some along the way. The objective is to attract more of your community to your organization. To do this, you need a bigger footprint on the web. If your differentiation strategy was primarily based on a blog, you may need to expand your strategy. There are several ways to do this. You might expand your blog from one topic to several topics staffed by several subject matter experts. You might commit to producing videos. A video content strategy is a bigger commitment of time, resources, and budget. For example, if you create a branded channel for video content, you can potentially expand your reach on the social web. You might commit to monitor and engage in discussions on the social web in groups. Groups are available in public-facing social networking sites such as LinkedIn and Facebook and can offer very easy ways to expand your reach. Similarly, you may find groups in industry-specific social sites where your staff can participate. By starting group discussions on the web, you expand your presence without leaving the office. This requires commitment, which carries with it some staffing implications, but this can be accomplished strategically when you map out your social media strategy and adjust your staffing requirements to meet this commitment. Cutting nonperforming marketing activities and reallocating staff resources to producing more social media content is certainly a plausible and popular approach to the staffing issue.

In the case studies section, you'll read examples of market share growth strategies including those from Blendtec and the Student Loan Network. Indium Corp. expanded its market share by adding more bloggers on more technical topics. It also added a video content strategy to its social media plan.

Brand Expansion

To expand your brand using social media requires a big commitment and carries some risk. Expanding your brand usually means you will also grow your market share. The tactics used for brand expansion can vary. Effective execution of brand expansion in social media is dependent in part on staffing and budget. It is also dependent on experimentation. You'll need to decide which social media platforms to use, who will create the content, and who will be the person presenting the content. The content strategy is the key to success in brand expansion. Presumably you've done your homework to find the audience you want to reach, and you're committed to producing the content that will reach them. You'll need to experiment with new content and content platforms such as social networks, blogs, video, or Twitter to find the right mix of content and platforms to reach your desired audience. You may find that some content is more effective than others in expanding your brand. You'll need to take some risk and measure results along the way to determine the effectiveness of expanding your brand through social media.

Brand expansion strategies are similar to market share growth strategies. The primary difference is the target audience. In brand expansion, you attempt to reach an audience that doesn't know much about your brand or perhaps perceives it differently. Blendtec was known among restaurateurs for its commercial blenders, but it was not well-known at all by consumers looking for a new blender for their kitchen. HubSpot has become known in the business-to-business industry as a software company that helps B2B companies manage their web strategies. HubSpot is also becoming known as a credible source of intelligence and advice for inbound marketing strategies. In fact, it is building a brand around the phrase, "inbound marketing," which it has popularized. HubSpot doesn't sell market intelligence services. However, brand expansion as a credible source of market intelligence leads to market share growth.

In the case studies section, you'll read examples of brand expansion including Blendtec, HubSpot, and Chris Griffith, Realtor.

Let Your Content Go

Remember that the fundamental purpose of developing a social media marketing strategy is to benefit from the power of communities. I've previously discussed the three types of social media platforms on the web:

sites offering published content, sites offering shared content, and sites offering opportunities for engaging in social networking. As a business, the most effective aspect of your strategy is to leverage all three of these platforms through your content. And to this end, I say just *let it go!*

One of the biggest cultural hurdles companies need to overcome is somewhat of a psychological one. We have been taught over the years to protect our content. Sentiments such as not letting our competitors see our content for fear of giving them insight into our strengths or weaknesses or (heaven forbid) our future plans, have driven this paranoia. Other than protecting what is truly proprietary content, forget that approach. To be blunt, that is old school. The new Marketing 2.0 approach is to let your content go.

The reality is that most of our businesses have more content than we know what to do with. We have white papers, news releases, websites, newsletters, and countless internal documents, not to mention the brilliant but undeveloped content residing in between our ears. The power of social media marketing lies in letting it all go. Share your content with the world. The truth is there is so much content floating around the web in social media platforms, the only way your content will get noticed is if it is as good or better than what already exists. So if you have good content for your community, share it, promote it, but most of all, just let it go.

This was just a warm-up for the next chapter. Now it's time to start thinking like a publisher.

THINK LIKE A PUBLISHER: CONTENT MARKETING

T hroughout this book, I have been evangelizing the concept of providing your community with good content. This chapter is devoted to the importance of content creation, as well as some content strategies that can have a big effect on your success in a Marketing 2.0 strategy.

In their book, *Get Content. Get Customers*,[1] authors Joe Pulizzi and Newt Barrett, when speaking about the revolution taking place between seller and buyer largely due to the availability of content made available to consumers online, make this point: "By the time customers are ready to talk to you—the seller—they are armed with information about your company, people, and products. ... In this way you have already begun a relationship that will make it easier for them to buy."

I find it amazing that this is obvious to us as consumers but less so as marketers. As consumers, we jump online to research products and services without even blinking an eye. As we find content about the products and companies we consider, we form opinions and we share those opinions with others both online and offline. Some of those opinions result in

---

1   Junta42: http://www.junta42.com/

either buying decisions or the elimination of products or companies as possible buying choices. In other words, when conducting our research, the content we consume online can influence our decision about which products or companies to exclude as much as it can influence those to consider in our buying decisions. *If we behave this way as consumers (at home and at work), then why don't we focus as much time, energy, and resource as marketers in producing quality content that our target audience can consume in order to begin their relationship with us before they even talk to us?* Notice how I've asked this question—it's about building a relationship with you before they contact you. Old-school marketing believes the relationship begins when the buyer contacts you.

Marketing 2.0 is about Building a Relationship with Your Buyer (Bridging the Gap Between You—the Seller—and Your Buyer) Through Social Media Marketing.

To address this topic, I will take off the gloves. Get ready—this may sting if you're still thinking in a Marketing 1.0 mind-set. If you are, you're still creating interruptive (outbound) marketing campaigns hoping for that 1 or 2 percent response rate. Your management team is still focused on measuring (only) leads and sales. You know by now that I care about measuring leads and sales. But when these are the only meaningful metrics, you're missing out on other valuable contributors to the success of your marketing plan.

The truth is that committing to a content marketing strategy requires a paradigm shift. It may even require revising your organization chart to adapt to the age of social marketing on the web. Making adjustments to your organization is crucial to your ability to adopt a content marketing (Marketing 2.0) strategy. If you're a sports fan, you know how important it is for a team to trade for players that fill holes in its team. A team is sometimes just one or two players away from being outstanding. Likewise, your marketing team may need some reshuffling to get the right talent in place for creating content in a Marketing 2.0 world.

On the social web, your content strategy is truly all about getting engaged with your customer. Let me put it another way. It's about getting intimate with your customer *before* he or she becomes your customer.

Let's examine the types of content we produce in our marketing efforts. For the purposes of this exercise, we will review GCA Technology Services, a provider of technical training services. GCA has a curriculum of courses on popular hardware and software platforms. It has a website that describes the company, its courses, where you can take the courses, the qualifications of its course instructors, and other details about its training services, as well as its value-added professional services. It advertises in search engines using Google Adwords to drive leads and registrations to its courses. Is has an inside sales force focused on calling into Fortune 2000 companies, all of whom are potential prospects for its technical training services. It sends regular email blasts to people who have previously attended its courses.

Does this sound familiar? These marketing strategies have produced relative success. The business is doing well. However, there is increased competition, and GCA feels it's not capturing as much business as it should. The potential is much greater than the current reality.

Enter the Marketing 2.0 mind-set. GCA decides to focus on building content around the most popular topics in technical training. It developed a dedicated website around one of those topics—identity management—and co-branded this website. However, it focused the main theme of the website around the topic of identity management and security, which all corporations are interested in. The website's content is focused on educating and informing corporations about the importance of identity management. Training solutions are offered but under the premise of educating site visitors on the crucial topic of identity management.

Additionally, GCA built its content strategy by researching the content found when searching on keywords such as *identity management training*. This research is crucial to its content strategy because it enables the company to simulate the process its prospective buyers experience. GCA learns what content will and won't be found and garners ideas from this research. It finds that most of its competitors are doing pretty much the same as it is with a website. So, it embarks on a content strategy that incorporates the following ...

Blogging. GCA initiates a two-part blogging strategy. It builds its own blog, which is headed up by Bill Nelson, vice president of professional services. He is well-qualified to blog on identity management topics due to his subject matter expertise. The approach in the blog is to offer tips and best practices on identity management. His exposure to client scenarios gives him nearly limitless ideas on content.

The other component to GCA's blogging strategy is to track other blogs in the industry that cover this same topic. Nelson tracks industry blogs using HubSpot and Technorati. He regularly comments on relevant blog posts. This helps to spread his influence on the subject of identity management throughout the blogging community. Whenever Bill posts a response to a blog post, he leaves a link back to the co-branded website, which is www.actionidentity.com. Many people research blogs when searching for services. Having a presence in the blogosphere builds credibility for GCA. Those who read the blog on the various topics about identity management are actually starting a relationship with GCA before they've ever talked to the company. If a GCA salesperson contacts someone who has read Bill Nelson's blog content, that contact is differentiated from GCA's competitors.

Forum. People sometimes confuse blogs and forums. In a blog, Bill Nelson proactively writes blog posts about relevant topics around identity management. Bill drives the content strategy. He comes up with the ideas for the blog content, and he writes each blog post. In a forum, the community can create its own *threads* around any relevant topic it wants. Others who join the forum can join in the threads and contribute to the conversation or ask questions. The main value of a forum lies in providing a platform for the community to serve itself by engaging with each other. Forum members are appreciative of the platform and give considerable loyalty to the host of the forum. A forum strategy doesn't require

GCA to create content; instead, it simply provides the platform for the community to enter and enjoy the conversations.

Frequently Asked Questions (FAQ). An FAQ section on a website is certainly not a new idea. Keeping your FAQ section up to date and comprehensive is important. Another aspect of the FAQ is using this content as feeder content into a blog by creating new blog content through inspirations garnered from the FAQ.

Newsletter. Like an FAQ, a newsletter is not a new idea. A newsletter developed under a Marketing 2.0 strategy provides a platform to link to other content platforms. It can link to the blog, the forum, the website, news releases, et cetera. A newsletter hosted on the GCA website is a great way for it to contribute to its SEO strategy because the content in the newsletter is indexed and shows up in search engine rankings. Therefore, what makes a newsletter a Marketing 2.0 newsletter is that it exists both as an email and a web-based digital asset, which helps broaden its footprint on the web.

News Releases. In years past, creating news releases required having major news to announce and typically meant hiring a PR agency to pitch it to the media in order to get coverage. On the social web, news releases take on a whole new meaning. Certainly a PR agency can still offer great value, but the social web makes it much easier to reach the media than ever before. In fact, the definition of the media is different than it used to be. If you consider the media just the news publications that cover your industry, you are only partially correct. You are restricting your reach by limiting it to just those publications.

Today, the media is anyone who is interested in your news and can access it online. News releases about anything that is of interest to your prospective customers should be distributed online. You don't need to wait until you ink a big deal to send a news release. Create news releases about the value of your services to your market. GCA sends out news releases about how identity management solutions help corporations protect their data, saving them money and preventing downtime. News releases have incredible potential to be indexed and ranked by search engines. People who read the news releases form brand impressions about GCA before they even have any contact with the company. They talk about their news releases in a human voice on the social web in their blog, on LinkedIn, Facebook, and on Twitter.

Website. The GCA website is an effective website. It's also a typical company site. It describes the company and its services and offers contact information, including links to register for its training courses. As described above, GCA has also created a website called Action Identity (www.actionidentity.com). This site focuses its entire content on the subject of identity management, also known as IDM. Building a dedicated website around one topic creates greater potential for developing search engine marketing strategies that drive traffic. The site's entire content focus is identity management, positioning GCA to attract more traffic on this topic. The dedicated website also positions GCA as an authority on the subject. While building a dedicated website in addition to a company website requires commitment and resources, the potential return on investment is huge. Consider how much more sales potential there is for people to find GCA not only through its corporate website or its blog, but also through the dedicated website on identity management.

Think of it this way. Rather than just one fishing pole with a baited line in the water, GCA has three. But, wait ... GCA actually has more than three.

Video. Far and away, my favorite form of content in Marketing 2.0 is video content. Why? Because video allows us to get creative and craft our message in completely different ways that are not possible with the printed word. Video requires a bit more planning, but it doesn't have to be expensive thanks to the availability of high-definition digital camcorder technology at price points under a thousand dollars. The most effective videos entertain us. Some of the most entertaining videos cover topics that would not otherwise be considered humorous topics. By adding some creative thinking, videos can communicate a message very effectively. At the time of this writing, GCA has not produced videos. But the creative juices are flowing about how people's identities in a corporation may be compromised. Imagine a video showing a guy in a T-shirt and jeans attending a board of directors meeting, listening in on confidential conversations. In the video, no one can see this person as he writes down details about the new product launch plans and pulls out his cell phone to call up the competition to tell them all about it. Are you starting to see the picture here? The same entertaining commercials you may have seen on television are possible in your business at a fraction of the cost—but with powerful reach potential.

Video content doesn't always have to be entertaining to be effective. Video content can be educational. If it's executed well and it's interesting to your target audience, it can be very effective. In the case studies, you'll read how HubSpot hosts a weekly Internet TV show that provides its audience with information—along with some entertainment value—about various web marketing strategies.

Podcasts. Podcasting is a very effective way to either create new content or repurpose older content into an audio (or video/audio) format. Often the most effective way to produce podcasts is to repurpose content. GCA has many instructors with great knowledge about their respective subjects. With so much knowledge between their ears, and limited time for writing new content, producing podcast content is a simple way to do this. By committing a limited amount of time, about two hours per month, instructors are interviewed by a podcast show host. With minimal prep time, mostly providing a list of questions for the interviewer, the podcast is produced using a TV news interview-style format. Since the instructor's content is in his or her head, the process of re-purposing this content is very efficient. The podcast content is then syndicated on various Internet channels including iTunes. It's also posted on the GCA website and blog for community consumption. Technical audiences are the most voracious consumers of podcast content, so this strategy a no-brainer for GCA.

Photos. Posting photos on the company website, as well as on other social media sites such as Flickr, can accomplish several purposes. While it's not traditional content in the sense of being educational, this form of content can provide a strong sense of culture and provide a human face to the company. Photos of students in classes, or instructors teaching and interacting with students, as well as other related photo opportunities, can truly provide some key differentiation for GCA.

White Papers. White papers are a common and popular marketing tool. GCA uses white papers on the social web by saving them to PDF format and optimizing them. Adobe provides optimization features in the current version of Acrobat, which makes PDF documents search engine-friendly. Additionally, discussing the content of white papers in a blog or forum with links to them also helps promote the content. The premise to successful white papers is, of course, to provide good content that addresses your community's interests and share it with your community on the social web.

PowerPoint Presentations. Many organizations have a library of Power-Point (PPT) presentations. While some PPT files are not intended for external viewing, many of them have content that can be repurposed and shared with your online community. At the time of this writing, a popular and free social media platform for PPT is Slideshare.[2] Simply open a free account on Slideshare and upload your PPT files. Slideshare converts the PPT to a URL that you can share with your community. You can link your Slideshare PPTs on other social sites including LinkedIn and Facebook. Slideshare's popularity is growing. Many people use Slideshare to conduct research. Your PPT content may become part of people's research, which gives you added exposure on the web and potential traffic to your website from yet another social web platform.

Consider the differentiation for GCA when prospective buyers of its training and professional services uncover various forms of content on

---

2   Slideshare: http://www.slideshare.net

the web ranging from blogs, websites, news releases, podcasts, video, and photos.

A content strategy similar to the one described above, which is a work in progress at GCA Technology Services,[3] requires two ingredients to be successful. First, the CEO must be willing to think like a publisher. I call this subscribing to a Marketing 2.0 mind-set. Without CEO commitment to this strategy, it won't succeed. Second, the team charged with executing this strategy must be the right team. Without the right people on the bus (to borrow from Jim Collins' best-selling book, *Good to Great*),[4] a content strategy won't succeed. Content marketing strategies require some out-of-the box thinking and creativity. Those who do it well seem to have a lot of fun with it and enjoy their success. Those who do it really well set themselves apart from their competitors. Those who do it well develop a strong understanding of the culture of the social web and how important communities are on the web. On the social web, feeding good content to your communities with regularity truly builds relationships with buyers before they ever contact you and creates winning marketing programs with measurable success.

---

3   GCA Technology Services: http://www.gca.net/
4   Jim Collins: Good to Great: http://www.jimcollins.com/

PERSONAL BRANDING

The very essence of a Marketing 2.0 strategy is based on people in your organization engaging other people and building relationships. Along the way, the transparency of the social web, coupled with its powerful reach, gives people an identity, which becomes their personal brand.

The term *personal branding* is relatively young, but the concept is nothing new. Before the advent of the social web and its many opportunities for personal branding, we just referred to our *reputation*. If you're old enough to remember building a career before the Internet, our reputations were something that followed us from job to job. We used personal referrals through the relationships we built to maintain and enhance our reputations. Our reputations were built by our achievements and supported by the relationships we built throughout our career. Those relationships included our peers, bosses, subordinates, customers, trade association colleagues, and people in our community. As we traveled around in the course of our careers, our reputations followed us through a chain of phone calls and live conversations, not to mention old-fashioned letters of referrals. Our reputations have never been limited to our performance on the job. If your colleagues also knew about your sense of humor, your community involvement, family activities, and hobbies, those aspects of your lives often were assimilated as part of your reputation.

Fast-forward to 2009, and our reputations aren't even called that anymore. Now it's called our personal brand. This concept of the personal brand is one that many people don't quite yet understand in a corporate setting. There are real dangers in not understanding the concept of a personal brand and how to develop and manage one. There is also a danger for employers to attempt to stifle employees from building their own personal brands. The truth is that an employee who builds a good personal brand has two benefactors: himself or herself, and his or her employer.

Let's start with the basics. To build your personal brand, start by filling out your online profile on social networking sites including but not limited to LinkedIn and Facebook. If you're willing to devote the time to Twitter, then go there as well (I recommend it). If you're willing to devote even more time to it, create a Flickr account featuring photos and a YouTube channel where you can aggregate videos about your favorite topics.

It's critical to understand one point though: before you set out to build your personal brand, remember that whatever you put online stays online. Your personal brand is you, both professionally and personally. If you think you can build a personal brand about your nine-to-five life and a separate personal brand about your life in the evening and on weekends, think again. Our lives have converged into one platform on the web. In this sense, our lives really have become open books on the social web.

Whether the economy is weak or strong, employers use the web as a key resource for researching prospective employees. They can easily read about your work experience, check your references without lifting the phone, and see your personal interests and community involvement just with a few clicks. All of this may occur before you even walk in the door for your first interview.

Buyers do the same thing. They research your company, your products, and your reputation in the market. They also take a close look at the personal brands your employees have built on the web, if any exist. This research is used as a basis for forming impressions about your business based on the personal brands of the people in your organization, especially those contributing content or commenting on it on the social web.

How can you help your staff build their personal brands while also benefiting your organization? Start by embracing this concept, understanding that you both have much to gain from it. Next, if you haven't already, set out to build your own personal brand, get started today. In most cases, whatever you do to build your personal brand, you should encourage your staff to consider doing the same, although you should give them some guidance in expressing their unique personalities. It's important to know the area of expertise of your team members and encourage them to build personal brands centered on those strengths. Start with the basics described above. Create a footprint on the social web by getting them actively engaged in social networking sites. Make sure their profiles are complete and up to date. At first, it's tempting to limit yourself to just one platform to get your feet wet. A popular place to start for business professionals is LinkedIn. Fill out your entire profile. Upload a current picture of yourself. Once you've filled out your profile, you're ready to get started connecting with people you know either directly or indirectly. Use the search feature to find people you used to work with or went to school with or who are from your hometown, and connect with them. Be aware of the unique terminology used in each platform. In LinkedIn, you connect with others. In Facebook, you friend others. In Twitter, you follow others.

Chances are you're already using at least one of these social web platforms. That's great! However, are you building your personal brand on each one and encouraging your staff to do the same? Perhaps your staff has a head start on you and they've been bugging you to get started. You've resisted either because you think it is for kids or because you're very busy and don't have the time. Well, Mr. or Ms. CEO, I've got news for you. Many of your peers are already there. Your absence is obvious. The train has left the station. Get on board!

Perhaps you belong to an association of professionals where a private online group is formed. The same principles apply. Even if LinkedIn or Facebook aren't your thing, chances are there is a place on the social web where you can connect with people that matter to you and where you matter to them.

Once you have your social profiles completed, how often do you upload content to your personal profile or to industry social sites? How often do you recommend others in your network? How often do you answer questions in online discussions? How often do you ask questions? How often do you check each of these platforms? Once per month? Once per week? Daily? More than once each day? In order to develop your personal brand, you must be active in the online social platforms. Think back to the networking examples given previously. If you show up to the networking club just a few times throughout the year, you will not build your personal brand or any meaningful relationships.

While we are all unique individuals with unique personalities and talents, establishing your personal brand online requires that you must be interesting. I didn't say you need to be funny or good-looking. Being interesting simply means you have something meaningful to say.

Here are some tips to consider in building your personal brand on the social web:

- *Be visible.* Whichever social web platform you choose to join, stay active in it. When you are active, you will be noticed more and you'll enjoy more opportunity to engage with others.

- *Be interesting.* Whatever your subject matter expertise, you probably have ideas to share. Think of creative ways to express your thoughts. Ask questions meant to get people thinking. Remember that, very often, what is obvious to you is probably not so obvious to others. Don't be shy about expressing your points and stimulating new conversations.

- *Be a contributor.* Similarly, share your insights. We live in an economy where our content is our marketing. When you have good content to share, by all means, share it! You'll get recognized for it. Don't be surprised if you get invited into more conversations or invited to speak or write because you have contributed good content.

- *Push the envelope.* This one requires discretion, especially if you are employed (as opposed to being self-employed) or you are the

CEO. You don't want to create controversy that can have a negative effect on both you and your company. Be provocative and
thought-provoking with your ideas or methods of getting things
done. Brent Britton (see the Attorney 2.0 case study later in this
chapter) pushes the envelope by creating his personal brand very
differently than most attorneys. This ranges from his nontraditional attorney attire to how he spends his time building relationships online and offline. In the end, his success speaks for itself.

- *Be real.* Authenticity is critical. The social web is not a place to
  act or be someone you're not. You may get away with it for a little
  while but not for long.

- *Develop easy ways for people to find you.* If you do a Google search
  on *personal branding,* the number one listing (in early 2009) is a
  blog called, "Personal Branding Blog by Dan Shawbel."[1] Dan has
  written a book called *Me 2.0* with a proven four-step process to
  building a personal brand. Develop your personal brand around
  something specific that you can use as your unique value proposition that will easily be found. Even if it doesn't boil down to a
  single phrase, as in this example, you can still become known for
  something like, *"the gal you want to hire if you need to launch a
  new product in the (fill in the blank) industry."*

Promote your personal brand by promoting your presence on the
web. Start with simple tactics such as including links to your social web
profiles in your auto signature, on your business card, on your website,
in your blog, on your T-shirt (okay, that one is a little farfetched, but you
get the point). If you have a blog, include graphic links to each of your
social web profiles and invite people to connect to you. Don't miss any
opportunity to invite people to connect with you on the social web in

---

1   Personal Branding Blog: Dan Shawbel: http://personalbrandingblog.wordpress.
    com/danschawbel/

your daily written or oral communications. Remember, Marketing 2.0 is a mind-set.

Even world-renowned people like internationally acclaimed marketing consultant, author, speaker, and blogger Guy Kawasaki[2] make it easy to connect with them. People like Kawasaki understand the value of both personal branding and connecting on the social web.

If you are going to make yourself available on the web, you need to be truly available. When someone connects with you or contacts you on the social web, you should respond. Sure, there are some obvious frivolous connections you could ignore, but you'll find that most connections are not frivolous. Generally speaking, do *not* make the mistake of assuming that someone is not worth your time. The person you ignore today just might be influential one year from now. You wouldn't want that person remembering that you thumbed your nose at her. Treat everyone on the web as if he or she were Guy Kawasaki.

Building your personal brand is too important a task to ignore. Businesses that understand the value of a personal brand do more than simply accept the concept. They embrace it. One of my favorite examples of a well-built personal brand is the one belonging to Matt Cutts of Google. His personal brand is very recognizable to people in the Internet industry. Google benefits greatly from Cutts' personal brand because he is so effective at conveying both who he is as a person and as a Google engineer. With Matt, Google has a very effective face in the community. Matt Cutts portrays Google in a very human manner. This is very effective considering how big Google as a corporation. Its ability to be represented by a plain, ordinary engineer with a friendly and intelligent demeanor is brilliant. Matt has become a rock star in the Internet industry. His personal brand is a great asset to himself and an equally great asset to Google.

I wrote this book for companies much smaller than Google. However, the Matt Cutts example should get you thinking. So, consider how you can achieve a personal branding success story similar to Google's by allowing really talented people in your business to develop their per-

---

2   Guy Kawasaki: http://www.guykawasaki.com/

sonal brand for their benefit and the benefit of your company's brand. If it frightens you that your employees may leave once they develop their personal brands, I believe you have other problems to address. In the age of marketing on the social web, such insecurities will backfire on you. A strong personal brand benefits both you and your employees, assuming other healthy employment practices are in place.

Personal branding is nothing more than the new media version of managing your reputation, only in a much more public and socially dynamic forum. You can't fight it. Instead, embrace it because it offers you exceptional value. Personal branding may not have a line item in your marketing budget, but it is still one of your strongest marketing assets. Yes, it takes time to develop it, and even more to maintain it. There is also a strong argument against preventing employees from developing their own personal brands. Understand this: one way or another, they will do it because the technology and the culture is in place. You may as well encourage them to do it in a manner that benefits both of you.

Case Study: Personal Branding with Attorney 2.0, Brent Britton, ESQ

I have witnessed firsthand the Marketing 2.0 style of a hip attorney named Brent Britton. I asked him to summarize his marketing strategy for this book. When I received his email, I decided to publish it unedited to give you insight into his personality and marketing style. Clearly, Mr. Britton understands the power of personal branding. Do a Google search for his name, and you'll find several links to him on the social web. Below is Brent Britton's firsthand account of his Marketing 2.0 strategy, which is summarized by building and fostering relationships both online and offline:

> *"I am a lawyer running a very busy technology law practice. I use the Internet to connect with my current and future clients and instill in them the necessary confidence that I am the right lawyer for all of their legal needs. I do this with my Web bio, emails, and*

direct messages of various types, as I have done continuously since I first began using the Internet in the early 1980s.

"More recently, however, I have been able to imbue my business development efforts with unprecedented breadth and scope using some of the new social networking tools, including my pages on Twitter, Facebook, and LinkedIn, and with my blog and my podcast.

"Few business people hire lawyers they do not know personally. Clients almost always hire a lawyer based on some history of personal contact; hence the adage, Clients hire lawyers, not law firms. In most cases, a law firm's brand is largely meaningless. Unless the dudes the firm is named after are hanging out in the lobby serving cocoa, they are absolutely irrelevant to my clients and me. *My* brand is far more important. And my brand is the aggregation of every interaction I have with my current and future clients.

"In this business, networking rocks the house; successful lawyers have always been great social networkers. The new tools available on the Internet today just make that process much easier and efficient, for those who are willing to adapt their client development strategies accordingly. Those who are unwilling to adapt will, as in nature, undergo attenuation in their capacity for survival. If you're not on the net, you have no brand. You do not exist.

"In the past, to build my brand equity, I had to meet new clients face to face and impress them in that context, often on the spot. Turns out I'm pretty good at that, but no one gets a slam dunk every time. Perhaps they would hear me speak at a conference or read a magazine article I wrote, but there was little else they could do to learn about me or get inside my head short of meeting me and spending time with me in person. And my bandwidth for that has been and always will be, regrettably, quite limited.

"Social networking tools have increased my networking bandwidth substantially. The power of these technologies is in how they increase the power and reach of my brand. My future clients can now time-shift how they learn about me and discover how I think

in a manner that is completely untethered from scheduling conflicts.

"Here's what I do when I am communicating with current and potential clients:

1. *I assume everyone is a potential client if they aren't a current one. Every caller, every emailer, every reader of every tweet.*

2. *I always answer emails and phone calls on the same day or the next.*

3. *I always answer text messages as soon as I see them.*

4. *I write/post/communicate with as high a level of authenticity as I can possibly muster. Nothing, absolutely nothing, will ruin you and your reputation on the net faster than dishonesty. And the truth always comes out. Everything is on the record and the record will be preserved and studied. On the net, dishonesty is a big fat CFIT.[3]*

5. *I tweet once or twice daily, on average. I try to keep my Twitter presence relatively constant, though I do experience highs and lows. I try to mix my tweets about 50/50 about the law versus about other things, even just silly puns. LinkedIn is my resume; Twitter is my personality.*

6. *I auto-direct my tweets to update my Facebook status. Lots of people read me on FB who do not use Twitter.*

7. *I join LinkedIn groups and participate in the conversations, especially answering substantive legal questions.*

8. *I try to blog every Monday morning, usually about entrepreneurship. If I do not have time to compose something thoughtful, interesting, or at least entertaining, I do not try to phone*

---

3   CFIT definition: http://en.wikipedia.org/wiki/CFIT controlled flight into terrain

it in. The minute your blog gets boring, no one comes back. It's got to be great every time.

9. *I accept nearly every FB friend request and I follow back nearly every Twitter follower.*

10. *I honor requests from other sites like Plaxo, but I do not actively participate in these communities.*

11. *I am fortunate to co-host a radio show—The CEO Lounge[4]— that gets posted as a podcast on iTunes. I am also working on others."*

Brent C. J. Britton
http://brentbritton.com
http://twitter.com/bcjb

---

4   CEO Lounge: http://www.tampabayceo.com/ceolounge.html

THE LIFECYCLE OF
INTERACTION IN SOCIAL
MEDIA MARKETING

n previous chapters, I spoke of social media as comprising online communities where people collaborate with each other, share content, and in general share a collective influence or a collective wisdom with and through each other. The popular cliché concerning the wisdom of the crowd—or *crowdsourcing*—is an apt characterization of this phenomenon in social media. Crowdsourcing refers to the act of seeking help, advice, or input from a community of people online who collectively qualify to provide the desired input from the asker.[1] Let's examine this in the lifecycle of social media interaction from a marketer's perspective. The purpose of this chapter is to give marketers guidelines to develop social media (Marketing 2.0) strategies while driving and measuring results.

In social media, there are four stages of interaction. These stages are not always linear. Rather they are iterative and dynamic. Nonetheless, there are distinct stages of interaction in social media:

---

1   Crowdsourcing definition: Wikipedia: http://en.wikipedia.org/wiki/
     Crowdsourcing

- Engaging

- Listening

- Interacting

- Measuring

Engaging. When embarking on a social media marketing strategy, the first place to start is identifying the communities that are meaningful to your business. In plain words, let's fish where the fish are. Once you find them, you must engage them. It's about connecting with them and giving of your time and talents. The first part—connecting—is not so hard to grasp. You go to social media sites, find people with common interests, and connect with them. Keep in mind that the social media sites you use may vary according to your industry and geographic location. In the United States, sites such as Facebook, Plaxo, and LinkedIn are popular social networking sites for business professionals. In Europe, Xing[2] is a popular social networking site. Twitter has rapidly been adopted as a popular tool for engaging people. Additionally, industry-specific social networking sites have been rapidly emerging. One such example is ITToolBox, which attracts interest from members of the information technology (IT) community. The key idea here is to seek out social networking sites in your industry and get engaged with those communities.

Engaging people starts with asking people to be your friend. If this sounds a little weird or even childish, don't worry—you'll eventually warm up to it. Remember our earlier discussion on social networking in the physical world? When you meet people in a social setting and you engage them, you are *friending* them. It's just an expression. It doesn't mean you have to become best friends or that you're inviting them over to dinner. Remember, these are your virtual friends. You'll find that most of your new virtual friends in social media are people you may never meet. And chances are good you may never even have a phone conversation with most of them. The friending relationships with most of your com-

---

2   http://www.xing.com

munity will almost always be online. This is part of the phenomenon in social media. For some of the people in the younger demographics, this is normal behavior. For others of you out there over thirty-five (like me), you'll grow accustomed to it quickly.

Don't be overly selective about the people you friend in social media. The general criteria should be commonality of industry or topic. For example, my common topics are social media marketing, Internet marketing, or search engine marketing, all of which are related. When I friend people, it doesn't matter how old they are, what they do for a living, or where they are located. In fact, I invite you to be my virtual friend on the social web. You'll find my social web links in the contact section in the front of the book.

Once you engage people, you must give of your time and talents. This is a concept, I have found, that many marketers don't understand. I believe this is because, throughout your career, you've been trained that Marketing 1.0 is all about pushing your message out to the consumer and asking for something back in the form of a lead or some other conversion that can be measured. Your boss requires you to measure results, and the lowest-hanging fruit in Marketing 1.0 to measure has always been the proverbial conversion, also known as a lead, or a sale. In social media marketing, we must first learn to give in order to get. In fact, I argue that you should not even think about getting anything! Now, c'mon, pick yourself up off the floor. You'll still be able to measure results. Keep reading …

When you give of yourself, you are getting engaged in your community. You are building relationships, which are intended to bridge that gap between seller and buyer. Again, I remind you of the discussion earlier about our social lives in the physical world. We engage in conversations, we offer our thoughts and recommendations, we volunteer for committees, and we do these things all the time. Giving of ourselves is the first place to start in any social setting. Remember, social media marketing is a natural extension of our human desire to be social creatures. The only difference here is that our desire is capable of being manifested online by the technology enablers discussed earlier and accelerated by a global audience willing to embrace it.

Giving of your virtual self in social media can look something like this. You select your favorite social media destination sites and visit them frequently. You respond to questions being asked by people. For example, in LinkedIn, there is a feature called Answers, where people ask for advice on various topics. You look for and find questions that you are qualified to answer and answer them. On Twitter, people ask for opinions or drop links to articles and surveys, and you respond with your insight, not with a plug for your product. You offer your opinions, your expertise, and your thoughts wherever and whenever the opportunity presents itself. However, you always do this in a giving way, expecting nothing in return. Do not—I repeat—do not ask for something in return. Remember, you would not do that at a cocktail party, so don't think about doing it in a social media situation. If you violate this basic tenet of online etiquette, you'll discover that online communities can be very unforgiving.

In summary, engaging in social media with an attitude toward giving will bring you many virtual friends. You'll build a good reputation for yourself and your company, assuming your identity is tied to your company.

Listening. Engaging and listening are very closely tied, but there is a distinction. I opened this section with a clear emphasis on the importance of engaging. I just explained the importance of giving of your time and talents, which is the art of offering *value* to your community.

Listening is also an important aspect of social media. In fact, I argue that one of the most measurable aspects of social media is what you learn online when you listen. Listening can be incredibly informative. Listening to your community is part of the wisdom of having a community. Often, there are thought leaders in your community with good insights. Your online friends will send you links to articles, blog posts, videos, photos, and other content that can give you valuable insights that you may not have otherwise found. Listening also lets you tap into market intelligence. Your company may be launching a new product, and if you listen carefully, you may hear something from your community that enhances your launch strategy. Now I'm not referring to one isolated comment. I'm referring to sentiments expressed by your community as a whole.

Remember that listening and engaging do go together. One typically leads to the other. When you hear comments from your community, you can engage the members in conversations about those comments. Be careful not to be argumentative with those whose opinions may differ from yours. If you encounter unwarranted disparaging remarks, consider recruiting the aid of other friends in the community to intervene on your behalf. It is more effective for others to defend your brand than for you to do so. Your defense should be a good offense with positive feedback and guidance. Don't ever fight against the sentiment of the online community. If your brand has a problem, admit it and discuss how you're addressing it. Such honest disclosure is more effective than trying to defend it. Dell learned this lesson the hard way when in 2005, customers complained about shoddy products and customer service. All the complaints were on the web. The phrase "Dell sucks" linked to a blog post ranked on page one in Google. Dell wasn't listening and took a beating. Eventually, they responded and set up online communities for customers to engage them, and they engaged them back. The backlash took some time to recover from, and to this day, it's known as "Dell hell" and is probably studied in MBA classes around the world.[3]

When you engage your community, you may try to take some conversations offline for further insight, but you must first earn that right. If you do take the conversation offline, do more listening. Don't sell. When you take it offline for a meet-up or phone conversation, the same social rules apply. Be giving and listen. If you start selling, you'll squander the value of the online relationship. There are many online communities who do meet-ups. Industry conferences are one great example of this. If you're traveling to a conference, it's always a good idea to let your community know and offer to meet-up for coffee to continue conversations and build in-person relationships. Often these meet-ups get mentioned online, and your reputation and relationships can grow more because of it.

In summary, listening to the wisdom of the online crowd can offer valuable insights into your market, your competitors, your products, your

---

3   Dell Hell: http://www.buzzmachine.com/2005/07/01/dell-hell-seller-beware/

employees, your opportunities, and your brand. Listening also can result in some of the most measurable results in social media marketing, which can impact the effectiveness of the decisions you make.

Interacting. When we engage our community, we share our insights and we listen to the community's insights, ideas, and opinions. When we engage our community, we *interact* with it. In this section, you'll discover ways you can interact in proactive marketing while playing by the rules of social media marketing.

In your career, you've earned the right to (finish this sentence according to your career specifics). Earning the right to do something in any business circumstance means you have the authority, credibility, or know-how. Let's sum this up by using the word *credibility*. When you begin interacting with your audience, you should have some credibility. You may be just beginning to build credibility within your community, or you may be fortunate to have it from day one based on your recognized accomplishments within your industry. Either way, interacting with your community can take several forms.

First, I'll touch on personal interaction, referring again to the cocktail party analogy. People interact with people in a social setting because they enjoy the personal interaction. We are not robots. We are people with interests and personalities. In social media, it is both common and advantageous to show your true personality. In fact, the genesis of social networking stems from being very personal. When you fill out your first profile, you'll display lots of information about yourself, including your gender, your location, marital status, interests, et cetera. I personally enjoy seeing comments from prominent people I follow online about the photos they've taken, their daughter's wedding, or whatever personal tidbit it may be. If you're wondering what this has to do with marketing— the short answer is everything! Remember, we're out to bridge the gap between seller and buyer on the social web.

If you've been involved in sales at any level, you know that entertaining clients is all about getting to know them personally in order to build stronger relationships. Opening discussions—sometimes called icebreakers—in business settings are often about something other than the business at hand. Social media affords us the opportunity to be ourselves while gaining personal insights into the people in our communities. Don't be all work and no play, or you'll be perceived as boring and only interested in advancing your business cause. In other words, allow yourself to have some fun with social media and allow others to enjoy their interaction with you.

Interacting with your community on the social web can be very effective, but it must be approached carefully. Proactively asking people their opinion on relevant industry topics is certainly one way to have meaningful interaction. Posting links to blog posts or articles and asking for reaction is another way. Even if people don't respond, you're still interacting with your community by sharing content. Don't worry about how many people respond, especially if you're a newbie in social media circles.

However, responding to other people's shared comments or content is another effective way to interact. This shows you have interest in them or their content. Respond with sincere thoughts and insights. Avoid sounding like you're a groupie.

Building awareness for cool and interesting things that you or your company are doing is a good way to interact, but you must earn the right to do that. If you are not a regular member or a long-standing member of an online community and you just drop in once a week and post a link to your press release about a product announcement, you'll bomb. You haven't earned the right to do that. It's akin to crashing a party. Trust me, it's a big mistake! Don't do it.

On the other hand, if you are a regular member of an online community, or you have a well-earned reputation, you have earned the right to share your content, even if it is a news release. However, you may not actually post a link to the news release. You may post a link to someone who wrote about the announcement in the news release. Remember, the power of social media lies in the wisdom and influence of the crowd. Anyone can write a news release. But we need to face the fact that a news release has no real credibility anymore. What matters most is what people think about the subject in the news release. So getting a reaction to your news release and posting a link to that reaction would be more effective than posting a link to the news release itself. This allows you to truly engage people in your community because the link is to genuine content, not a canned news release.

In the personal branding chapter, I wrote about Matt Cutts[4] from Google. Matt is a senior engineer at Google who has become the face of Google. He regularly blogs, attends conferences, speaks, participates in panels, and generally communicates Google's position on a variety of technical and policy matters. The fact that Google has personified their company through a regular joe like Matt Cutts is a brilliant marketing strategy. Matt's interaction with the community is genuine, not canned or corporate. He wears T-shirts and jeans and doesn't ever sell anything. He just interacts with his community from a position of credibility and passion on search engine topics, something he is imminently qualified to speak about. When Google distributes a news release, Matt is asked by his community to comment on it. Matt usually proactively comments on news releases in his blog before being asked. For example, when Google announced that Adobe was making Flash content more search engine-friendly, Matt wrote a blog post[5] about it in which he offered his opinion and insights.

Here is the good news: you don't have to be Google to effectively interact with your community. But you can take a page out of its book. Google's strategy is to use one employee who acts as the primary point of contact for the company within the online community. In the end, Google's interaction with its community is more effective because it is interacting using social media. Any company of any size can do this—including yours.

The fourth element in the lifecycle of interaction on the social web is measuring. Measuring results is one of the most controversial and widely discussed topics in social media marketing. And therefore, it warrants its own chapter.

---

4   Matt Cutts blog: http://www.mattcutts.com/blog/
5   Matt Cutts blog post about Adobe/Google announcement: http://www.mattcutts.com/blog/google-gets-better-at-flash-with-adobes-help/

MEASURING RESULTS IN
SOCIAL MEDIA MARKETING

M easuring results is one of my favorite topics in marketing. Since the invention of marketing (I couldn't find that date in Wikipedia), executives have wanted to measure the effectiveness of marketing dollars against sales in order to determine their *return on investment,* or ROI. I've worked for bosses in my career, and in more recent years for clients, who are very intent on measuring the ROI on their marketing spend. So I'm very comfortable with the whole idea of measuring marketing results.

The reality is that in recent years, measuring marketing results, at least at the quantitative level, has become increasing sophisticated through tools and techniques. There also is a qualitative element to measuring marketing ROI that is somewhat more difficult, though it is still possible. In addition to quantitative metrics, measuring qualitative results can be just as valuable. Let's first look at measuring quantitative results.

Quantitative social media marketing measurement is very similar to measuring other web marketing results. Therefore, let's start with a look at the conventional web marketing metrics tools, beginning with some free and simple tools. You may be familiar with some or all of these tools.

To my surprise, I often meet marketers who are not harnessing these tools to their full potential.

Google Analytics[1]—a free web analytics service that provides website owners valuable insight into website traffic details including visitors, sources of visitor traffic, pages visited, time spent on website, keywords driving website traffic, geographic location of visitors, conversions based on predefined goals, and much more. Setting it up is as easy as adding some code to your website. One way Google Analytics can be used to measure social media marketing results is by observing the sources of traffic to your website. When you see that traffic to your website comes from social media sites where you and your staff spend time, you gain some insight into the effect of your social media marketing strategy. You can also measure "goals" that you define. For example, visitors who reach a certain page such as the "thank you" page after completing a form can be a goal. Such insight admittedly represents only a high-level view, but it remains worthwhile nonetheless.

Google Webmaster Tools[2]—another set of free tools from Google, these provide another level of detail in studying traffic data for your website. Here you can see the last date your website was crawled by Google. It provides many other valuable metrics, including the top keywords used by searchers coming to your website (including where you rank for each one), which keywords are responsible for driving traffic to your website, how many links Google recognizes coming to your website from external sources, and how many internal links Google recognizes within your website. Since external links play a crucial role in your search engine rankings, Google Webmaster Tools lets you see if people are linking to you from certain social media sites where you have been actively participating. Sometimes you'll find external links from sites you don't visit but some of your community members (your friends) do, and they posted a

---

1   Google Analytics: https://www.google.com/analytics/
2   Google Webmaster Tools: https://www.google.com/webmasters/tools

link to your website from there. Ah! Now that's a valuable thing to know and measure! Maybe you should spend more time in that community.

Google Alerts[3]—another free service that will alert you by email each time Google finds a relevant result for a topic you've set up to track. Common examples include tracking a person's name, your company, your competitors, et cetera. One word of caution, though: the broader the term you track, the more email you will receive from Google with alerts. Google Alerts will find results that are recent and some that are not-so-recent. It's a good tool for tracking specific terms; plus, it's easy to set up and manage. So if you want to stop tracking a term, or track a new term, it's simple. Google Alerts is commonly used to track individual names and brand names. As mentions occur in social media, your alerts will keep you in the know. You'll see how your content travels on the social web through Google Alerts.

Google Blogsearch[4]—a free search engine subset of Google's search engine geared to display blog posts. When you search on a phrase, Google displays recent blog posts for that phrase. You can use this to track how well your blog posts are displaying in Google as well as to find blog posts on topics of interest to you.

The Grader[5] tools from HubSpot offer simple and free tools to measure the inbound marketing effectiveness of your website, your Twitter profile, your Facebook profile, your press releases and other aspects of your inbound marketing presence.

As social media has exploded, so has the landscape of tools and services designed to help companies optimize their productivity. The modern-day clipping service has evolved into a cornucopia of tools allowing marketers to track and measure data about their social media activities.

---

3   Google Alerts: http://www.google.com/alerts
4   Google Blogsearch: http://blogsearch.google.com/
5   http://www.grader.com

Admittedly, many of these tools are blog-centric. Let's look at some of the popular free blog monitoring tools.

Blogpulse[6]—a free service from Nielsen Buzzmetrics that acts as both a blog search engine and blog tracker. Bloggers can track conversations taking place about topics of interest, as well as discover where their blog ranks in relation to others covering similar topics. Web surfers can use Blogpulse to find blogs of interest to them, and use features such as Buzz-Tracker and ConversationTracker to track blogs by topic.

Trendpedia[7]—a free service that functions mostly as a search engine that helps web surfers find blogs and social media sites by topic. Its main feature involves helping people find the most popular trends in social media across a variety of topics and tracking the trend of the topic over a three-month period. It's a valuable tool for monitoring the popularity and trends of your blog or any other content you have posted in social media. It also functions well as a tool for finding other people online who have the same interests you do.

Trendrr[8]—a free service that adds a real sense of analytical measurement through its use of trending graphs. Trendrr lets anyone *track, compare,* and *share* trends on any topic across blogs and other social media. You can compare trends and draw your own conclusions based on the trend data. However, this tool is not intended to tell you the meaning of trends. Instead, the tool allows you to see the trend graph on favorite topics so you can form your own opinions. I recommend you use this tool in concert with others, not as a stand-alone utility. There are other free tools that allow you to follow content trends. They include the following:

---

6   Blogpulse: http://www.blogpulse.com/
7   Trendpedia: http://www.trendpedia.com/
8   Trendrr: http://trendrr.com/home

Technorati[9]—a free service that functions as an Internet search engine for blogs, competing with Google and Yahoo. As of December 2008, Technorati has indexed 133 million blogs.[10] You can track your blog content in Technorati as well as all other tools described here.

Junta42[11]—a social media site where marketers can post their content and search for more content on various marketing topics. The popularity of each post can be voted for, much in the same way that users vote on Digg. Junta42 also publishes a list of the top content marketing blogs. This list is updated quarterly.

Sphinn[12]—a social media site focused on the Internet marketing industry. Anyone with an interest in web marketing and social media strategies can submit blog posts and start conversations with others, as well as read content submitted by others.

The free tools listed here are not meant to be an exhaustive list. However, these tools are some of the most popular and readily available tools used to track, measure, and monitor social media and web content. They are all free to the user community. I encourage you to use as many as possible to measure and track your social media marketing results.

In addition to the free tools listed, there is an ever-growing list of fee-based tools to measure social media results. I chose not to list any of them here because they are changing frequently. In the Resources section, I provide a link to social media monitoring tools. If you explore fee-based tools, be sure to give them a good trial period before making any commitments. In most cases, you should be able to sign up for a tool on a month-to-month basis so you can test it to determine if it meets your measurement needs.

9   Technorati: http://en.wikipedia.org/wiki/Technorati
10   State of the Blogosphere: http://technorati.com/blogging/state-of-the-blogosphere/
11   Junta42: http://www.junta42.com/
12   Sphinn: http://sphinn.com/

Now let's examine measuring qualitative results. I find that many executives do not place as much value in measuring the qualitative results of a social media marketing plan.

Measuring Brand Equity on the Social Web

The economy in which we live and work as we close out the first decade of the new millennium is in a paradigm shift. During this decade, we've seen the web evolve and grow faster than in the previous ten years. We've also begun to experience a younger workforce that is accustomed to using the social web in both personal and business ways and with lines blurring between the two. This workforce is already in leadership roles, as proven by Mark Zuckerburg at Facebook and others like him. These workers place a huge value in brand equity with little regard for spreadsheets to prove it. I argue that these workers understand the value of brand equity more than many of the members of the management crowd over age forty. The new workforce would rather have buzz about their brand over response rates and conversion rates.

At some point in the coming years, the current management breed with MBA degrees earned in the 1970s and '80s will be retired. In the meantime, we are in an interesting time with a hybrid workforce.

No one would argue that brand equity is important.

Large companies place a lot of importance in measuring brand equity. However, most companies are not Nike. So how do the rest of us measure brand equity in a Marketing 2.0 strategy?

In social media marketing, there exist new opportunities to positively affect and measure your brand equity. It all starts with the people in your company who actively engage in social media communities. Previously, I used the example of Matt Cutts from Google. When someone from your company takes a visible position in a social media community, as Matt does, and he or she effectively communicates meaningful stuff that the community truly appreciates, you are positively affecting your brand. Later in the book, you'll read a case study on Chris Griffith, a successful

Realtor in Bonita Springs, Florida, who has branded herself as the go-to person for anything real estate-related in this region of Florida. How do corporate brands or personal brands measure brand equity on the social web?

Let's not overcomplicate this. Using some of the tools described above can help you measure your brand equity. However, I'll offer a simple tip that takes ten minutes, doesn't cost a dime, and is so often overlooked that I'm blown away by its simplicity. Go to your Google Analytics account or equivalent website traffic analytics program. Assuming you have had your analytics in place for more than one year (which you should have), look at the visitors that came to your website from the keyword (insert the name of your company or your name here). Study the visitors to your website from your company name over different spans of time, starting with a period before you became active in social media marketing. Likewise, using Google Alerts, study how often your content travels on the social web. Your content can also include mentions of you or your company (or your employees). If you are actively engaging, listening, and interacting with your community in social media, you will see an upward trend in visits to your website coming from some combination of your company name or you or your employees who are actively involved in your social media strategy. For example, I've experienced this firsthand as both *Find and Convert* (my company name) and *Bernie Borges* are two of the top five keyword phrases that drive visitors to my company website. Likewise, the Find and Convert blog[13] home page is in the top three most frequently visited pages as shown in Google Analytics. I frequently receive Google Alerts with links to my blog content referenced by others around the world. These data points alone tell me that my efforts in social media are positively affecting my brand. In my case, the "show me the money" results are mostly tied to invitations to speak and guest write, which results in more business to my web marketing agency. But, there is also a "buzz" factor ....

---

13   Find and Convert blog: http://www.findandconvert.com/blog

What is Buzz and How Do You Measure It?

In social media marketing, we often hear people refer to "buzz" when describing a successful social media strategy. *Buzz* is simply unsolicited chatter about something, usually a brand or story. Buzz is a very good thing, assuming the buzz is positive. Negative buzz is another story. Positive buzz is one of those qualitative attributes that is very desirable but hard to measure, at least in conventional means, such as a spreadsheet report. When you have positive buzz, you have more interest in your brand, more job applicants, more sales prospects, more media interest, and an easier time for your sales people to get appointments and tell your story to prospective buyers. In essence, positive buzz is in part telling your story. If you have sales staff, its job is not only easier, but also it evolves to a role that must support the positive buzz. Your sales staff must pick up where the buzz leaves off with a positive experience. *Contemporary Marketing 2.0 doesn't close a sale; it facilitates the buyer's buying experience.* Buzz can set the stage for your buyer to buy because you've already begun to bridge the gap between you (the seller) and the buyer.

While some tools such as Google Alerts can help you measure buzz, my favorite way to measure buzz is by observing the volume of conversations about a brand or story on the social web. The frequency of mentions, along with the influence of the communities talking about your brand, can have a huge financial impact on your results through buzz.

But still, there are CEOs and business executives who insist on measuring results through conventional data points such as the number of new customers, customer retention rates, customer complaints/service call trends, employee turnover, market share, revenue, and profit. I submit that the most compelling way to measure all of the above in Marketing 2.0 is to compare results over time in comparison to your Marketing 1.0 strategy. In due time, a Marketing 1.0 strategy is going to die a slow death. Implementing your Marketing 2.0 strategy and measuring both quantitative and qualitative results over time is not only doable, but also it is very practical using both free and fee-based tools.

A social media marketing strategy is not a point-to-point straight line. Instead it is a continuous loop. The good news is that when you apply the measurement principles discussed here, very good things can happen to your brand equity and they can be measured. But, notice I described it as continuous. If you discontinue participation for any length of time— even a few weeks—you can lose some or possibly all of the brand benefits your efforts have accrued.

If I could summarize this chapter into one point, it is that Marketing 2.0 results are measured in brand equity. When you move the needle in your brand equity, you can move the needle in all other metrics you care about.

RISKS IN SOCIAL MEDIA MARKETING

A s organizations begin rolling out social media marketing strategies, there are risk factors that require consideration. Organizations of all sizes and types, from profit to nonprofit, can use social media. As with most things in business, there are many potential benefits and, of course, there are a few risks. Let's begin with the risks.

Having No Strategy. Perhaps the biggest risk in social media marketing, and one of the most common mistakes companies make, is diving into social media without a strategy. Too often, companies jump on the bandwagon without first developing a plan. A social media plan must begin with an objective, followed by a strategy and a list of tactics, as well as a definition of the resources, the budget, the tolerance for failure, a timeline, and measurement strategies. Begin with research to define your objective. Study your competitors and all members of your market segment to identify how they participate in social media to give you insight into how you should approach social media. When defining the timeline, be flexible. You'll initially be entering unchartered waters. What you think may take three months will probably take six. There is much that is unpredictable in social media marketing, and that is also part of the risk.

Here is the key: the stronger your brand, the stronger your potential to launch a plan capable of producing measurable results. Just don't make the dangerous assumption that you'll that have overnight success. And don't go into it without a plan.

Having The Wrong Strategy. If having no strategy is the riskiest proposition in social media, having the *wrong* strategy is almost as bad. A social media marketing strategy requires research, observing, listening, and planning in order to develop a plan that can succeed and still be measured. This warning is meant to dissuade marketers from producing new content in popular new media forms such as a blog, forum, wiki, podcasts, or social networking tools without first planning it out. Listen to your community and learn what is important to them. Planning your objectives, understanding what your content will be, who will produce it, who will maintain it, who will measure its effect, and who will manage it are all essential to your success. I am a strong advocate of diving into social media first as a listener. I'll discuss this in the next section.

Ignoring Social Media. Another risk marketers run comes from ignoring social media. I often hear marketers say, "We don't have time to devote to social media," or, "We plan to get into social media somewhere down the road." Devoting time to listening to online conversations is very important. I assure you there are relevant conversations occurring on the social web right now in most industries, including yours. But if you are totally ignoring them, you are potentially ignoring threats and opportunities that are readily within your grasp today. You just may wake up one day and realize you are missing out on valuable opportunities and run the risk of diving in too fast with either no strategy or the wrong strategy. If your competitors are already active in social media, the perceived urgency to begin a social media strategy may dangerously accelerate your planning.

It is well-known in B2B that searches for products and services are conducted by staff reporting into a final decision-maker. These staffers have two objectives: 1) make good recommendations based on diligent research; and 2) not get fired for recommending a vendor who performs poorly. When they conduct their research, do you honestly think they limit themselves to reading your website? Don't you think they seek out opinions and input from others who have already selected a vendor in this category? Where do you think they turn for this advice? The answer is the social web. There is no shortage of websites with content from peers and industry opinion leaders who have something to say about your industry, your products, your customer service, and your employees. Maybe they'll even find your employees, or competitors, blogging out there. Do you really think you can ignore this? Being totally absent from these conversations (social media abstinence) is like suggesting you refuse to use a computer. Sounds absurd, doesn't it? That's what you sound like if you really believe you don't have the time to at least listen to the conversations on the social web.

A Little Here and a Little There. Another risk I see stems from companies taking a fragmented approach to social media. I consider this a management problem. If different people in your organization get involved in social media without a cohesive, planned approach, you could easily step on each other's toes. Worse yet, you could cannibalize each other's efforts, overlap each other, damage your brand, or simply miss out on the potential leverage of *one plus one equals three*. A cohesive strategy with division of labor is important to get meaningful results from a social media strategy, but this will only be effective if senior management is committed to the plan.

Bull in a China Shop. Another risk companies take is moving ahead full speed into a social media strategy, and ending up doing too much too quickly, thereby creating negative results. When implementing your social media strategy, you'll learn what works and how to use certain platforms, and you'll understand what skills you have and what skills you need to acquire. And, you'll make some mistakes. Don't dive into the pool headfirst. Dip your toe in the water in the shallow end and get used to the water's temperature. Plan out the first ninety days, and roll it out with meticulous attention to details pertaining to staffing, content, listening, and measuring.

Abandonment. If you take the bull in a china shop approach, you run the risk of doing too much too soon and producing negative results. Or, if the strategy you develop is not realistic, or not well-staffed, or not well-executed, and you don't see quick results, the outcome can be the abandonment of your social media strategy. In addition to the lost opportunity, you can also cause extensive damage to your brand. Given this, it behooves most organizations to venture into social media conservatively, and only after developing a workable and realistic plan.

I Just Don't Get It! I believe one of the biggest risks any organization faces when considering social media marketing is a lack of understanding of its potential benefits along with the (mostly) unwritten rules of social media marketing. The interesting thing about this comment is that social media is a young and evolving platform, yet there are fundamental rules of engagement already in place that are very black and white (with only a few shades of gray). Organizations that understand the social, viral, and technological characteristics of social media have the greatest potential to achieve positive experiences. Understanding social media doesn't require a technical bent, as much as understanding the natural evolution of the use of computers in the Internet age, made possible by innovations resulting in tools that are being embraced by people and businesses of all demographics around the globe.

Organizations must understand that these social media tools are being used for both personal and business purposes. In fact, the lines are blurring between personal and business purposes. The social aspect of this new media heightens the awareness of people interacting with others to get real productive work done. The interaction experience has created a culture of collaboration among people who work well together, regardless of whether they are inside or outside the company. People want the freedom to choose with whom they will collaborate on their work. Social media makes that possible. The adoption of social media is changing the landscape of some of the business community's most traditional and mainstream functions.

Here are some ways organizations can use social media to shift old paradigms into new ones:

- Product development people can communicate with each other internally through blogs and microblogs.

- Marketing departments can conduct customer feedback forums (e.g., focus groups) faster than ever before, and do it on an ongoing basis, instead of limiting it to special projects.

- Marketing departments can spread the word about products and services through conversations and good content, not by shouting to the masses in one-way messages.

- Customer service departments can tear down the walls of customer interaction, thereby reducing customer frustration.

- Sales teams can follow each other's activities and share best practices every day in near real-time, not just in sales meetings.

- Executives can join private groups to keep in touch with peers sharing best practices, without having to travel.

- Market intelligence personnel can study the competition through RSS-enabled content easier than ever before.

- Operations people can likewise subscribe to RSS-enabled content in order to keep abreast of the latest best practices and technology advancements.

- Human resources management can conduct research on best practices as well as monitor people's activities by following them in social networks. Note: this isn't intended to sound Big Brotherish, but the fact is that it's now easy to check people's activities using social networks.

- Staffers at all levels can subscribe to blogs, groups, webinars, podcasts, wikis, and social networking sites, and conduct research and stay in touch with peers around the world, making it easier to do their jobs.

- Staffers can enjoy the benefits of social media without having to throw parties or provide other expensive perks. I'm not suggesting the abolition of perks. I'm merely pointing out that staffers should be permitted to enjoy social media as long as they don't abuse it and they get their jobs done. Remember, the lines between personal and business are blurring.

A lack of understanding social media at the top level of any organization large, midsize, or small is very risky. Frankly, if you run an organization and you have been resistant to social media, there is a good chance your staff is exploring new employment opportunities. If you don't visit social networking sites, you won't even know they are marketing themselves and looking for a new job. The risk of not understanding the role of the social web in engaging your customers, listening to them, and providing them with valuable content is huge. The risk of not allowing your staff to use the social web to get their job done is just as big.

No Top-Down Support. Understanding how to use social media to your company's advantage starts at the top of your organization. Isn't that usually true of most new business ventures? For a large corporation with thousands of employees, it's not totally necessary for the CEO to be active in social media for successful experiences. However, it is imperative that the CEO be supportive of any new social media initiative. Staffers can experiment with social media, but they risk getting embarrassed if something goes awry and the CEO isn't on board. In fact, due to its pervasive nature, the possibility of the CEO learning about a negative experience from social media is extremely high. So while I believe the CEO doesn't necessarily need to actively engage in social media, his or her approval is a must. In social media, you can't do it right and stay anonymous. And if you screw up, the CEO can know about it in minutes.

I read that IBM has more than ten thousand internal blogs. It's safe to say that senior management endorses these blogs, whether or not they ever participate in them. In fact, at IBM, success stories are plentiful. They range from reducing inefficient email clutter to increased collaboration among a global staff. In an organization such as IBM, with a global workforce, imagine the possibilities of tapping into various skills simply by using a social media platform such as a blog.

The CEO must understand the risks inherent in a social media strategy. By far, the biggest risk that the CEO must accept is that a conventional return on investment may or may not be measurable (in a spreadsheet anyway), and it may not happen quickly. In fact, the first social media venture may not yield any measurable results at all. Or it may fail. Top-down support includes support for the plan, beginning with the objectives and the tactics and a ninety-day initial plan. Any early failures should be accepted as a learning experience upon which you can build and take new and decisive actions.

Misallocation of Time and Resources. Another risk in attempting to make your social media strategy work is not spending enough time at it. This is one of my pet peeves. The single biggest objection I hear from marketers to using social media is, *We don't have time for it.* To that I ask, *Do you have time to come to work?* If you just woke up from a thirty-year nap, would you say, "I don't have time to learn to use a PC?" Admittedly, I get irked when I hear this comment because the marketing paradigm has unequivocally shifted. Using social media as a viable mechanism for engaging your customers simply can't be ignored. How can you say that you don't have time to speak to your customers? If you don't, your competitors will be glad to do it for you. By now, you know that I am an advocate of starting out by engaging and listening on the social web while developing a proactive social media plan that is truly practical for your company. But I never said it wouldn't require a commitment of time and resources. How much unproductive time are you allocating in your current marketing strategy? If you want success, just do it. Make a good thing happen.

Organizations that embark on a social media strategy must allocate time to it. There is no other option. When it is considered an add-on activity with no change to current activities, the risk of abandonment is high. There's a statement I like to use: *work takes work*. Pretty profound, eh? Here's my point. Any organization deciding to experiment with social media must go into it with the understanding that it requires a dedicated commitment of time and resources. If a new blog is part of the strategy, quitting the blog after six months simply because you didn't capture any new business from it is the most shortsighted decision you can make. If you're going to start a blog and you don't spend a reasonable and consistent amount of time updating the blog and promoting it (yes, in most cases you must promote your blog), you won't achieve measurable success. Social media marketing takes time and resources. But doesn't everything in business take time and resources to achieve good results? This is one of the most common struggles when a business launches a social media plan. You're already accustomed to spending eight-plus hours a day doing stuff, some of which may be unproductive or no longer effective. Allocating time to social media seems additive. That's often the first mistake. Social media has the potential to replace certain other aspects of your current marketing strategy, especially if you're still shouting at your target customers.

I liken social media marketing success to surfing. I have never personally ridden a surfboard, but I understand the concept. A surfer goes through the investment of buying the board and perhaps a wet suit. He or she gets up early in the morning, drives to the beach, and paddles out to a certain point. The surfer may spend hours waiting for the perfect wave, which may begin to feel like totally wasted time. A good wave may never come on any given day, resulting in hours of just floating on a surfboard. Or it may come within five minutes, or it may come after four hours. When the surfer catches the perfect wave, there are only two results.

The most obvious result is the glory of the ride, which looks and feels effortless. Oh, it requires great skill to navigate the ride on the board, but the wave is doing all the work. The surfer is using the energy of the wave to enjoy the ride by applying his skill to get the maximum thrill of that ride. A lot of practice went into acquiring the skills to ride that wave. The surfer understands it takes a lot of persistence and hard work to gain the skills necessary to ride the biggest waves. Along the way, there will be some wipeouts that may sting a little bit, but they are valuable learning experiences. As long as each crash is not fatal, it is a productive learning experience that, in the end and over the long haul, pays dividends.

The other benefit of riding the wave is the satisfaction of the achievement because of all the hard work that went into making that singular activity pay off. A dedicated surfer understands and appreciates that hard work and persistence make the whole surfing experience a worthy pursuit. And he understands that sometimes you catch a good wave and sometimes you don't. On top of that is the realization that some waves provide a better ride than others.

Surfing's correlation to social media marketing is this: when marketers prepare well, allocate the time and proper resources, and apply them with patience, not expecting immediate results, they will eventually enjoy the exhilaration of catching a wave. Just as the force of the wave propels the surfer, the momentum of viral social media success can produce great results. When a marketer experiences that, after months of applying time and hard work, the satisfaction is great and the inspiration to continue to build on that positive momentum wave is reinforced.

Improper Measurement of Results. As your social media strategy progresses, you'll want to begin measuring not only your progress, but also your results. A big risk here involves measuring either the wrong metrics or not measuring any at all. As discussed previously, measuring results can include easily accessible details such as website traffic (visitors), keywords referring website traffic, referring sources (search engines, directories, et cetera), pages viewed, time spent on pages, time spent on the website, bounce rates, landing page conversions, and other well-known web marketing analytics. It's true that some of these same metrics can be applied to measuring social media marketing, but they are either not always obvious or not always easily accessible. Measuring sources of website traffic from social media destination sites is one obvious metric. By using tools such as Google Analytics (free) or HubSpot[1] (fee-based) to measure the source of leads by tracking the original source of the visit, you can clearly measure lead intelligence and new business back to the social media platform responsible for the lead.

As you might expect, social media marketing success is defined differently for each business, depending on its objectives. In the end, most businesses want more of something, whether it's more sales, improved collaboration among staffers, customers, suppliers, or more members or subscribers to a newsletter. One metric many companies should set as an objective, but do not, is improved brand recognition. Unfortunately, too many CEOs don't understand that improved brand recognition eventually results in more sales. Most CEOs are focused only on measuring more sales. I was taught early in my education that when you can affect the behavior that produces your desired outcome, you can produce more of your desired outcome. This principle applies to many aspects of life, not just in business. My point here is meant to illustrate that when a business achieves stronger brand recognition, it strengthens a behavior that ultimately leads to sales. Too many CEOs think this marketing mantra is limited to the Nikes and Ciscos of the business world. A twenty-person company in a market niche can profit greatly from great brand equity, just like the big companies do. The reason I'm stressing this point again and again is because social media marketing often positively affects a company's brand.

Whether it's brand equity or leads, the key is to develop a strategy that allows you to measure something that is meaningful to your stakeholders. Measuring metrics that don't correlate to your strategy or to your stakeholders is potentially dangerous. Likewise, attempting to measure results prematurely is also potentially dangerous. Depending on your social media strategy, it can take months before any results begin to develop. Measuring results over a sustained period of time is important. Remember, it starts with your plan, and your plan must align with the vision and

---

1   HubSpot: http://www.hubspot.com/ a popular inbound marketing software platform.

mission of the company. Your stakeholders in executive, sales, marketing, finance, and IT must all be on board with your plan. In many cases, it's not possible to have everyone on board due to the realities of internal politics and other internal factors. But if you align with the stakeholders that matter the most, you measure results, and communicate those results often, your chances of success improve exponentially.

Shifts in the Wind. Remember that social media is still a relatively new development. At the time of this writing, the adoption curve is still in the early adopter phase moving toward early majority and mainstream among bigger businesses but less so among most small businesses. There is already discussion of Web 3.0. A client once asked me if his company should consider skipping Web 2.0 and just wait for Web 3.0. The question alone implied that this company didn't understand Web 2.0, comparing it instead to a software version.

Social media tools and platforms are continually emerging and evolving. Some may thrive and some may die. Twitter, for example, is very popular (in 2009). As a microblogging platform, it shows much promise. But I also remember how popular WordPerfect was in the 1980s. It was the dominant word processor on the PC. Yet Microsoft's Word took over this position. And while the comparison isn't apples to apples, the point is that potentially shifting winds in social media suggest that we don't put too much emphasis on any one aspect of a social media strategy. Staying informed of trends and risks in using specific platforms is part of the game. There are numerous webinars and conferences you can attend to stay informed. Plus, the online communities to which you belong should not only help keep you abreast of developments, but also they should enable you to see when the handwriting is on the wall.

The shifts in the wind do not just pertain to the public social platforms such as Twitter or Facebook, any of which could fall out of favor almost overnight and be replaced by something else. Private social communities in industry niches also deserve much scrutiny. I advise you to know who is behind a private social community. Are they on solid ground? Are they reputable? Who is maintaining it? These shifts have the potential to do serious damage to a community and to your social media strategy if you are overinvested in a specific platform. If this sounds similar to the principle of having a diversified investment portfolio with risk spread over several investments, it is. In social media marketing, over time you'll find some aspects of your plan can be more effective than others. Be careful that you don't get the rug pulled out from under your feet if you are overinvested in one social media platform and the wind shifts away from it. Diversify your plan.

There are many risks involved in launching and maintaining an effective social media strategy, but the potential benefits are outstanding. The risks outlined here should not dissuade any marketer from harnessing the collective power of the conversations and community in social media. In the next chapter, we'll explore these powerful benefits.

Engaging with the Wrong Communities. I've stressed the importance of getting engaged in communities on the social web. And I've also stressed the importance of starting out by listening to conversations on the social web. One risk factor is getting involved in communities that may not align with your interests or value proposition. You should visit several online communities and spend some time in each before deciding if they are right for you. Study them to see if they are growing. Are the conversations relevant to what you offer? Are the same people dominating the conversations? Are there influential thought leaders in these communities? Is there an opportunity for you to become a valuable member of these communities? Eventually, you will find several online communities comprising people whose interests are common to yours.

Building the Wrong Communities. Similarly, when you set out to produce your content to build communities willing to consume that content, it's important to attract people who are aligned with your objectives. If you're an established business, start out by inviting your customers to read your content. Approach select customers privately and ask them to support your social web efforts by consuming and commenting on company content, as well as telling others about it. Express your appreciation to them by inviting them to comment or contribute their own content to your strategy. Customer content contributions can be very effective in helping attract more members to your community who are aligned with your interests and objectives. If you're not an established company, the same advice applies. Instead of inviting customers (because you don't have many), invite people with whom you align professionally on the social web, starting with your network. You'll find others in groups, blogs, and forums on the social web. Seek out these social groups by relevant categories or keywords. For example, if you manufacture medical supplies for hospitals, don't limit your community focus to broad categories around health care. Get as specific as possible using category segment keywords such as surgical supplies, cardiac equipment, et cetera. Depending on what you find, you should invest time to determine which communities are worthwhile. You'll likely find plenty of them to engage with, and *hang out* for a while before you determine which groups are aligned with your objectives. Eventually, you can invite people to read your content or contribute content to your social media community—but only after you have established some credibility in your communities. If you've built the right communities, you will have bridged the gap between you (the seller) and your buyers.

Types of Communities to Explore

I characterize the types of communities on the social web as *peers, marketplace,* and *authoritative.* Let's explore the characteristics of each community and what you need to understand about how they can serve your social media strategy.

Peers. A community of peers generally comprises people who do something similar to you. If you are a marketing manager, a peer group is made up of other marketing managers. Regardless of titles, these people generally do what you do. Engaging with this community is an opportunity to share best practices, network, and get references to good content, reliable vendors, and other people, including people in the other two categories as well as employee candidates.

Building rapport with your peers has always been an effective way to learn, grow, and network. Doing so online eliminates the geographic restriction of accomplishing these objectives with peers in your town. Finding your peers online is not as difficult as it may sound. Depending on the social media platform, you can search using keywords such as your title or other relevant topics, including industry-focused topics. In social networking sites such as Facebook and LinkedIn, it's easy to find peer groups. The real work comes in engaging them. If you are job hunting, use discretion because most online conversations are public. If you are networking for other purposes, use the principles discussed throughout this book to sincerely get involved in conversations where you can contribute and build relationships. Remember, it takes time, but like the surfer who catches a wave, the results can be terrific.

Marketplace. This group generally refers to the people who are involved in your company's selling and buying process. It may comprise customers, prospective customers, consultants, suppliers, your employees, and the employees of your competitors. This group of communities can be the most effective place to have success, but it also carries with it the highest degree of risk. If you make a mistake in this community, it becomes very visible very quickly. This community is not for social media beginners. Most mistakes are often made by social media newbies. This is a community that thrives on transparency. Shameless marketing will not be tolerated here. The people with the most to contribute gain the most. Remember that both your current and potential customers can be here, listening and watching. In fact, everyone in this community is watching each other's behavior, and it's all about transparent conversations—meaningful conversations, not sales conversations.

These communities are harder to find and even harder to build. Finding them is usually achieved through a referral from someone else you know in another community, whether online or offline. Facebook and

LinkedIn may have these groups, and they may even be closed groups where membership is by invitation only. Sometimes, they are focused on a particular industry niche. Some communities distinguish vendors from users, though both member types are wanted. Some niche community examples include ITToolBox.com, a portal for the IT community; Healthworldweb.com, an online community for doctors and patients; Lawlink.com, a social network for attorneys; Mspmentor.net, an online community for IT services companies who provide managed services; and Furnituredealer.net/Manufacturers.aspx, a portal for furniture dealers and their customers. This list grows every week. If you don't find a social web destination in your industry, keep searching. But if you're willing to work at building the community, you can start your own group on LinkedIn or Facebook or on another dedicated social website.

The marketplace community requires considerable commitment to achieve good results. This is a community where starting out by listening is always a safe strategy. Selecting the right people on your team to engage in this community is also critical. If you understand the do's and don'ts of social media, but the people on your team who engage this community don't, that could mean big trouble.

Authoritative. This community is generally composed of people with subject matter expertise in your desired area. The most challenging aspect of engaging in this community is that it can be found within either of the peer or marketplace communities. You may not immediately recognize authoritative members of a community. The best advice is to assume that these people can be anywhere. Never assume people in a community are not authoritative. The day-to-day titles and functions of authoritative communities can be all over the map. They can be competitors. They can be subordinates. They can be located anywhere in the world. They are authoritative by their domain expertise. Their reputation makes them authoritative. They are usually frequent contributors of content and opinions in a group. They have something meaningful to say, and they say it often.

The best aspect of engaging with authoritative community is the opportunity to learn. These people tend to share great content. They read articles, attend conferences, and speak and write on topics of interest to you. They often share their great content and great insights with you and their community. In some ways, authoritative community content is a form of free consulting. Subject matter experts often give away pieces of domain-specific information for free in online social communities, even if they get paid well by clients for this same content. Chris Brogan[2] comes to mind as an example of an authoritative person who shares his expertise extensively with his community on a daily basis.

If you are an authority in some discipline (and most of us are in at least one area), I encourage you to be generous with your knowledge. By freely sharing what you know and whom you know, positive benefits will come full circle.

Let me briefly outline my personal experiences with these three types of communities. I use Twitter, LinkedIn, and Facebook to engage with peers, many of whom are authoritative. I have built many casual relationships, including a few that have migrated offline. The general theme of these relationships is that we help each other out by sharing content and best practices. My web marketing blog at Find and Convert reaches a community in the marketplace. These people tend to be combinations of customers, prospective customers, and industry peers, many of whom are influential. The nature of my blog and podcast content[3] makes me an authoritative contributor in the area of web marketing content. I benefit from the brand recognition and business opportunities realized in part from these social media activities.

Understanding your community is pivotal to reducing the risks in social media marketing. By understanding the makeup of your community, you can better understand not only how to engage that community, but also the benefits that are available to you in the communities you engage. The benefits of your social media marketing strategy far outweigh the risks. The best you can do is to have some understanding of the risks.

---

2   Chris Brogan: http://www.chrisbrogan.com/
3   Find and Convert Blog and Podcasts: http://www.findandconvert.com/blog/

BENEFITS OF SOCIAL MEDIA MARKETING

The risks described are not meant to scare you away from social media. On the contrary, all marketers know there are risks involved in the implementation of any marketing strategy. And with the continual maturity and evolution of social media, the risks are better dealt with when laid out in the open and understood. The risks I've described may apply more to some businesses than others. You should examine the social and political culture of your organization and your markets before deciding to what extent a social media strategy is needed.

Having said all that, there are still many benefits to using social media in your marketing strategy. The benefits I describe below pertain specifically to using social media for marketing purposes. While this book is not meant to cover in any detail the internal benefits to a business that uses social media, one such example is SpaFax. Arjun Basu, editorial director, keeps its two hundred global employees informed when he travels to conferences by using Twitter to communicate key points during the conference. Most people consider the social media benefits as marketing-centric. While that's true, the technology truly provides many communication opportunities for even small businesses to enjoy internally.

Let's look at the primary marketing benefits of social media marketing.

Low Cost. Rolling out a social media strategy is not an expensive venture. In fact, it can be done on a downright low budget, especially in the beginning. Many of the social media platforms you can leverage monetize themselves through advertising. Therefore, the use of many of these tools is free. The primary benefit to using social media is in the relationship value of the community you create or join. So the cost of using many social media tools is free or low. The biggest cost in the beginning of a new social media strategy is the staff's learning curve associated with using various tools and destination social platforms. There are also the associated costs of doing research to find communities, building a community, and maintaining the relationships. As mentioned earlier, building online relationships is similar to building offline relationships. People need to develop a sense of trust and credibility in you. That may take considerable time. So chalk up people's time as the biggest cost in developing a new social media strategy.

Some may argue that the time cost factor is equivalent to hard costs associated with other marketing expenses that cost real money. I say that doesn't matter because there is a cost to go to work every day. The biggest cost is not using that time wisely to produce results. So go ahead and make the argument, but it falls on deaf ears with me.

Eventually, you may choose to invest in commercial tools to help you manage and monitor your social media strategy. In most cases, I don't recommend doing that in the beginning of a social media strategy for several reasons, not the least of which is the need to perform a few trials in the beginning of your social media plan. Building some organizational history, as well as understanding what works and what doesn't, is a key task for your organization. Once you have some understanding of the key components required in your social media strategy, as well as your staffing requirements, investing in fee-based tools may make sense.

Brand Building. I've mentioned in previous chapters the importance of building your brand, whether you're a large company with household brand recognition or a twenty-person company in a niche market. I am truly of the opinion (shared by many contemporary marketing pundits) that brand equity is the most valuable marketing asset we can achieve, regardless of the size of our company. Social media provides a platform like none other in modern history to build our brand.

There is much talk and recognition of social media as citizen journalism. This concept refers to the fact that journalism has been redefined. Journalism used to be confined to people whose vocations were in print, radio, or television, and were responsible for producing and delivering content through those media. Journalistic content has traditionally ranged from news, business, social, sports, editorial, and other categories as defined by industry periodicals. The people who produced the content were in control of the content. When this crowd was in control, brand building was largely a function of advertising and PR-generated press coverage. Well, much to the chagrin of those media companies, those days are dead and gone. Social media allows all of us, regardless of our socioeconomic status or title, to create good content that can be consumed by anyone. It is available to anyone, anywhere, at any time because the Internet is the platform.

When we speak of building brand in social media, it is often synonymous with creating buzz. I have mixed emotions about this expression. How do you measure buzz? I measure buzz as improved brand. How do you measure the value of improved brand recognition? Increased sales (or your equivalent)! When your target market perceives your brand to be associated with your value proposition, your sales results will benefit, provided you have effective sales processes in place.

There are many well-known examples of large companies using social media to promote their brand. They include names such as Nike, Dunkin' Donuts, Microsoft, Proctor & Gamble, and JetBlue. And there are a growing number of terrific examples of companies who serve niche markets, whose names you will not recognize, using social media to build brand and increase sales. There is an entire section later in the book dedicated to case study examples of progressive small and medium-size companies implementing social media marketing strategies with great success.

Staffing Advantages. In the previous section, I suggested some staffing considerations. You may be able to leverage existing staff, and you may not. In some situations, you can awaken a sleeping giant in your organization. I am referring to existing talent that is underutilized in a role that could be leveraged in social media. It's not uncommon to tap into someone's domain expertise and put it to great use in social media.

One of the most common requirements of social media marketing is producing content. Whether it's blog content, podcast content, wiki content, photos, videos, et cetera. Producing content and sharing it with your community to inspire good conversation is the name of the game in social media. Producing content with regular frequency is the key to social media success—as long as your community agrees that it is good content. Using existing staff with domain expertise can often be the best place to begin. Unless your entire staff is extremely averse to a social media plan, you should be able to repurpose some or all members of your existing staff to contribute to your social media strategy. Some staffers may become active online participants, and others may operate behind the scenes. If you effectively paint the vision for them, they should all be able to contribute something of value to your new media plan.

Generally speaking, marketing staff should embrace social media. Simply put, using social media gives your staff the opportunity to produce good results using contemporary tools in an enjoyable work environment. Marketing staffers who embrace social media tend to really enjoy it, especially as they begin building a personal brand. The demographics of the up-and-coming workers are in our favor. These workers are already accustomed to maintaining a social networking profile. In short, they already get it. Social media is the norm to them. To say this in another way, if your company isn't using social media, you may have difficulty recruiting marketing talent, depending on your industry. In many industries, the people who apply for jobs are competing fiercely. And your company is competing just as fiercely to attract the best available talent. The talent pool of people capable of helping you successfully implement your social media strategy is growing every day. That's the good news. The bad news is that you may not be able to recruit good talent if your marketing strategy is stuck in 1999—or even 2005—with no plans in social media. Given the choice of working at a company with exciting social media campaigns under way, or a company barely thinking about social media, the best talent will run from the latter and go with the former.

Loyalty. Producing content considered useful by your community produces loyalty and can also produce viral marketing value. Loyalty is very powerful, no matter the source or the medium. It's very common for people in online communities to pass around links to blog posts and other content they find useful. Social media community loyalty is such a valuable asset that you will ask you your accountant to find a way put it on your balance sheet. Unfortunately, that's not possible (as far as I know). We often speak of the collective wisdom of community. We also need to acknowledge the collective loyalty of community. The surfer analogy used earlier speaks to this. Once you achieve loyalty, it is like catching a wave. The force of the wave is all-powerful and self-propelling. Social media loyalty has that characteristic. You can't buy that type of loyalty through advertising, at least not in contemporary marketing.

Level Playing Field. Essentially, social media levels the playing field for most marketers. Small businesses can create loyal communities online just as large companies can, though perhaps not at the same pace or to the same extent. One of the greatest benefits to social media is the ability to leverage these communities by harnessing the power of their loyalty. And you harness their loyalty by feeding them good content, giving selflessly of your time and talents, strengthening the community through collaboration, expressing gratitude to your community, and showing benevolence to them. In other words, give to your community while asking for nothing in return. If you do ask for something, tie it to their loyalty and not to your sales goals. For example, if your company is nominated for an award, asking your loyal community to vote for you is very reasonable.

A well-planned social media strategy, executed with good content by good people, can build loyalty in community and achieve excellent results. This picture I'm painting is true of a five-person company, a five hundred-person company, or a fifty thousand-person company. The difference is the extent of the social media plan and the reach of the brand, which is a limitation of the resources applied. At some point, there may be diminishing returns. But we don't know where that point is because social media is still evolving. A company such as Cisco or Oracle, known as aggressive marketers with deep pockets, can apply more resources in social media than a twenty-person company.

If you are a small company competing with large companies such as those mentioned here, a social media strategy truly has potential to level the playing field—maybe not literally, but to some extent, there is a lot of truth to this. A smaller company can potentially do a stellar job of building a loyal community through great content, or a great service made popular through social media. Just look at 37 Signals.[1] This small software company has a global customer base for its web-based project management and collaboration software. Some of its competitors are large software companies including Microsoft. Word-of-mouth loyalty spreads on the social web and continues to build its customer base.

Another company doing a spectacular job of building a loyal community is Twitter. I've devoted an entire chapter to Twitter. This is a company that (at the time of this writing) has done no advertising or marketing of any sort. Twitter is a microblogging service that was adopted early by influential new media types in the San Francisco bay area. The loyalty factor has exploded rapidly for Twitter like nothing we've seen since the rapid adoption of Apple's iPod.

Perhaps if Apple had launched a microblogging platform, it would've grown just as rapidly. But what if Oracle launched it? Or Microsoft? I don't have the answer. But I would speculate that the fact that Twitter is a first-mover with incredibly loyal fans is part of its appeal.

I'll even suggest that established companies with long-standing

---

1   37 Signals: http://www.37signals.com/

brands might have more of a challenge using social media because their brand is already so well-known. The loyalty of established brands is likely to have a preconceived perception that is difficult to change. When I think of Microsoft, Oracle, and Cisco, I have very definite impressions of each brand, created from many years of watching how these brands behave in the market. When a newcomer such as Twitter or Facebook comes along with no history (or baggage), the playing field is level. The newbie has the opportunity to create an impression by building an online community.

But let's look at the flip side. If a newbie starts out strong by building a loyal community, then makes a big mistake without 'fessing up or correcting the mistake, the online community can be very unforgiving. Facebook had such a near fatal mistake in 2007, when it launched an advertising platform called Beacon that used an opt-out option rather than an opt-in approach. The community erupted in resentment, resulting in a huge backlash from the Facebook community. Fortunately, Facebook CEO Mark Zuckerberg apologized for this mistake, and the online community forgave and forgot. It's interesting to note that Zuckerberg's apology was in a blog post in Facebook,[2] not through a mainstream news release. Zuckerberg used the social media platform to apologize, relying on its vast reach rather than the old-school wire distribution services and print media. Zuckerberg understood the power of the collective influence of the Facebook community. Apologizing on Facebook was, for him, the right way to go.

Even though Facebook was not a newbie when this embarrassment occurred, in comparison to the then-leader of social networks—MySpace—the company was still considered an up-and-comer. If Facebook had decided not to own up to its mistake, alienating its online community could've sucked all the wind out of the brand's sails. I say this with conviction because that is how powerful online communities can be. They can literally make or break a company. So while the playing field for newbies may be leveled, understanding the potentially devastating repercussions of a mistake is crucial to your success in social media marketing.

---

2   Mark Zuckerberg apology blog post: http://blog.facebook.com/blog. php?post=7584397130

The simple rule of thumb to follow is this: deliver great content and listen to your community. If you hear your community complaining about something, and you agree that the sentiment is legitimate, and not just the voice of one or two disgruntled people, take action immediately. The same online community that gives you trust and loyalty can be quick to take both away if its members feel you have violated them.

Building Trust. Companies that communicate with a human voice and build relationships online do well in social media. Companies that behave as *companies* don't do as well. Social media is all about sincere conversations and building relationships. When a company hides behind a corporate voice, it alienates itself and its people and doesn't reap any of the potential benefits, including that all-important loyalty and trust.

Typically, loyalty and trust go hand in hand, but this is not always the case. In social media, it is possible to build a loyal community that doesn't necessarily trust you. There are many who are loyal to using Microsoft, IBM, Oracle, or Apple products without necessarily trusting that the companies will treat them well. I'm not implying that any of these aforementioned companies don't treat their communities well. I'm simply using them to illustrate that having a loyal community may result in a community that trusts you, but not necessarily.

One sure way to build trust is by empowering your communities. How do you empower your communities? By delivering good content to them and by engaging them in a manner that shows you have their best interests at heart. Empowering your community to accomplish more, enjoy more value, and be equipped to demonstrate their value to others results in empowerment. It's no different than when an employee is put in a visible situation by her manager that allows her to shine in front of peers and superiors. If the manager provided the employee with the opportunity, advice, and even the content to allow her to shine, and the full credit goes to the employee, that employee will trust her manager and be loyal to her. On the other hand, if the manager takes all the credit for the exceptional work of one of his employees, and the employee receives no credit for her fine efforts, trust goes out the window. That employee is very likely to tell others about that negative experience. The word soon spreads how the manager manipulated the situation to his credit. Mistrust spreads like cancer. That manager's reputation will eventually be destroyed, and deservedly so.

Online communities work the same way. The main difference is that online reputations are built rapidly. And they can fall apart rapidly if the sincerity and continuity of content aren't sustained.

Convergence of PR and Social Media for Viral Marketing. As social media awareness has been rapidly increasing, the role of PR has quickly been intertwined with it. Effective social media strategies can and should be part of your PR strategy. Creating content that has viral potential is at the heart of a social media PR strategy. Give your loyal community access to your news and let them be your media channel. Let your loyal community promote your news. Going viral with your news can run the gamut, from exposing it to a few loyal fans to getting your news to the first page of Digg.

When you have news, tell your online community about it. However, sharing it with your community requires that you adhere to the communication protocols of the medium. For example, sharing news in a blog should be done in a manner consistent with the blog's theme and personality. Do not merely regurgitate news on a blog. Discuss it and invite your community to comment. If you're just starting out and still building a community, sharing news in a blog is a good way to invite people into your community. Invite people you know to comment on the news, but make sure they aren't perceived as payroll comments. Remember, the online community is extremely intelligent, and it is quite capable of ferreting out insincerity at a moment's notice. Get people to offer their honest and sincere opinions on your news, what it means to the industry, et cetera. The viral potential of spreading your news this way is potentially very strong and very powerful.

Positive SEO Benefits. Another benefit of social media is the effect it can have on your organic search engine optimization (SEO) strategy. When you produce good content online in social platforms, you increase the possibility of attracting links to that content, which can also link to your website. In turn, those links help give your website authority to the search engines, especially Google, which places most of its ranking criteria on the link popularity of your content. It's widely known that the more content you produce on your website, the better the chance of attracting links. And the more links you attract, the more authority Google will give to your website, which in turn produces a positive effect on rankings for certain keywords relevant to your content.

(Not So) Quantifiable Metrics. As discussed previously, some social media results can be measured quantifiably, and some can't. The following are some examples of things that can be measured in social media marketing. Please note that this is both a partial, as well as a general, list. Chances are not all of these will apply to all organizations.

- Visits to your website from social media platforms

- Requests for information for (fill in the blank)

- Sign-ups to your (fill in the blank)

- A growth in your community

- Improved communication among customers and others in your community

- Invitations to speak or contribute to an event, blog, or other online platform

- Receiving recommendations from your community (unsolicited)

- Customers openly defending you if someone is critical online

- Increased visits to your trade show booth due to social media exposure

- Improved awareness of your company's brand as noted by the sales staff

- Improved awareness of your company's brand as noted by media

- Improved awareness of your company's brand as noted by online measurement tools

- Recognition of thought leaders in your company

- Being recognized for an award based on your blog, podcasts, et cetera

- Growth of online communities (or groups) started by your company

- Learning something meaningful about your customers, market, competition, et cetera

- A noticeable positive sentiment in how your company is perceived

- Becoming a sought-after employment destination for highly qualified candidates

- Shortened sales cycles due to improved brand strength

- More sales opportunities due to improved brand strength

These are just a few possible ways to measure the positive results of your social media strategy.

Educational. One of my favorite benefits of my involvement in social media is the ability to learn something new every day. I categorize learning in two ways: learning and market intelligence. The availability of good (and not-so-good) content in blogs and other social media destinations is nearly endless. So many people in your community can offer tips, ideas, insights, and links to content that is informative and educational. Using bookmarking and social voting tools like Delicious and Digg allows you to find good content easily and share good content just as easily. Additionally, industry-specific destination sites offer valuable and highly educational content. For example, marketers can trust Junta42[3] to consistently deliver good content. As an added bonus, marketers can both submit their own content as well as review content submitted by others.

The other key aspect of education involves market intelligence. For years, industry analysts such as Gartner, Forrester, and BearingPoint made good livings by acting as reputable, dependable sources of market intelligence (and they still do). I'm not predicting their demise, but I do believe their business model is being affected by social media's ability to capture and deliver differing levels of market intelligence. There will always be a need for detailed research accompanied by quantitative metrics. But industry analysts are not the only smart people in the world with access to industry insights. Industry conferences, webcasts, blog posts from industry thought leaders, and even Twitter posts (with links to articles) are a valuable and reliable source of market intelligence. The insights you can gain about your markets, your customers, your competitors, and even your employees are impressive and sometimes surprising. The collective wisdom of the crowd in social media offers incredible amounts of information, and business intelligence that was not readily available prior to Web 2.0 applications is going mainstream.

Here is one example. In years past, focus groups were used as a primary mechanism for gathering market intelligence. Today, focus groups still exist, but I question their contemporary value when all you have to do is spend time in the online communities that matter to your business to learn what people are saying. You can ask questions and get honest responses from the community. One long-standing objection to focus groups is the potential for people to be less than sincere because the entire scenario is purposely staged for input on a particular product. Even when the sponsor of the focus group is not disclosed, it is still a staged situation. By contrast, the people in online communities generally give their input

---

3   Junta42: http://www.junta42.com/

in spontaneous situations, inspired by a conversation. The lessons learned from online communities can be invaluable.

Show Me the Money

All of the benefits described in this chapter add up to the new way of marketing to produce sales results (or equivalent). When you listen, you learn. When you engage your online community, you build trust and relationships. When you communicate valuable information, you build brand. When you make offers to your community in a compelling way (ebooks, podcasts, videos, photos, et cetera), you get better responses than the outdated, traditional Marketing 1.0 methods. When you use software marketing tools to measure activities, sentiment, buzz, and leads, you can track the effect your social media marketing strategy has on your sales. When you consider the alternative to a Marketing 2.0 strategy, you just might be compared to a music store trying to sell records in a digital world of CDs and music downloads. The music industry could not ignore the interruptive technologies and culture shifts. Neither can you.

The primary benefits of a social media marketing strategy can be summed up as building relationships that can bridge that gap between you (the seller) and your buyers.

Staffing for Social Media Marketing

One of the benefits I described is the ability to tap into staff members wherever they may be in the org chart. And, staffers should enjoy their work when they are instrumental in building and maintaining your social media strategy, especially as their personal brand also begins to grow. But, how do you develop your staff to get great results?

Having the Right People on the Bus. Successful social media marketing requires people who understand it, embrace it, and know how to work within the culture and technology. People need to understand the life-cycle and the types of community involved in social media to better understand the opportunities and the risks.

Roles should not only be well-defined and documented, but also they should also be discussed in depth. Everyone on the team must be on board with his or her roles and responsibilities. Then, the heavy lifting begins. In some cases, heavy lifting has been in place for some time, but now you are in a better position to turn it up a notch with better clarity of roles. Ongoing discussions about roles and responsibilities should occur as your social media plan matures. Changes may be needed.

However, what if you realize you don't have the right staff for social media marketing? The fact is some people just don't understand social media. Sometimes the barrier is demographic, but most often, it's just an "I don't get it" attitude. Worse yet, some may resist it for any number of no good reasons. There are still many people who are stuck in the traditional marketing paradigm, and they are not ready to shift to the new social media paradigm. Remind yourself that when the Internet became available to the public in the mid-1990s, many companies at first resisted setting up their websites for a few years. Today, a website is considered an organization's calling card to the world, and every serious business has one. Don't fret—the laggards will eventually get on the social media train because the forward momentum of the culture and the technology will sweep them along. The real problem is this: what if they're holding you back today? If you face that scenario, here are some ideas to consider.

Don't force everyone to jump into a social media strategy overnight. An overnight commitment with a take-no-prisoners mentality can produce corporate culture shock. You run the risk of becoming a maverick, which can trigger counterproductive results. The best way to win people over is to approach them gradually with small but highly visible wins. Assess the people on your team and determine who is best suited to contribute to your social media strategy. People have strengths, weaknesses, likes, and dislikes. It's your job to recognize who may embrace using social media and who may shun it. If you are not the manager and you want to convince management to begin using social media for marketing purposes, you may have a tall order ahead of you. Consider some of the advice I offer here.

People who embrace social media tend to be social. If this sounds a bit trite, hear me out. Being social doesn't necessarily mean being gregarious, boisterous, or the life of the party. Social people are self-confident people, even if quietly so. Their self-confidence may be limited to a specific area of expertise, but they are confident about something. I've noticed that some people who might otherwise shun a public social setting are often very social about something in online social media situations. The key is to recognize the personality attributes of the people in your organization, as well as to recognize their domains of expertise and passions, and then convince them to dip their toes in the social media waters. Asking someone to display his or her expertise or passion in a way that helps your organization meet its strategic objectives is giving that individual an opportunity to shine. For some, it's a new opportunity he or she may embrace willingly. Find the people who will embrace these opportunities and recruit them to your team. If necessary, move people around on your team. Along the way, giving people new opportunities where they can achieve tangible results and be recognized by peers and management will be part of your job as the manager. People who like to write about specific topics and have some level of creativity or technical acuity are good candidates for your team. The bottom line is this: if you don't have the right people on the bus, your social media strategy will not go very far. Defining the roles of the people on your team is my next point.

Definition of Job Roles. At some point, it will be wise to redefine job roles so that they reflect your commitment to a Marketing 2.0 strategy. If you consider social media marketing additive, to which employee's plate do you add it? This will be different in each organization. In some companies, the CEO embraces social media by blogging or being active in a social network. This is a best-case scenario, because the CEO can set the tone for the rest of the organization. In most cases, you'll need to allocate time away from one activity in order to allow time for social media marketing activities. In the beginning, always start small. It may not be difficult to decide to cut back on some activities that don't yield results. Don't continue doing something just because you've always done it that way or because it always produces the same results. You do know this is the definition of insanity, don't you?

A commitment to a social media plan requires a formal review of people's job descriptions and in some cases revising job descriptions to reflect allocation of their time. Here are two examples. The first is for a chief marketing officer under the traditional marketing paradigm. The second is for the same position, but reflecting the Marketing 2.0 paradigm. Note the differences.

CMO: Old Job Description

The chief marketing officer's primary role is to produce leads for the sales department by creating marketing strategies and executing marketing programs with the primary purpose of producing measurable sales leads. Responsibilities include setting up and managing trade advertising, trade show participation, direct mail campaigns, telemarketing, seminars, webinars, and design and production of printed marketing collateral. Web marketing strategies include maintaining the website and using SEO and SEM to drive sales leads from the web.

CMO: New Job Description

The CMO's primary role is to develop marketing strategies and execute marketing programs that strengthen the company's brand while creating strategic opportunities for growing market share and profitability. Strategies should leverage the talents of the executive team and relevant staff members, reinforce the company's core value proposition, and maximize customer evangelism. Tactics should include a combination of some traditional marketing activities (at the discretion of the CMO) and new media, providing our team with the most effective ways of reaching our current and potential customers. Success is measured by strengthened brand equity and improvements in the sales processes that directly result in market share growth.

If you were applying for a CMO role, which job description is more comfortable to you? If you have not yet embraced social media marketing, the old job description is probably familiar to you. However, if you want the freedom to use social media in ways that make sense for your employer, the new job description is a better fit. The revised job description is more strategic and much less restrictive. Notice it does not measure success by sales leads. Rather, success is measured by strengthened brand equity and improvements in the sales processes that directly result in market share growth.

Notice, too, that the new job description doesn't specifically name social media but instead uses the term new media. Throughout this book, I describe marketing on the social web. However, in this case, I refer to *new media* as a form of marketing that leverages media without specifically naming the web as a platform. This leaves the door open to anything that achieves the stated goal. If that includes producing an Internet TV show and syndicating it on the web, so be it. Also, this job description defines the primary role as strengthening the brand and creating strategic opportunities that grow market share profitably. Producing sales leads may be a tactic responsible by members of the CMO's staff through webinars, SEO, SEM, et cetera. But success will be measured by improved brand equity and profitable market share growth. This requires the CMO to have a staff that can produce marketing programs with the right content for the right reason. Rather than putting the emphasis on the tactics, the emphasis is on the strategy, which drives the tactics.

The social media platforms the CMO would use to do the job should not be specified in the job description, in order to avoid confusion between strategy and tactics. During the interview process, I'm sure any qualified candidate would discuss potential strategies he or she might consider using.

Creating strategic opportunities is a terrific way of setting tangible and measurable criteria by which to measure the CMO's performance. This may include conventional sales opportunities, but it may also include opening new markets, new distribution agreements, or strategic alliances. This may also open doors for thought leaders in your company to speak at conferences or simply to achieve peer recognition or build peer relationships. You may also achieve differentiation from key competitors that can allow the sales team to compete in opportunities not previously available. You may extend the use of your products in the same market or in a different market that opens new opportunities. You may improve the reputation of your company or simply create more awareness or credibility for your company.

The revised job description gives the CMO the freedom to pursue the stated goals using his or her chosen tactics in achieving these goals. But don't risk using the revised job description as a blank check to do anything you want. Communicate plans to the stakeholders, and approach it at the right pace according to the resources available. Check in with stakeholders often to make sure you are always in alignment with them. It's difficult to always be in perfect alignment, but if you know who the critical stakeholders are, you can remain as aligned as you need to be. If you find you are way out of alignment with key stakeholders, either find out why and address it quickly, or update your resume because you're likely to be looking for a new job.

The best way to rewrite a job description is to propose it. Don't wait for the boss to come to you and say, "Hey, we should rewrite your job description so you can use social media!" Be proactive by recommending a revision to the formal job description. Draft the revision and sit down with your boss to discuss it. You may have to negotiate the wording. Make it clear that your ultimate objective is to help the company meet its strategic objectives. Your revised job description should not be a departure from the company's mission or goals. If you can sell that, and your boss is not stuck in 1997, you have a good chance of rewriting your job description.

If you have managed to get your job description revised, then discuss what it means with your staff. Discuss it vertically, horizontally, and across the hall. Don't assume just because you revised the job description that everyone else understands what it means. Each organization is different. Depending on variables such as company size, culture, industry, and other characteristics unique to your organization, you may need to do a lot of educating and evangelizing before you start rolling out social media plans in support of the company's objectives. Encourage your colleagues to read what you read, and attend webinars or events where they can get exposed to ideas and successes involving social media marketing.

In many circles, social media is commonly referred to as new media. Let's face it, the evolution of the jargon is unending. Don't get hung up on the jargon. Be diligent about evangelizing your social media plans with your team. But do it at the right pace. Don't overexpose your plans before they have matured. You don't want to promote new social media plans prematurely and have them blow up on you. Build some experience and confidence with social media relationships, and roll out your plans according to the cultural and political norms. Work toward exposure that minimizes your risk internally while maximizing your success in getting recognition for good results, earning credibility and garnering more resources to do more of it.

Once the CMO has redefined the job description successfully, it's time to look at the job descriptions for the marketing staff. An obvious risk is not revising the staff's job descriptions. In some cases, once social media marketing has gained traction, redefining staff job titles also make sense. I've seen some progressive marketing teams assign titles like manager of online communities, community evangelist, director of customer conversations, and chief blogger. Use your creativity to come up with whatever makes sense in your business.

Social media staff skills require a blend of creativity, writing, organizational skills, analytics, and teamwork. A social media plan should leverage the individual talents of staffers while orchestrating them to work as a team to achieve results.

As your social media strategy evolves, so should your staff's skills, titles, the way they spend their time, and the way you recruit new team members. In the years to come, social media skills will be prominently displayed on resumes. In fact, they already are.

THE SOCIAL GRAPH: SHOULD YOU CARE?

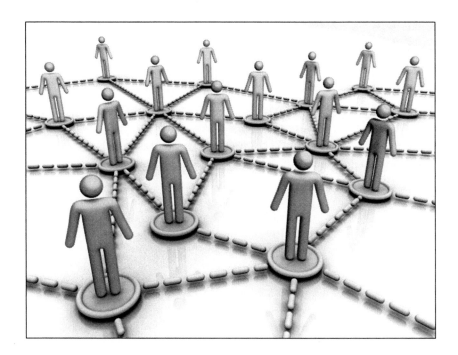

There is much being written about the *social graph*. Let's define it and discuss its relevance to marketers. A social graph is simply a graphical representation of your relationships on the web. The concept is an attempt to visually represent your online relationships in order to help you manage them and get the most value from them. The premise is that if you have an understanding of your online relationships—including the influence of the people in your social graph—you can more effectively manage your efforts at building relationships. As you connect with people, understanding your social graph can potentially suggest others with whom you might build mutually advantageous relationships.

There are, however, many challenges with the social graph, many of which are being addressed actively through the OpenSocial alliance, led by Google.[1] This effort aims to create a set of open standards allowing any developer to a build social graph application that can be used on any social network. Such an application would allow us to build and maintain our individual social graphs without regard to, or restriction by, any social networks. The current problem is that most of us maintain multiple social network profiles on different social networks. So maintaining a social graph is currently a bit cumbersome because their formats are unique to each social network and therefore of limited value collectively. Both Facebook and LinkedIn provide their version of a social graph, but the insight is limited to your relationships within each respective social network. Ultimately, our goal is to manage our relationships on the web, not just on one or two social networks. For example, if we connect on LinkedIn, I should also know how to connect with you on Twitter, Facebook, or other social networks independent of the platform.

The ideal scenario is that, eventually, we will have a neutral trusted third-party resource outside of our social network platforms. This resource would allow us to import and maintain our social graph and determine who we allow into it, as well as who can view our social graph. Ideally, we will be able to prune our social network by removing people we no longer want in our social graph. Ideally, the social graph should travel with you from social network to social network. In time, as we consolidate the social networks in which we participate, the social graph should become more manageable.

What is the significance of the social graph to marketers? Before answering that, allow me a little detour. Whenever I explore and discuss

---

1   OpenSocial by Google: http://www.opensocial.org/

tools or concepts in social media, I always like to ask, "How can we make money with it?" Of course, this isn't the only question you might ask. If your goal isn't to make money, just revise this question to whatever matters to you in your business or organization. Having said that, why should you care about your social graph?

The social graph allows a visual representation of our connectedness to others, presented in such a way that it allows us to understand and determine what that means to us in our relationship-building. Therefore, as a marketer, you can assess your online relationships and determine if you are reaching the people you want to reach. For example, if you are aware of people in your target community who are influential and desirable to your online relationship-building strategy, but who are not currently in your social graph, you might be able to identify other people in your social graph who have access to these people. You can then seek to connect with them in hopes of eventually connecting with your desired relationships. In my opinion, this is one of the greatest potential strengths of a social graph. However, while the social graph does possess tremendous potential value, I caution you not to place more merit in it than it warrants until the third-party application technology is available.

Throughout this book, I've been writing about social media as a marketing strategy. Using tools to achieve our marketing goals is simply a means to an end. Tools will always evolve and improve. It's imperative to study the evolution of available tools. Rely on trusted connections to recommend useful tools. If you consider the social graph as a tool that potentially assists you in achieving your marketing goals, you're looking at it logically and the way I recommend you look at it.

Much is being written about social graphs. I suggest you visit your favorite search engine to research the social graph for current status on its availability in an open and portable format.

I'll close this chapter with this thought. We are social in every aspect of our lives. In a previous chapter, I wrote about the three types of online relationships we maintain: personal, specialized, and virtual. Our ability to visually understand the map or landscape of our online relationships is, at the very least, interesting and at its best, extremely powerful. Be careful not to put too much merit in the social graphs found on social networks that don't matter much to you. Place merit in your social graphs found on social networks where your most meaningful relationships exist. Invest time studying your social graph to maximize the value of the relationships you build and minimize unproductive relationships. Of course, it's up to you to define "productive" and "unproductive" relationships. However, remember that until trusted third-party applications exist, you may not be able to see your social graph outside of a private social network. Therefore, watch the OpenSocial movement carefully for significant developments on this topic.

SEO AND SOCIAL MEDIA MARKETING

S earch engine optimization (SEO) is a practice that has become a mainstay in web marketing in recent years. Even the SEO acronym is considered mainstream among marketers across all industries. There are some who are still leery of SEO due to stories or experiences with mal-intentioned practitioners, known as *black hat* organizations (so called because they use ethically questionable practices). In this chapter, I discuss the best practices of SEO, also known as *white hat* SEO practices (so called because they are ethically sound), and demonstrate the advantages of weaving SEO into your social media strategy.

I have been involved in the SEO industry since 2001. Some of my colleagues have been involved in SEO since the stone age of the Internet, which dates all the way back to the early 1990s. As you might guess, the differences in best practice SEO techniques from the '90s compared to today (2009) are considerable.

Let's start with some SEO basics. Search engines are robots. If this conjures up an image of a machine on an assembly line, think of another type of robot. Search engines send out mathematical crawlers, also known as bots or spiders, across the Internet to visit your website. In essence, they are algorithms which crawl every website they encounter on the Internet.

When the crawler hits your website, it moves through the content, storing your web page URLs in its database for retrieval when a user enters in a search phrase. This is called a keyword search.

When a search engine crawler visits your website, it sees your content, but not in the same way as humans see it. Search engines see your source code, which is the underlying programming of your web pages. This is akin to the way an X-ray machine sees our body. It doesn't see our clothes or skin. It sees our inside skeletal structure. Likewise, search engines see the internal structure of your website and examine several aspects of it. They examine your content and your link structure. These are the two most significant factors search engines consider. Let's examine each one.

Web Site Content

When a search engine visits your website, it attempts to read your content. Remember—a search engine does not see your content the way humans see it. Search engines do not see any of the visual aspects of how content is laid out for the human visitor. Search engines essentially come in through the back door of your website. They *crawl* your web page(s) in an attempt to read your content so they can index it and store it in their databases. If your website contains a lot of images that are not tagged appropriately with text describing them, those images are completely invisible to search engines. If your web page has very little text-based content, the search engine is not able to determine the main theme of the web page. If the words on your web pages are words embedded in an image (because your designer created it that way without regard for effect on your SEO), the search engines cannot read those words at all. This is known as *image-based content*. Please understand that this type of content is totally and completely invisible to search engines.

As a marketer, your goal is to enable the search engine crawlers to easily find the content on each web page. Your content must begin with a clearly written title tag, which is a tag specifically written for search engines. This Meta data serves a simple purpose—to communicate to search engines the main content theme of each page. The Meta data on each web page should be unique. Each page on your website serves a unique purpose, and it should therefore feature uniquely written Meta data. The most important component of the Meta data is the title tag, because it defines the main theme or topic of the web page. If you manufacture or resell industrial equipment and you have a page about earth-moving equipment, the title of the page should include the phrase "earth-moving equipment." It is not enough for the title tag to say "industrial equipment" because it will not show up in search engines for earth-moving equipment. Each page on your website should be uniquely described in the Meta data and in the content in order to help search engines determine the theme of each page on your website.

Link Structure

Prior to Google, search engines primarily determined how to rank website content by analyzing its content as described above. Those who put some effort into their SEO plans were able to *game* the search engines with relative ease by writing content and creating well-written Meta tags. A popular black hat technique was to produce a lot of repetitive content on a page that was invisible to the human eye (white text on a white background) but it served the SEO purpose of achieving high search engine rankings for the website. While both content and Meta data are still important, Google's perspective and practices on how search engine rankings are achieved has brought about dramatic changes.

The founders of Google, Larry Page and Sergey Brin, came up with another method of indexing content. While working on their graduate studies in mathematics at Stanford University, Page and Brin came up with a way to measure the popularity of web page content. Their premise was that ranking web page content in search engines strictly by Meta data and page content didn't necessarily serve the user's best interests since it was fairly easy to manipulate ranking results in the search engines at the time. During this time (1996 to 1998), the two most popular search engines were Yahoo! and Alta Vista. Page and Brin determined that if other people had linked to your content for legitimate reasons, then it must therefore be better than other content that is not as popular, so to speak, because fewer people have linked to it. So they created a new algorithm based on the mathematical googol equation, which is an expression of the number 1 followed by a hundred zeroes. It is also symbolic of their quest to organize a seemingly infinite amount of information on the web. Page and Brin initially called their search engine Backrub.[1] The Backrub name was based largely on the method they used to measure back links to website content as the primary source of indexing website content and determining search ranking results. After changing the name of their business to Google, it didn't take long for the new search engine on the block to catch on. Its popularity—and its use—soon exploded, and today, Google is one of America's best-known success stories with revenues in excess of $15 billion and more than fifteen thousand employees worldwide.

In addition to link popularity as defined by Google, there are other factors in how search engines determine rankings. I won't go into further detail, but if you want to know more about this, see the Resources section for more about SEO.

This background on SEO and Google's link-centric methodology is intended to give you insight into how your social media marketing can significantly contribute to your SEO strategy. Now that we've covered some of the SEO basics, let's turn our attention to understanding how social media and SEO fit together. There are two main ideas to discuss when we look at SEO and social media: *content* and *links*.

Content is still very important for SEO. In fact, you may have heard the familiar saying that content is king. Well, my sentiment is that content is *king, queen, president,* and *prime minister!* I am amazed at how this simple concept is seemingly so misunderstood or even ignored by many marketers. If you ever hire an SEO firm, assuming it uses white hat best practices, you'll be asked to either revise your content to match your keyword strategy, and/or write additional new content to support your keyword strat-

---

1   Google history: the Backrub story: http://www.google.com/corporate/history. html

egy. Many marketers do not devote a lot of time adding new content to their websites. One of the reasons a website may not rank well for its desirable keywords is because the content is *stale*. Search engine crawlers can determine the frequency of content updates occurring on your website. If they determine you have not been updating content on your website, they score you negatively. Adding new content to your website regularly is one important ingredient in your over all SEO strategy. So how can your social media plan contribute to your SEO content strategy?

Once you have a firm understanding of the importance of adding new content, sit down with your team and determine the types of content you can produce. If your website is built out as far as you think it should go in terms of company and product/service information, here are some other ways to add content and how social media can help you.

Synonyms and Antonyms

To get fresh ideas, do some web-based research using search engines, blogs, and other social media sites to find topics that are relevant to your business. You may find ideas that are similar to yours or some that are very different. Don't hesitate to make use of a good idea as long as you don't *plagiarize* its presentation. I often get ideas from other blogs. I take the idea and put my spin on it, creating original content. The point is to find inspiration on other websites, blogs, or social groups. You'll find that, with just a little effort in research, it's easy to do.

Resources

Review your website content and look for ways to rewrite the content with a similar view. For example, if you offer a software product that fits different industries, consider repurposing the content to fit each of the industries. In the main section of your website, your product page may list the industries your product fits. Then, create another section of your website titled Resources or whatever you want to call it, and repurpose the content for each industry. Be sure to name the URL of each of those pages with the theme of the page. It should look something like this: www.yourcompany.com/accounting-software-furniture-dealers.aspx

In this example, your product page may include furniture dealers on the list of industries you serve. But this page is written specifically to address your accounting software for the furniture dealer market.

The resources section is a catchall for adding new content that you don't want to place in the main navigation of your website. Once this content exists, you can promote it in blogs by linking to it. Participating in social groups about this industry can produce natural links to your website. The search engines will score you positively when they find relevant content linking to your website because (in this example) they know that accounting software for furniture dealers is relevant to your website.

FAQ

Creating a frequently asked questions, or FAQ, section in your website is a viable method of adding content. Over time, new questions can be added. Each question should be converted into its own unique web page. Listing all the questions in one FAQ page is not optimal. It's best to have each question link out to a dedicated page, enabling you to be able to create a dedicated URL such as www.yourcompany.com/how-to-track-project-billing-costs.aspx. As you participate in social media communities, you can potentially reference relevant pages from your FAQ section as long as they are relevant to a conversation and truly provide answers to a question. Others who read your FAQ content may also link to it, resulting in more organic links.

White Papers

Many companies have written white papers on various topics of interest to both customers and prospects. Leveraging white paper content for SEO is extremely valuable. Make sure your white papers are not too long. Depending on your industry, it's a good idea to keep white papers under ten pages. You can list all your white papers on one page in your website, but each white paper should link out to a dedicated web page URL using the same guidelines explained in the FAQ section. If your white papers are in a PDF format, use the most current versions of PDF conversion that permit SEO tagging. These PDFs are search engine-friendly and will be indexed properly by search engines. Also, be sure your white papers have text links to relevant pages in your website. White papers likewise can support your conversations in social web communities providing both good content and resulting in organic links to your website.

News and Events

Most company websites have a news and events section. In terms of its SEO value, this section is frequently overlooked. The same concepts apply here. Each link to a news release or an event should link out to a dedicated and descriptive URL. Add text commentary to describe the announcement or the event. Similarly, the content in this section can be socially discussed in online communities as long as you do so in a relevant manner and in human voice, not in corporate jargon.

Testimonials

If you have a section in your website where you list customer testimonials, you know how influential this content can be in your marketing strategy. Testimonials help sell the credibility of your company. But don't overlook the SEO value of these testimonials. Ask your customers to include important keywords in their testimonials. A testimonial such as, "ABC Law firm has been a terrific resource to us," is not nearly as valuable as, "ABC Law firm has been terrific in helping us protect our intellectual property legal rights." In the second example, the customer quote can help the law firm to be optimized for *intellectual property legal rights*. Likewise, repurposing this content in online conversations can have a positive effect on your SEO results.

Blogs

One *very* powerful way to add great SEO content to your website on an ongoing basis is adding a blog to it. One way to get SEO value from your blog is to connect your blog to your website. For example: www.yourcompany.com/blog. The content on this blog will be part of your website because it is connected to your top level domain name.

If you consistently maintain your blog, you will be adding content to it on a regular basis. Since it's your blog, you can write content on any topic you deem appropriate. Most blog software platforms allow you to define the permalink of each blog post. The permalink is the URL of the blog post. Since you can create the permalink, you can define it according to your SEO keyword strategy. For example, the law firm wanting to be optimized for keywords related to intellectual property legal rights can write blog posts using a permalink such as www.yourcompany.com/blog/common-legal-mistakes-intellectual-property.aspx. In this sample blog post, the blogger could write about some of the common mistakes to avoid with intellectual property. Note how the words *legal, intellectual,* and *property* are listed with dashes separating them. When search engines "see" that your website has many pages focused on the main theme of intellectual property law with derivatives of this phrase, the search engines give your content high scores.

Blogs allow you to write content without having to figure out where it fits in your website. Just concentrate on writing content that is relevant to the theme of the blog and, assuming it is relevant to your business, you will receive SEO value. Of course, your blog is also a source of community- and relationship-building with people who visit your blog.

Links

In SEO, the link value credited to your website by search engines is the single largest factor. It's been estimated that links count as much as 70 percent toward your potential search engine ranking. Just so you know, Google, the current industry leader in search, has never published this ratio. Therefore, this is not a scientifically derived percentage; it is instead an estimate made by several leading industry pundits, including yours truly. However, this ratio is a little misleading. I have said many times that in order to get the full value of the 70 percent weight placed on links, a website must have a sound foundation of content that is friendly to search engines. In other words, the 30 percent of weight placed on good content, is foundational. In other words, without a strong foundation of good content, you do not receive the full SEO value of links. The reason this is important is because you can't shortcut your SEO strategy by building links without also providing good content to link into.

I've been asked many times how are links created. Many marketers don't understand how links to their websites originate. There are several common ways that links form, and social media offers an accelerated opportunity for links.

First, consider that the web is in itself a vast link structure. After all, it is called the World Wide Web. The web metaphor is no accident. The web comprises content connected to content. There are no technical barriers to linking from a web page to another web page anywhere on the globe. So the first concept to grasp is that content attracts links naturally (organically). I call this the *weed phenomenon*. Weeds grow in a pile of dirt without any attention or any watering. Don't try to explain it. They just do.

Over time, the more content a website contains, the more links it will attract (naturally). I've often told clients they probably wouldn't need to engage our SEO services if their website had thousands of pages of relevant content, assuming the website's technical architecture is search engine-friendly. Websites featuring page after page of good content naturally attract links and the high search engine rankings that go with them. However, the reality is that most SMB websites have a range of twenty to one hundred pages, not thousands.

So how can websites like these attract links? The first way is to write great content that is truly meaningful to your target audience. Like those weeds in the dirt, links will occur naturally. Again, unless your website has thousands of pages of content, those natural links may not be enough to secure a high ranking in search engines for all your desirable keywords. Below are some other strategies you can use to ensure your website attracts links. Each of these can be shared appropriately on the social web in sincere and authentic conversations:

- *Tools.* Are you in an industry where you can create a page of content featuring a tool that is of interest to people? A good example of this is a real estate industry website featuring a mortgage calculator. In the heating and air conditioning industry, a web page might offer a means of calculating the energy cost saved by purchasing a new heating or air conditioning unit. In the telecommunications industry, a web page that calculates savings between differing types of telecommunication systems is attractive to site visitors. Whatever the details might eventually be, if you can offer a web page of content that people will share with others because it offers a valuable tool, people will link to it.

- *Blogging.* There are two ways of using a blogging strategy to produce valuable links to your website: 1) When you leave comments on someone's blog, you are usually provided the ability to include a link to your website. Your website link can be your home page, your blog site, or a particular page on your website or blog. As you leave comments on blogs you visit and you provide these links, they start to add up and create SEO value; and 2) Embed links in your blog back to a specific page to your website. You should *anchor* the text link from your desirable keyword phrase such as *intellectual property law.* This passes the authority of the link for this keyword phrase to a web page with similar content in your website, and the search engines score this favorably.

- *News Releases.* A press or news release is an easy way to produce links. Using any of the major wire distribution services such as BusinessWire, PRNewswire, and PRWeb, you can distribute news releases with text links anchored to your selected keywords. Just be aware that there is a cost associated with distributing each release. Anytime you send out a press release, you should always use the SEO package from any of these wire services to create back links to your website from your most desirable keyword phrases.

- *Article Syndication.* Consider syndicating articles you've written by submitting them to websites offering syndication. There are two ways to identify syndication sites. Certainly, you can search for them in your favorite search engine and you'll find plenty of them. But I prefer to focus on industry-specific websites. Concentrate your search within your industry and seek media and news outlets, including blogs that allow you to submit your content. I regularly submit my blog posts to Junta42 and Sphinn, which are both destinations for content on web marketing and social media topics. Be selective about your syndication sites. Some syndicators turn your content into billboards for their advertising while sabotaging your link.

- *Content Sharing Social Sites.* There are several content sharing sites where you can submit articles and other relevant content. I mentioned two pertaining to my industry. Additionally, there are dozens of content sharing sites you can submit to. Here is a partial list: Reddit, Delicious, Digg, StumbleUpon, Technorati, FriendFeed, Xanga, ma.gnolia, Propeller, Newsvine, Mixx, and Simpy. Do your homework and look for content sharing sites that pertain to your industry.

- *Social Media Promiscuity.* This is a sensitive topic, but not for the reasons you may think. This concept refers to the *pimping* of your content on the social web. It is a fairly common practice. Social media promiscuity suggests that you and your friends promote your content on social media. Here is a common example. I wrote a blog post about how the lines are blurring among the social media sites. I submitted it as a guest post to HubSpot. They published it, promoting it to their sizeable community. They also promoted it via email through Twitter and Facebook. Their daily email blast contained a link to the blog post. There are several people at HubSpot who maintain active Twitter accounts and they each sent out links to the blog post through Twitter. They also mentioned it on their Facebook page, which is seen by their Facebook friends. I recorded a podcast discussing the blog post in detail and posted it on my blog with a link to the blog post. I submitted the blog post with my podcast to Junta42, Sphinn, and several other content sharing sites. I asked several friends of mine to send links to my podcast on this particular blog post as well. Through these combinations of friends, and some social media pimping, I managed to get this blog post considerable exposure, which in turn drove considerable traffic to both my blog and website. When promoting content using social media promiscuity, you will naturally produce links to your content. This tactic should be used sparingly, or you run the risk of spamming your community. It's important you feel strongly that the content you are pimping is good content. A general rule of thumb is not to pimp all your content. Save only your best content for this tactic and you should feel confident you've earned the right to do so.

- *Link Juice.* The background provided previously on Google's history will help you grasp the concept of *link juice.* As Google scores your links and your content, it is essentially giving your website a certain level of authority. This authority is largely measured by your PageRank,[2] which uses a scale of one to ten (in whole numbers). As your website gains authority, your PageRank increases. As your PageRank increases, it becomes increasingly important to protect it. One way you can drain the link authority (link juice) of your website is to link from your website to another website that is not relevant to yours. If your outbound links are excessive or not linking to relevant content, the result is draining authority from your website. This is known as draining link juice. The

---

2 PageRank definition: http://www.google.com/corporate/tech.html

opposite occurs when link juice is passed along to your website from a high PageRank website with relevant content. The most common resolution to prevent draining link juice is to place a piece of code on your links which tells the search engines "not to follow the link," and therefore you don't drain any link juice from your website. This is known as a *no-follow tag*. The point to understand is that you can prevent leaking valuable link juice from your website by using no-follow tags in your outbound links. However, you should know that the recipient of your link will not receive any SEO value from your link. Adding a no-follow tag is purely to tell search engines not to credit this link for SEO value. It has no effect on the visitor's ability to click the link to the destination website. In other words, it's strictly behind the scenes and transparent to your website visitors.

SEO is evolving. Google isn't going away anytime soon. However, people don't limit their research on the web to Google and other search engines. Don't limit the ability of potential buyers to find you by only concerning yourself with search engine rankings and results. While these are very important considerations, the whole purpose of this book is to encourage you to broaden your footprint on the web through social media. Buyers across all industries are fast becoming diversified in how they use the web, where they seek information, from whom they seek it, whom they trust for opinions and recommendations, and how they find suppliers of products and services. Be accessible on the web through a combination of conventional SEO and social web strategies, and you'll bridge the gap between you (the seller) and your buyers.

Blogging

A business blog is one of the most effective methods of developing a community in social media. However, creating a blog and succeeding with a business blog are two entirely different things. Technorati delivers an annual State of the Blogosphere report.[1] The statistics are mind-boggling. There are more than 100 million blogs worldwide, though many of them are not actively maintained. In May 2005, *Business Week*[2] wrote a cover story saying that business blogs are mainstream. More recently, blogs have crossed over into social networks, complementing stand-alone blogs. A business blog can be a very effective element of your social media marketing plan, yet it can also be a high source of failure if executed poorly.

Many small and medium-size businesses express distrust in a business blog. Another common objection to business blogging is the time required to make it successful. Before you get discouraged, let's examine business blogging by looking at the opportunities and the risks. However, first consider that the success of a business blog starts with your strategy.

---

1   Technorati State of the Blogosphere 2008: http://technorati.com/blogging/
    state-of-the-blogosphere/
2   BusinessWeek: Blogs Will Change Your Business: http://www.businessweek.
    com/magazine/content/05_18/b3931001_mz001.htm

As stated previously, setting your strategy is crucial to the success of your social media marketing efforts. In fact, the most common mistake people make in business blogging is starting a new blog with little consideration for a strategy, the objectives, resource allocation, and how they will measure success.

When considering a blog for your business, I strongly recommend you start by studying other blogs in your industry. In fact, it would behoove you to study blogs both in and out of your industry, as you may learn something very valuable from blogs outside your industry. Using blog search tools such as Technorati and Google's Blogsearch, as well as Digg, StumbleUpon, and Reddit, you can find blogs on relevant topics in your industry. Search for blogs using keywords relevant to your company's products, your industry segment, people's names, issues, trends, generally anything relevant to your business. Experiment with your search using many different keywords.

You will likely find no shortage of blogs to study. Initially, I recommend not spending a lot of time reading each blog that you find. Start out by building a list of blogs that you will go back and study later. As you initially visit the blogs, read the title of the blog. This is important because most blogs are titled according to their primary purpose or theme. Scan the blog post dates to ensure it is maintained and kept current. If you notice that the last blog post was more than a month ago with previous posts spread out over weeks or months, I don't recommend putting it on your list. You should only study blogs that are actively maintained and kept current. There are many blogs that have been abandoned due (at least in part) to an ineffective blog strategy. Don't limit yourself to blogs that are updated daily. Look for consistency of blogging, not entries spread out sporadically over time. A blog with sporadic entries is a sure sign of a blog with no commitment. Such blogs are updated whenever the blog owner gets around to it. This is a sure way to alienate your blog community and fail at business blogging. As you select blogs to study, bookmark them using your favorite web-based bookmarking tool. You may want to create categories in your bookmarking for ease of review later. Don't overanalyze the blogs at this stage. At this stage, your focus should be on building a long list of blogs to study. Your objective at this stage is to identify and observe relevant blogs that will help you set your blog strategy.

Developing your blog strategy is not much different from developing a product strategy. You wouldn't consider building a new product without conducting market research to understand current product offerings, their strengths and weaknesses, and the demand for a product in a segment with which you are familiar. Your product strategy would be to find out where the opportunities are and build a product that suits the market opportunity. Researching business blogs to determine your blog strategy is akin to doing market research for a new product.

Your list should include approximately twenty blogs. After you have developed this list, go back and read them. At this stage, your focus is to devote more time with your list, seeking to observe two primary attributes of each blog: *theme* and *personality*. Observe the main theme and topics(s) of the blogs you've selected. Make a list of these topics to see if you can develop any patterns or observations meaningful to you. Look for holes. Are there topics not covered in these blogs that could be covered by your company? Again, similar to setting a new product strategy, seek ways to be different with your blog strategy. You may find blogs not adequately covering a topic in which your company has domain expertise. Therefore, you may decide you can develop a more effective blog on the topic or a blog with another perspective on the same topic.

The other observation you should focus on is the personality or voice of the blog. Personality in a blog is very important. Sometimes a competitive blog doesn't have an interesting personality; that is an opportunity for your blog. A good business blog should reflect the personality of the company or the blogger(s). Sometimes, the personality of a blog can affect its success as much as any other factor. Consider our personal tastes in television news anchors, radio show hosts, politicians, and certain actors.

Once you have reviewed each entry on your blog list, if you have devoted adequate time to this exercise, you will likely start to develop some ideas about your new blog. I urge you to resist the temptation to finalize your blog strategy just yet. Take your long list and trim it down, creating a short list. In developing your short list, use criteria unique to your situation. Perhaps certain blogs have very good personalities, or some blogs have really great content. Whatever the reason, your short list of blogs should be the best of the best on your long list. Then let the dust settle on these blogs by either engaging in blog conversations or just by observing them a little longer. The idea is to let the cream rise to the top; allow yourself time to digest your research and begin to form your blog strategy.

Regardless of how many blogs you have identified, one recommendation I make without apology is that you spend ample time reading blogs and observing the conversations. This is also known as listening. I once heard someone jokingly refer to this as lurking. This description was used in the context of visiting blogs and reading the content, but not engaging in conversations. If you do nothing more than listen to the conversations in relevant blogs, you can learn a lot that can contribute to your business blog strategy. Remember that once you set your blog strategy, it should live for a reasonable period of time. So, don't rush the process to develop your blog strategy.

Depending on the resources you have, this research exercise can take a week up to a couple of months. The duration depends partly on your time and resources, as well as how many blogs you research. I urge you not to shortchange this exercise. Once you set your blog strategy, it is akin pointing your ship down a channel. It's difficult to change direction once you've started. Many businesses that have failed at blogging didn't do their homework. Is it any wonder they failed at business blogging?

If you give this exercise the time and energy it deserves, you'll likely have many good ideas for a blog strategy. You may even have more than one good idea. Your greatest challenge may be choosing a single strategy. Even if you have the resources for more than one blog, resist the urge to start more than one. In giving this advice, I understand that the circumstances of each business are unique, so realistically consider both your resources and your ability to commit to a blog strategy. Even if you have the ability to allocate significant resources to the new blog strategy, I still believe starting with just one blog is best so you can learn from it and concentrate on building a community. Expect to make a few mistakes along the way. Expect the blog's audience to grow slowly. Your actual experience may be spectacular out of the gate (not the norm), but don't have high expectations over the first few months of a blog. In short, give it time to mature. Stay committed to adding quality content on a consistent basis. Don't deviate from your strategy unless enough time and results have passed to indicate failure. Stay on topic with all your blog content. If you follow the strategy outlined here, your chances of success with your blog are far better and in fact very strong.

Another approach to consider is to listen to your customers and create a blog that addresses their needs. Perhaps your customers want to learn more about your development cycle. If your engineers are apt to being effective bloggers without giving away the keys to the kingdom, just giving your customers access to your engineers could be a successful blog. This is just one example, of course, but in this example, the engineers must understand their role is to engage customers in conversation about certain topics, not to disclose proprietary information. Sometimes giving customers access to people inside a company with whom they don't ordinarily interact can create a valuable customer experience as a blog strategy. You'll read about a great example in the Indium Corp. story in the case studies section.

Setting the Strategy. Once you've completed your research and you are full of ideas, consider the opportunities you have for your business blog. Here is a partial list of the types of blog strategies you may consider:

- *Technical.* Discuss technical aspects of your products or your industry in ways that give your customers and prospective customers valuable insights.

- *Marketing.* Promote good content through your blog, but do it with a human voice, not through corporate marketing jargon. Discuss the meaning of your announcements. Offer links to other good content, both yours and others within your industry. Discuss your marketing strategy in plain language. This can help your customers and prospective customers understand it better, which isn't always possible with corporate-sounding news releases and websites. If you're concerned about your competition understanding your marketing strategy, let it go. They still have to outperform your strategy. Clarity of message is critical in marketing, and your blog is a good place to give clarity of message.

- *Thought Leadership.* If you have one or more people in your company who have strong vision and a passion for communicating it through a blog, a thought leadership blog can be a home run. Thought leaders are created organically. Sure, PR agencies can help, but in the age of content marketing, visionaries need only to communicate their visions using the broad reach of social media to gain recognition. Thought leaders can blog about issues, trends, ideas, best practices, et cetera. For example, Dan Schawbel is a thought leader on the subject of personal branding as illustrated by his blog, Facebook fan page, and his book *Me 2.0.*

- *Best Practices.* A blog about best practices can be authored by a thought leader or by domain experts whose blog contribution is limited to best practices. An example is an engineer who blogs about performing quality assurance testing.

- *Entertaining.* Remember that a successful blog must have a personality, a human voice. When a blog has entertainment value, it has great potential. It is possible to combine entertainment within the context of a business blog. Sometimes the entertainment is in the form of a creative design, or the use of clever and creative videos, or simply a blogger who has the gift of humor in his or her writing style. We all enjoy being entertained, and a business blog can be a source of entertainment, of course in good taste, and in a relevant way. You can embed humorous video in your blog that has a relevant relationship to your blog content. It doesn't have to be your video. If you find a video on YouTube, you can embed it in your blog simply by copying the code and pasting it into your blog. Video content producers want you to share their video. Video has proven to be one of the most (if not *the* most) viral forms of content on the web. Entertaining video can help spread your blog content like nothing else in social media. Rick Short, director of marketing communications at Indium Corp., maintains a blog about B2B marcom.[3] Short shows his sense of humor using video. Check out his post on October 23, 2008, in which he discusses billboard advertising and suggests that shaved heads can be potential billboards. Short uses his own shaved head to illustrate this point. It's quite humorous.

- *Controversial.* This is probably the most difficult to pull off. A business blog that asks questions designed to be thought provoking is one possible way to be controversial. Effective controversial blogs will be unique to each industry. Similar in perspective to the entertaining blog, someone gifted with the ability to create controversy without damaging your brand should maintain a controversial blog. A controversial blog is often tied to an individual, not a business. An individual who has strong opinions, yet communicates them in non-offensive ways, can build a loyal following. Glenn Beck[4] comes to mind. But, few people can pull off this strategy effectively in business. There is risk to this strategy, but it can still be effective of executed properly.

These are but a few blog strategy examples. If you do your homework, your blog strategy may be a combination of these or something entirely different. I urge you to do your homework and then select or develop a blog strategy that has a high probability of success.

Risks in Business Blogging. When setting your blog strategy, other important factors to consider include the main topic, or theme, of the blog, availability of bloggers in your company, the intended frequency of blogging, who will respond to blog post comments, and how you will handle

---

3   Rick Short: Director Marketing Communications, Indium Corp.: http://www. indium.com/blogs/Rick-Short-B2B-Marcom-Blog
4   Glen Beck: http://www.glennbeck.com/content/blog/stu/

them, particularly when they are negative comments. Of these factors, the one with the highest risk factor is the selection of the blogger in your business. Let's assume you've done your homework and you have selected a topic and theme. Do you have someone inside the four walls of your company who has the domain expertise to blog about it? Does he or she have an interest in being a blogger? Does he or she have the skills to write in a human voice? Although effective blogging doesn't require a degree in journalism, a blogger certainly needs a decent command of grammar and a writing style that will succeed in a blog. Above all else, an effective business blogger doesn't sell! An effective business blogger tells a story.

The single biggest risk in business blogging is setting the wrong strategy, resulting in discouragement and abandonment of your blog. For this reason, taking the time to study the blogs in your industry and selecting a strategy that you believe is suitable to—and workable for—your company and its available resources is so important.

Be sure you select a strategy that aligns with your available resources. The selection of a blog theme and producing content that goes with it must be supported by people in your company who can and will commit to writing good content for the blog. If you choose to use outside resources, be careful to select resources with a backup plan. If your external resources become unavailable, you need to have other resources lined up to keep your blog going.

Another common risk and concern among businesses is the potential for negative comments on your blog. I have a glass-half-full attitude toward this issue. In most cases, negative comments can turn into something good. Of course, it depends on the circumstances. If your company dropped the ball on something very big, the outcry from the community can be harsh. However, even in these situations, you can usually turn lemons into lemonade.

When people post negative comments on your blog, there are several actions you can take. One possible action is to do nothing. Sometimes, it's just not worth fanning the fire by responding. Consider just letting the post run its course and move on. However, I advise you use this approach only in minor situations where you feel the post is just one person's point of view and not significant in the grand scheme of things. Anything major absolutely warrants a response, the absence of which will be perceived very harshly by your community. If your company has a positive history, there is a good potential for loyal followers to come to your defense by acknowledging your fault in the situation and suggesting that, based on your history of doing the right thing for the customer, there is confidence you will make the situation right.

A common and often effective approach to negative comments is to respond in a very positive and professional manner. If the negative posts are accurate because you have done something worthy of the criticism, the best reaction you can have is to thank the community for caring enough to write about it and acknowledge that you have work to do to fix it. If you can, spell out exactly what you are going to do to fix the situation. Speak in a human voice; sounding like a corporate robot may hurt you. Even if the fix involves standard corporate procedures, respond with a plain language description of how you plan to resolve the situation and, if it makes sense, identify the people who will resolve it, again showing the human side of the business.

Sometimes negative comments are not warranted. If someone posts a negative comment about something that doesn't involve your company's failed effort at something, consider these remedies:

- As mentioned previously, not responding is certainly an option. This is a good option if the blog post is ridiculous and widely recognized as such. Your community would recognize a knucklehead post that doesn't warrant a response. In most cases, your community may self-police such comments.

- If negative comments are unwarranted, reach out to some of your loyal community members and privately ask them to write a response to the negative comment. Don't script it for them. Just ask them to respond in their own way. It's often more effective for your community to respond to negative comments than for you to respond. If you feel compelled to respond, do so in the human voice of your blog.

- Be careful not to become confrontational unless it is truly deserved, which in a blog is almost never warranted.

I can't effectively provide advice for every possible situation. A rule of thumb is this: remember that your community is watching. Show it you are listening, that you care about its members, and that you are committed to serving their best interests. Show them you are human.

Many business blogs use the option of moderating comments on their blogs. By using this option, you greatly reduce the possibility of negative comments on your blog. Using this option is a decision that should be made independently for each blog. In my own case, I started out using this option and turned it off after about six months. The advantage to using this option is that you can see the comment, review it, and edit it before you post it. However, you run the risk of angering the blogger if you edit his comment, if you don't post the comment, or if the delay in posting the comment is significant. The nature of blogs is to post content quickly. Comments should be available quickly.

Another big risk in business blogging is not taking it seriously by not allocating the time and resources to it. You should never start a blog as a project. If you make a commitment to a business blog, it should be because it has become a part of your overall marketing strategy. By definition, a project has a start and a finish. If you don't properly allocate the resources to your blog strategy, you run the risk of either not building a community or losing the interest of your community. If you can't commit the resources to your blog, your strategy should be to read other blogs and not start your own. In short, don't start your own blog until you can make the commitment.

What if your blog doesn't build a big community? What if no one posts comments? These are legitimate concerns, but don't expend significant energy fretting over these. Depending on your company's reputation, size, market awareness, and other factors, the reaction to your blog may or may not matter. Allow your blog to be a one-way communication tool from you to the outside world. It may appear that no one is listening because perhaps there are few, if any, comments to your blog content, or perhaps your subscriptions are very low. Remember that your blog content can spread throughout the web and can have other benefits.

What if you are in an industry where people don't visit blogs? I argue there are very few industries where people don't visit blogs. I don't suggest there are none, just very few. In most cases, you may be surprised to learn about blogs in your industry and the people who read them. Even if the numbers are low, there is a good chance that those people are influential. Do your homework by using the blogging strategy plan described earlier in this chapter. If you determine there really is not a significant blogging community in your industry, congratulations. You have either identified one of the few communities who don't blog or a previously undiscovered alien species. Consider becoming a pioneer and starting a blog for this community. Don't be surprised if you become a celebrity in this community.

Benefits of Business Blogging. There are truly many benefits to having a business blog. The effort to develop a blog strategy and the risks described above should not discourage you.

Depending on the strategy you select, one great benefit is that you can achieve the objectives of that strategy. For example, if your strategy is thought leadership, you can achieve this and be recognized in your industry as a thought leader. Along with achieving this, you may open up new doors and opportunities for your business in ways that can't be predicted but can be measured. Because the blogosphere is a vibrant online community, the reach you can have is impressive and sometimes amazing.

One of the greatest benefits of a business blog is the effect it can have on your ability to communicate to your existing customers. We are often so focused on new business development that we overlook the importance of sustaining valuable relationships with our existing customers. Whether or not your products or services have multiple cross-selling opportunities with existing customers, having a positive communication effect on your existing customers is invaluable. A blog strategy allowing you to engage in communication with customers—whether directly or indirectly—in a human voice can be very effective and implemented at a reasonable cost. Blog communication takes place all year long, whether it's daily or weekly. By providing customers with your insights or access to people in your company, you give customers a benefit that has great potential to strengthen their loyalty to your business. This alone is a huge benefit. Customers talk to each other and often to prospective customers. Your blog has potential to strengthen your brand with current customers. And your blog can also build brand awareness, brand loyalty, reach to new customers, and your credibility in your market segments.

I now turn to another huge benefit of having a business blog. Blog content is very influential in search engines, and I mean *very*. Your SEO efforts can be very positively affected by your blog content as discussed in the SEO chapter. Search engines, especially Google, score the authority of your website based on its content, relevant incoming links, and the extent to which your website's technical architecture is friendly to search engines. Why? First, you can add blog content anytime. Plus, you can hyperlink words within your blog content to other websites or blogs as well as to your own website. While search engines care most about those who are linking to you, when you link to others, you are sharing the authority of your website with those you link to. This concept is known as *link love*. Here's how it works. In the content of one of your blog posts, you link to another relevant blog or website. Assuming your blog post had good content, the receiving blogger will be grateful for your link. Most bloggers track all incoming links through tools such as Google Alerts and HubSpot's Link Grader. The reaction to your link can be favorable and can result in a new relationship, a return link, or some other unpredictable positive outcome. If your blog post is good, the link recipient may pass it along on Twitter, LinkedIn, or Facebook to share it with others, giving your blog post further exposure. There are many different ways your blog post can gain exposure to others giving it more potential for viral growth. All of this exposure increases its reach among online communities and search engines.

The best way to gain exposure with your content in search engines is to write blog posts where the name of the URL uses relevant keywords that are part of your SEO strategy. For example, on the Find and Convert blog, I have written blog posts containing the words *Internet marketing* and *social media marketing* in the URL, with these words separated by dashes. A blog post may look something like this: www.findandconvert. com/blog/2008/internet-marketing-hosting-nightmare or http://www. findandconvert.com/blog/2008/the-risk-factors-in-social-media-mar-keting/.

By using these terms in the URL, I contribute to the authority of my website in relation to these terms. When people search for these terms or variations of these terms, my blog entries and my company website search results have better ranking potential. In fact, some search results using derivatives of these phrases are on page one and some are on page two (at the time of this writing). The authority given to my website by having so much content on my blog using these keyword phrases in the URL and supported by good content is very strong.

The most effective SEO benefits are derived from a blog whose do-main includes your company's web domain. For example, http://www. findandconvert.com/blog/ tells the search engines that the content on my blog is part of my website. On the other hand, if I used a blog domain like http://blogger.findandconvert.com or http://typepad.findandconvert. com, the search engine authority would go to blogger.com or typepad. com, not to findandconvert.com. If SEO is a major part of your social media marketing objective—and it probably should be—these latter ex-amples are not the recommended approach.

How do you promote your blog? Oh, you didn't know that you'd have to promote your blog? Yes, you will. Remember that Technorati counts more than 100 million blogs. While most of them are not similar to yours, there still are many blogs out there. The number of blogs that are com-petitive with yours will vary according to your industry. Even if there are not many blogs in your industry, you still need to promote yours.

Promoting Your Blog. In some ways, promoting your blog is similar to any other marketing activity in your company. If you have developed a solid blog plan using some derivative of the strategy guidelines outlined in this chapter, and you have identified the internal blog resources, and you are truly committed to your new blog strategy, you should issue a news release announcing the existence of your new blog. There is one caveat to this, though: I suggest you hold off issuing a news release until after your blog has been launched and you have posted a reasonable amount of content. The news release will probably direct people to the blog, and it's important you have some content to show for it.

Before you announce your blog, you should preannounce it. Tap into a loyal following of customers and partners early in your blog strategy. Call them, email them, and generally recruit them to subscribe to your blog and to participate in blog posts to create conversations and buzz about your blog. When you issue a news release, use a wire distribution service such as PRWeb or BusinessWire, both of which offer SEO features allowing you to hyperlink selected keywords to a page on your website or blog. Choose your keywords carefully according to your SEO strategy and drive the links back to your blog site. When you write the news release, do not focus on yourself. Frankly, I don't care about your new blog. Tell me why your new blog will be useful to *me*. You may have heard of the old principle *WIIFM*, also known as, "What's in it for me?" Write the news release to explain the benefits of the blog, who will benefit from it, and ideally include a quote from someone who is participating in the blog. The quote should support the strategy of the blog with a testimonial. Use the WIIFM principle in announcing the blog and in ongoing promotional efforts. For example, I regularly tell people about my Internet marketing blog, and I stress that it is 100 percent focused on tips and best practices in web marketing strategies. I stress that subscribers will stay current on trends and ideas to use in promoting their business on the web at the Find and Convert blog. In fact, my blog was once ranked in Junta42's[5] top ten for content marketing blogs.

Once you've distributed the news release over the web using one of the wire services mentioned above, write about it in your blog. Don't repeat the news release in your blog. Remember that a blog should be conversational and reflective of the personality of the blog's theme and host.

---

5   Junta42: http://www.junta42.com/

Summarize the news release in plain language with commentary about the release in a human voice with personality. Elaborate on the news release. Invite people to comment on it. Forward the blog post about your news release to people in your community, including customers. The idea is to let the word spread using social media platforms.

Other ways to promote your blog include placing a link to the blog site in any or all of your marketing communications. Create a link or a button or a graphic image link from your website for easy access to your blog. Be sure to always explain the purpose of your blog. Remember, people don't care that you have a blog. They care why it's meaningful to them. List your blog address in your auto signature, in your presentations, on your business card, in your LinkedIn profile, and any other social media profile you have. When you update any marketing communications materials, include a link to your blog. Make sure you set up your blog feeds to automatically display in your social networking profiles.

As your blog matures, consider assigning new titles or alternate titles to the people in your company responsible for maintaining the blog. A fairly common title is chief blogger, or director of blog community. Create your own titles, and share them with staff and the outside world. If you're that serious about your blog strategy, be passionate, be vocal, and be visible. Whatever you do, don't keep it a secret!

As you create new blog posts, share some of them with others. As discussed previously, content sharing sites exist to share and propagate content. Ask someone to submit some of your blog posts to content sharing sites such as StumbleUpon. Make sure you have social media sharing buttons at the bottom of your blog posts so people can share your content easily. These social buttons are available from most blogging software platforms.

If you have a Twitter account, sparingly drop links to some of your blog posts when posting updates in Twitter. Have members of your staff do the same. If you have identified portals or blogs within your industry that exist to share and propagate content, use them. That's why they exist. Be aggressive in submitting your content to vertical industry social media sites. If you have profiles in social networking sites, add links to your blog posts in your profile. Your friends will see them and possibly share your content with others. If your blog has an email subscription feature, each subscriber will receive an email each time you add a blog post.

Consider inviting people into your blog conversations by posting questions and offering a poll or survey. A good blog is conversational and invites conversation.

A *blog roll* is a feature in blog software that allows you to list links to other blogs. The blog roll is listed off to one side, usually the right, and allows visitors to see links to other blogs that you endorse as relevant to the content on your blog. It's another way of saying that if you like the content on my blog, you will probably like the content on these blogs. Don't hesitate to do this. It is considered a common courtesy to share good blog content with your community. And by doing this, you pay a compliment to these blogs when you list them in your blog roll.

Another way to promote your blog is by branding it separately from your company. This approach is a strategy all unto itself. It involves selecting a meaningful theme and creating a dedicated blog around the theme. In essence the blog becomes a dedicated website, although it is a blog site. Personally, I like this approach a lot. It does require a big commitment of resources and in most cases doesn't warrant going this route out of the gate with a business blog strategy. The resource commitment is significant, but it can also have a big return if executed well. Your company size, market presence, and availability of resources may be factors in going this route. Still, it's an approach that can be effectively executed by any company with the commitment and the skills to make it happen. In the next section, I give an example of this approach through IdeaStorm, a dedicated blog site from Dell. It is a sterling example of execution using this approach.

Dell's Big Idea Blog Strategy

According to a September 2008 *Fortune* magazine article,[6] supported by research analyst comments, Dell has devoted a forty-plus person team to using blogs, forums, and other social media to build and maintain relationships with its community. Dell has realized that people spend the vast majority of their time online when researching PCs, and just a small percentage of time actually making the purchase. By devoting significant resources to social media communities, Dell is able to get involved in conversations and potentially thwart negative comments, particularly when they are based more on opinion than fact. Its involvement is not limited to the forty people at Dell. The community is involved. Dell evangelists are sought and enlisted in proactive ways to help defend and strengthen the Dell brand. One way in which Dell uses the community is to seek their input on new product features, which has resulted in adding new features (according to the *Fortune* magazine article) such as backlit keyboards for use in the dark.

The primary social media platform for Dell is IdeaStorm, a dedicated social media destination site that emulates the Digg model whereby people post comments and then vote on them. The community—or anyone else—can visit IdeaStorm, type any keyword, and find out what people are saying about that topic. Dell's goal is to use the input from IdeaStorm to build more competitive products as a response to this community input. Another area of focus for Dell's Team Web 2.0 is monitoring conversations on Facebook and Twitter. By actively listening and participating in these conversations, Dell is able to more quickly glean the sentiment of the collective wisdom of the crowd. Dell is also using tools from Radian6 and Buzzlogic to monitor and measure the discussions to help guide it in taking decisive actions. Considering the size of Dell's market and global presence, industrial strength tools like Radian6 and Buzzlogic are warranted to monitor such sentiment. For smaller companies, such tools may or may not be needed. Such a decision should be made on a case-by-case basis.

---

6   Fortune Magazine, September 4, 2008

Measuring a Business Blog's Success

When measuring business blogging, success begins with your objectives. If you've clearly defined and documented your objectives, you will have benchmarks against which you can measure. The metrics tools you use can vary. I will describe your possible measurement strategies in three possible scenarios using simple terminology: *low-tech* and *high-tech*.

Low-tech. A low-tech measurement strategy involves gaining agreement among the key stakeholders in your company about the objectives of your blog strategy and the ways in which you will measure success. Therefore, the first criterion for measurement is alignment with all the stakeholders in your business. Alignment is important regardless of the measurement method you use. In a low-tech approach, you can use combinations of free tools and assumptions. For example, using tools such as Google Analytics to measure traffic to your website and blog site, you can track which web pages are getting the most traffic. Your blog posts are individual pages, so this is a simple and quantifiable metric you can easily track with any web analytics tool. You can also track which keywords are driving traffic to your website or blog. One metric to explore is the increase in traffic to your website from your blog, or increase in traffic to your blog over time. Since each business is unique, I can't realistically offer advice that suits every reader.

The key to low-tech measurement is to dive into your web analytics and compare history to the present and the future. Study the trends and patterns in traffic to your site. For example, you may observe that traffic to your blog increases more for blog posts on certain topics. This would be a good indicator of interest in such topics and may suggest you write more about them. However, before you do that, study the bounce rates for those visits. A bounce is measured when a visitor to your website or blog visits only one page then leaves your site without navigating any further. A bounce implies the visitor was interested in the topic that attracted them to your site but was not interested in visiting any other content on your site. There are several ways to address high bounce rates, including offering more content to keep the visitor on your site as well as links to other relevant content within your blog or website. Don't hesitate to link one blog post to another blog post or to your website, as long as the link is relevant and useful to your blog visitors.

Measuring results in a low-tech manner involves mostly studying web analytics and drawing conclusions. You should have some assumptions based on history. For example, if you assume that about 10 percent of the visitors to your website become leads (or your desired outcome), your goal is to drive more traffic from your blog to your website and use that assumption. However, I caution you to carefully scrutinize your assumptions. You may find that those assumptions may not apply in a positive or negative way from blog traffic. In other words, your conversion rate may increase from your blog traffic or it may decrease. There are many factors that may affect this, including the quantity and quality of your blog visitors. Remember that anyone can visit your blog, and some visitors may like your content but may not be viable prospects for your business. This leads to another important factor: these visitors who are not viable prospects should not necessarily be written off. These people are potentially loyal to your brand, and they have the potential to be word-of-mouth referrers to people who are viable prospects to your business. While this is very much a possibility, it poses a problem in measuring results. For this reason, I suggest, as do so many of my peers in social media strategy, that measuring social media results is not the same as measuring all other online marketing strategies. Both quantitative and qualitative factors must be considered.

Another low-tech approach is to study the increase of traffic to your blog or website from people who searched your company name. A blog often has the benefit of increasing brand awareness, and that can be reflected in increased visits to your website from your company name.

Low-tech metrics involves using free tools such as Blogmarks, Blogpulse, Flickr, Google Blog Search, Google News, Google Alerts, Digg, Delicious, Feedburner, Ice Rocket, Technorati, Trendpedia, Yahoo News, and YouTube. Some of these tools also offer a fee-based version.

I argue that if your blog traffic grows over time, that alone is worth measuring and counting as a success. Your CEO may argue that the only ROI that counts is leads or sales, but your counterargument is that building brand awareness through a good blog leads to money. Measure sales trends before the blog and the trends during the life of the blog. Online conversations starting on your blog can move to offline conversations resulting in sales. Make sure you measure that.

Measure website traffic referrals attributed directly to specific blog posts. Measure search engine rankings from specific blog posts. Measure the viral effect of blog content by where it gets picked up and the potential reach of your blog content. For example, if one of your blog posts gets linked to, or summarized and linked to another blog in your market, measure the reach of that blog. To satisfy the CEO's ROI issue, equate it to the cost of advertising to that audience and remind her that, other than the time it took to write the blog content, it was free.

High-tech. A high-tech approach is to use fee-based measurement tools to measure the quality of traffic on your brand as well as conversions to leads or sales. In this approach, you still use elbow grease to measure what you can measure but you increase the use of tools as aids in arriving at more scientific metrics. High tech metrics tools include Brandwatch, BuzzLogic, ComMetric, Dow Jones & Company, HubSpot, Lexalytics, NetEquity, Nielsen Online, Radian6, ReputationHQ, ScoutLabs, Socialware, Visible Technologies, and Whitevector. This partial list of fee-based tools offers different feature sets. Some are designed to help you better measure your overall brand strength and improvement, some measure sentiment and buzz, while some offer detailed metrics including lead conversion details and closed loop metrics into CRM systems. These tools are not limited to measuring your business blog; they can help measure *all* your social media marketing efforts.

The mention of any of the tools discussed in the low-tech or high-tech sections should not be construed as an endorsement on my part. There are indeed many tools available and more coming out every week. You should do your homework to select tools that best fit your situation.

Blogging for Business Summary

Business blogging can be a very effective component in your social media strategy. Setting your blog strategy should begin with research, listening to conversations on other relevant blogs and eventually committing to a strategy that is realistic from a resource perspective. Your blog strategy should be focused on a theme or topic. Create several blogs if you have several topics to cover, but I caution against this in the beginning to avoid being spread too thin. Writing blog content in a human voice with personality is a must for a successful blog. Promoting your blog is necessary to attract a loyal following to your blog. Following SEO best practices, including linking your blog to your company website and creating search engine friendly URLs (permalinks) will help boost your search engine rankings. Linking from your blog content to other relevant blogs is an effective way to share your blog's authority with others, recognize their good content, and make a few friends along the way. Social media is social, and linking is an integral aspect of being social on the web.

Blog with passion and with consistency on subjects in which you have authority or expertise, and good things can happen in your business. Measure these things using low-tech or high-tech tools and measurement strategies. Whatever your measurement strategies, it's critical to have alignment with your key stakeholders for agreement on the achievement of success.

Above all, don't sell on your business blog! Let your good content be your marketing. A well-planned and well-executed blog strategy will contribute to bridging the gap between you (the seller) and your buyers.

Case Study: Blogging at Indium Corp.

Indium is a seventy-five-year-old manufacturing company headquartered in Utica, New York, with facilities in Korea, China, Singapore, and the United Kingdom. There is absolutely nothing sexy about Indium's products. Many of us have likely used its products without ever knowing it. Indium makes solder-based electronics assembly material products that are purchased by a diverse group of multinational manufacturers that make products such as consumer electronics, military products, medical devices, mobile communications, phones, LCDs, circuit boards, flat panel screens, and infrastructure products. If you use a PC, you may be using Indium's products. Simply stated, Indium's products help make the electronic connections in these products better. This is a very simple, non-technical way to describe what Indium's products do. Considering that Indium's customers are very technical, it's sort of ironic to simplify Indium's products so much. But that's exactly what Indium has done through its blog social media strategy.

Indium has five hundred employees. Many of them produce valuable content as part of the company's marketing strategy. About fifteen employees host one of the company's ten company blogs, all contributing to the central theme, "When Connections Count." I think this is a very clever theme.

Under the leadership of Rick Short, director of marketing communications and a twenty-five-year veteran of the company, Indium is implementing a social media marketing strategy that rivals some of the most progressive on the web. What is most impressive about it is that the company is largely made up of very technically oriented engineering minds. You don't often see midsize, private engineering-oriented companies get marketing right, but Indium is the exception. The secret lies in Short's understanding of the key ingredients involved in using social media effectively, as well as his leadership in harnessing the in-house talent to implement it properly.

Short is quick to point out that Indium's target customer is an intelligent, technical person who despises hype. These are very sophisticated people located throughout the world. As Short says, they are "some of the world's smartest people." In order to build great products for very smart people in the electronics industry, Indium has focused on hiring smart, technical people. Short understands that a technical buyer cares about making an informed, educated decision. Engineers who perform product evaluations take great pride in executing incredibly detailed research initiatives and sharing their findings with peers so they that can make informed decisions that serve them well. Indium's marketing strategy is to provide transparent information that is both understandable and credible. It's not hype. As a result, Indium has drastically reduced the amount of glossy marketing materials it uses by 70 percent in the past five years. Trade show exhibits have been reduced by 60 percent.

Recognizing the shift in recent years to the buyer's propensity for searching the Internet, Indium is emphasizing organic search engine results and social media. It accomplishes this by positioning its employees as thought leaders within the industry through its blog and video content.

When Short started blogging about five years ago, he slowly got other engineers involved, asking them to talk naturally about their interests. Those same engineers embraced blogging because they were not asked to become marketers. They were simply asked to be transparent. They were asked to let their natural voices be heard through the blog. These engineers embraced the opportunity to write about technical topics they really enjoy because they know them very well.

This blog strategy has been the centerpiece of Indium's social media marketing strategy. The goal has been to position Indium engineers as thought leaders in their industry. Indium currently maintains ten blogs, each hosted by one or more engineers and focused on a specific discipline. They are: electronics assembly (English), electronics assembly technology, electronics assembly (Chinese), solar assembly materials, thermal interface materials, engineered solders, semiconductor packaging, tech support, and B2B marcom (Short hosts this one).

Again, the overall objective for Indium's social media strategy is thought leadership. Short understands that producing intelligent, transparent content is the ticket to successful marketing results. In addition to producing blog content, the other aspects of Indium's marketing strategy include producing video content, chairing panels at industry events, contributing articles to trade magazines, providing training at customer sites and within the Indium research and development center, delivering technical papers at trade shows, technology conferences, and customer sites, and guest blogging on other relevant blogs.

What results can Indium point to? Since the corporate blog launched in 2004, Indium has seen search engine results improve dramatically and website traffic has become a dominant source of incoming sales opportunities. Indium has recently broken through the level of fifty thousand blog page views per month. Remember, the content is technical materials, science, and electronics assembly information. This blogging program is not attracting too many casual onlookers. Their visitors are the real deal. When inquiries come in from the web, they are from people who have spent time researching specific content, and they are often very serious about their buying intentions. They often turn out to be a very good fit for Indium's solder-based products.

Rick Short views his team as being accountable for delivering qualified contacts (leads) to the sales force. The primary quantifiable metric he uses is the number of qualified leads produced. The blog has unquestionably contributed to producing qualified leads. Over and over again, people from large manufacturers around the globe contact Indium about issues discussed in its blogs. Often, the contact is made directly to the Indium blogger, and the resulting conversation often leads to a sales opportunity. When people in this industry search relevant keywords, the Indium blog posts show up, which in turn lead to more sales opportunities. Short uses many third-party tools and metrics to measure and guide overall effectiveness of his social media strategy.

Since Indium maintains open dialogue with all members of its community, it often hears comments like, "We read about you everywhere." There was once a request from a competitor's CEO to be a guest blogger. In the spirit of transparency on the social web, the request was obliged though the competitor ultimately never followed through.

Considering that engineers are often introverts—they are at least viewed that way by many—I asked Short how he was able to get so many people at Indium to embrace the social web. He quickly pointed out that Indium engineers are accustomed to interfacing with customers on technical topics. Anyone who is comfortable communicating in any of the formats previously described has that option, but no one is ever required to do so. Indium hires people who are naturally available to customers to speak about any topic. As Short says, "The social web is nothing more than a platform that allows us be ourselves. It's genetic. We get out of their way. We let them be themselves. We provide some corporate guidelines, but we never ask employees to do anything that is not natural to them."

I asked Short for some of the lessons he learned from his social media marketing strategy, particularly as it relates to blogging. Here are some of his most compelling tips:

- Bloggers are bloggers, speakers are speakers, and sometimes the two are not the same.

- Some engineers just don't blog, and that's okay.

- You can blog about whatever you like, but if you're not talking about what the customers are interested in, nobody cares.

- We want to be the answer to the question being asked by the customer.

- Be pervasive and ubiquitous. Be everywhere in the industry (with your content).

- Talk about everything relevant, the whole package. Talk about what you do, what your customers are saying, what your industry is saying, et cetera. You are received as credible when you talk about everything.

Short's favorite story goes like this. Indium's vice president of marketing was in a meeting at a large computer manufacturer, and its engineers said, "Everywhere we go, your name pops up." That story doesn't show up in a quantifiable statistic, but it's obvious proof that Indium's marketing strategy of producing great content through the social web is working and bridging the gap between them and their buyers.

SOCIAL NETWORKING

I n the past three years alone, social networking has truly exploded. The explosion began originally among students, artists, and generally a younger demographic. As you read this book, there are now examples of three generations in a family, from grandparents to teens, connecting in social networks, and this is fast becoming the norm. Business social networking is still young and emerging, but doing so at a fast pace. At the time of this writing, the most popular public social networking sites among business users in the United States are LinkedIn and Facebook, with user communities measured in the tens of millions for each. Some also consider Twitter a hybrid social networking platform. What they have in common is that they are open to the public, they are free, and they offer the ability to connect and network with people online. Beyond that, there are distinct differences among them.

I will discuss the benefits and risks of using these popular and public social networks as well as guidelines for business social networking. Then I will discuss the merit of considering private, closed social networks.

Public social networks offer the ability to create profiles and connect to others. A business can benefit from any or all of the popular social networks in several ways. Individuals within your business can create their profiles and express all their interests to include their professional achievements and interests. They can also express their personal interests, which offer people a human view or insight into you and your employees. I frequently like to remind you that social media is *social*. Businesses must come to understand and embrace this social mind-set in order to gain the full value of online relationship-building.

When an individual maintains an active profile in a social network, the effect can be a co-branding experience. People actively maintain their profiles in social networks, connecting to others and sharing their life experiences, posting photos, links, and videos, while offering commentary on topics of interest. Since one aspect of social media is the convergence of personal and professional life experiences, social networking platforms offer good co-branding opportunities for both employer and employee. Of course, one obvious risk is the lack of control you have over employees who can post photos of a party where their conduct may be considered risqué or contrary to the image your business seeks to portray. Discussions should take place with employees about using good judgment and common sense when posting photos to their social network profiles. Some employees may push back if they feel you are imposing on their personal lives. Remind them that the social web has torn down the walls of the office. You're just asking them to use common sense. Remember the effect of party photos of Olympian swimmer Michael Phelps. It was a private party, yet the photos of him smoking an illegal substance, which showed up on the Internet, damaged his business relationship with some of his sponsors, not to mention his brand as a clean-cut athlete.

Social networking has become popular largely due to three drivers discussed previously: 1) technology advancements; 2) easier access to the Internet; and 3) social and culture shifts, which includes work/personal convergence. People in social networks are merging their public and private personas with their work personas. Some try to resist this convergence, but I argue that it's very difficult. Even if you maintain a LinkedIn profile strictly for business and a Facebook profile strictly for personal use, anyone who wants to connect to you in both platforms has a lens into your business and personal personae.

We identify our professional lives and our personal lives as if they are one and the same. Our life in modern economics is not merely a function of working at anything that produces a paycheck, but rather working at something we enjoy that involves subject matters for which we display real passion and expertise. This phenomenon is not really much of a phenomenon when you stop to think about it. People have always been social creatures. We've always had a personal and professional life. Long before the proliferation of the personal computer and the Internet, people socialized at clubs and events, discussing politics, sports, and the workplace. The ever-popular work cliché refers to people at work who gather around a watercooler chitchatting. Today, though, a stream of social media has replaced the watercooler, and social networks top the list of places where virtual watercooler conversations occur.

The most common question businesses ask when considering the use of social networks is, *Why bother?* Why not just do our social networking on the golf course? In many industries, the golf course was the preferred social networking platform. And, it was effective. It was also expensive and time-consuming, and also very limited. In a company of five hundred employees, how many of them can do effective social networking on the golf course? Ask this question in a down economy, and the answer is even more difficult. Yet the value of golf course social networking is not in doubt. Fast-forward to a Marketing 2.0 world, and the platform for social networking has shifted from the golf course to the Internet from any connected location in the world, without regard for titles, economic status, or even credentials. If someone has something of interest to say, they can say it and be heard.

Similar to golf course social networking, online social networking takes time. It differs from blogging in that it is truly more like socializing. At least when you maintain a blog, you are writing and that feels more like work. For this reason—and no doubt a few more—many businesses have resisted embracing social networking for business. It just doesn't feel like work. The roadblock is connecting the dots between the social and cultural shift to gain an understanding of the business benefits.

The growing reality is that many business individuals have embraced social networks. When I speak at conferences and events on social media, I always poll my audience to see how many people have created social networking profiles. Time and again, well over half of each audience (comprising business people, most in management roles) have created at least one profile. However, when I ask how many of them actively socialize, network, or otherwise proactively use social networking sites, the numbers fall off a cliff. And, when I ask how many of them have achieved any measureable return from their social networking—read: received business—the response is usually very few, and often none. While these informal polls admittedly do not constitute statistically valid market research, in my opinion, the frequency of similar responses does point to a consistent pattern among business managers about the lack of business performance using social networks. The dots haven't been connected yet. For this reason and others like it, I believe the younger demographics that understand the business value of social networking (as well as older demographics like me who get it) are anxiously awaiting the retirement of the Marketing 1.0 manager.

Public social networks can indeed pay dividends for businesses, but few companies are willing to devote the time and energy required to reap the rewards. Social networking for business is a little like going fishing. Even the most experienced angler can spend the entire day fishing and catch nothing. However, an experienced angler knows that, over the long term, by investing in the right tools, using best practices, and applying time and persistence to it, catching fish is definitely going to happen. In this metaphor, catching fish is akin to making money (or your equivalent) in business by social networking. So how can a business make money by being active in free and public social networking sites?

Let's begin with the premise alluded to in the preceding paragraphs: social networking for business takes time and persistence. Therefore, if using social networks for profit is truly something you want to do, you must first make the commitment to do it with persistence, consistency, and genuine intentions. Remember, we're talking about building relationships. Don't expect quick results. As in blogging, develop your strategy using the same strategy-setting guidelines discussed previously. Search for people in social networks with common interests and friend or connect to them. I must admit that I used to be very selective about accepting friend invitations from people I had never met. I eventually learned that the real benefit to developing friends in social networks is to expand your network and your social graph as long as there are common interests. I won't accept an invitation from a student in Belgium. But, I will accept one from a marketing manager in Israel or Cleveland. Geography notwithstanding, the common interest is the criteria.

To get real results from your social networking efforts, you must work at it. Sit down with your business development and marketing team and map out a plan. Start with your business development strategy. Consider the businesses you are targeting and study the connections in your social graph to find connections that can open doors. Find people who may provide a connection to a new business opportunity in a social network and contact them through the social network platform. You have a much greater chance of contacting someone through a social networking medium than you do through a cold-call or direct mail piece. The social graph is the key to finding the people who may offer your business potential new opportunities.

This approach to new business development using the social graph takes time. I get very frustrated when I hear business executives say they don't have time to do this. Whether they really mean they don't have time, or they won't allow their staff to make time for it, it just doesn't make any sense in a contemporary marketplace. Often, these are the same executives who allocate people and budget to cold-calling, direct mail, and other forms of intrusive marketing that are increasingly on the decline. The reason you don't have time for social networking is because you're too busy managing these 1990s-style marketing programs producing marginal results. If that offends you, I offer no apology. If you are having success using these intrusive marketing programs, either they won't last much longer, or you're fudging the metrics to kid yourself of their success. A 0.5 percent response rate in direct mail is not success. A 5 percent call connection in cold-calling is not success. How about a 20 percent response rate from a community that follows you online? How about an introduction to a key contact through a social network that would not have happened otherwise? That's what I'm talking about! It's about developing a loyal community and getting results from that community.

The Power of Groups

Another successful way to use business social networking is using the "groups" function in your favorite social network. You can either start a new group or join existing groups. A group is like a club or association. Groups exist around almost any topic. People start groups to build communities for sharing, collaboration, discussions, and networking. If you create a group, promote it and grow it, then nurture it with good topics of conversations. Help others in your group shine by providing a platform for their expertise. Encourage people to use the platform to share their expertise and start discussions. When you join groups, you should become active by joining in on discussions. Form a team of people from different functions in your business to devote time to groups. Spread the responsibility around as well as the topics to study and participate.

Make Friends

The purpose of building a *friend* network in a social network is to build your social graph so you can network with them—get it? That's why it's called *social networking*. Remember, the platform is online, so geography and time zones are irrelevant. The primary common denominator for friending in social networks should be common interests.

Let's be honest, to be my friend in a social network doesn't really mean you're my friend. In business social networking, we enter into relationships to build our network. Building our network allows us to become part of an online community. Providing something of interest to our virtual friends is what it's all about. Be a thought leader or a comedian or somehow interesting in your unique way. There will come a day when you want something from your community, and that's where the money is. Virtual relationships, not unlike personal and casual relationships, must be genuine, and that includes sharing good ideas, tips, and links that can build sincere relationships in social networks. If some of the tips and content you share with your virtual friends includes your own content, you can use that to create tangible and measurable returns in social networks.

Throughout this book, I've been stressing the importance of building community and giving to your online communities. That includes giving them access to your content, whether your content is words, audio, or video. Good content is good content. It should not be shameless promotional content but rather educational, informative, and entertaining. If you provide your social network with any of these forms of content, you are serving your online community and you will attract more virtual friends. Another form of content is introductions or referrals. A common practice in business social networking is to provide a testimonial or an introduction. Since these are done online, the value when it comes from a trusted source can be very powerful. In social networking, the trust factor is everything!

Social Networking Business Example

Here is an example of how to use social networking for business. When you create a new blog post, a new podcast, a new video, or a new photo session, any of which can pertain to your business, share it with as many people as possible for maximum exposure. Using virtual relationships in social networks, you can share your content and have it spread among your community and beyond. If you consider that any one person knows dozens or hundreds of other people that you don't know, there is always potential for your content to be shared with others, providing you with potential exposure. If your market segment is narrow, and I often see it, don't think this principle doesn't apply. If you are building your network among people with common interests, the same principle applies, no matter the numbers.

I caution you not to spam your social networking relationships by hitting them with your content too frequently. Make sure your content is truly good content as judged by those best qualified to judge—the members of your community. If the members of your community are telling you that you are producing content that provides value and serves their needs, share it sparingly so that your virtual relationships don't perceive you as abusing their trust. It is just as important to send your virtual friends good content from other sources to demonstrate genuine interest in your network. If you earn a reputation for sharing good content with your virtual relationships, when you begin sharing your own content, it will be well-received. But when it's always your content, it is likely to be perceived as entirely self-serving and spammy. Consider that your virtual friends want true relationships, not a one-link stand.

Private Social Networks

A private social network is essentially the same as a public social network. The obvious difference is that is it private. A common example is a social network developed within an industry, such as ITToolbox in the IT community. Another common example is private groups formed within a public social network, such as LinkedIn and Facebook. Anyone can form a group in these social networks and invite people to join it. The group administrator moderates and controls acceptance of new group members as well as the content policies. A group within a social network should be branded and should clearly describe its purpose. A group can be built around a topic or a business. Nonprofits often create groups to get people involved. Businesses form groups around a topic or theme. An example of this is user groups for specific products. The general idea behind a group is to create a sort of private club organized around a topic that is of interest to your community.

Using private groups in social media marketing can be very effective if you develop a sound strategy and work at it (sound familiar?). The first objective of a new group is to have a clear message. Make sure people understand whether they qualify for your group. Then, create the group using clear messaging to attract people. Use a logo to brand the group, whether it's a company logo or some other relevant image. People respond to a graphical image of any entity, and a group is defined as an entity made up of a collection of people. Have a content strategy for your group based on its theme. And have a promotional strategy for your group based on membership requirements.

Let's consider two groups. One is a nonprofit group with a local presence. The other is a topical group with a global presence. The nonprofit creates the group, brands it with a logo, and invites members. The purpose of the group is to promote dialogue among its members, extend its reach, and expand public awareness. The ultimate objective of the nonprofit group is to grow its membership base while promoting its cause. By working at building loyalty within the group and promoting good content, the group will reach beyond its current membership to people who can get interested in the nonprofit. The group will discuss events held by the nonprofit. The group members will create buzz around it, inspiring others to attend the events and get involved in the nonprofit organization, thereby achieving its objective.

Recall that the other group is built around a topic. The brand of the group is the company that sponsors the group, but the content of the group is limited to the topic. The group is promoted in a social network by inviting connections in the social graph and by posting content about the topic in Twitter and other social web platforms where like-minded communities exist. The content posted in this group is intended to share relevant content to its group members and get them talking about it. The group can grow in two ways. First, the group administrator can continue to invite people to join the group. Second, the value of the content and the conversations happening within the group can spread virally, attracting new members.

Creating a Private Community Destination

Let's turn our attention to *private social networks*. These are social networks created by people, businesses, or associations with the intent of building a private community. This is no different than private clubs or associations that require a membership, along with certain criteria or rules for membership. Building a private social network is a growing trend among businesses and associations. This approach has a lot of upside, but it also comes at a cost. First, it requires a software platform to build a destination website similar to Facebook or LinkedIn. The functions found in these two social networking sites alone are robust and the result of millions of dollars spent in development, not to mention market research. Platforms such as Ning[1] and Neighborhood America[2] offer any business the ability to create private social networks. Costs aside, other considerations include content ownership and availability (uptime).

A private social network or group can work very well if your business has an existing loyal community with the potential for growth. Another advantage to private social networks is preserving your market share through the private online community.

I don't believe that most small businesses can justify the cost of building a private social network, especially when so many free platforms are available in social networks. Nonetheless, the landscape for private social networks will continue to grow. As with most technologies, the costs will eventually drop, and the website of tomorrow is likely to be a social network. Google already offers free software through FriendConnect[3] as an add-on module to offer social networking features to a website. We can expect to see website redesigns for the average business to take on the look, feel, and personality of a private social network.

Social networking is not a new phenomenon. It is simply an extension of what people have done for centuries, including golf course social networking. Our businesses can benefit from a social networking strategy by developing one and working at it persistently. Planning should involve the relevant functions in your business, such as marketing and business development, to divide up relevant topics and online locations. There is no way to shortcut the process. Invest time in it, monitor progress, and take a long term view of relationship and trust-building. Those businesses that apply time, talent, passion, persistence, transparency, content, and a mind-set of relationship-building through social networking will bridge the gap between themselves and their buyers.

---

1   Ning: http://www.ning.com/
2   Neighborhood America: http://www.neighborhoodamerica.com/
3   FriendConnect: http://www.google.com/friendconnect/

TWITTER (MICROBLOGGING)

You've probably heard of Twitter. Twitter is a hybrid social media platform. It's part microblogging and part social network. *Microblogging* is a reduced form of blogging. Actually, microblogging is a little like blogging, a little like social networking, a little like instant messaging, and a little like participating in a giant chat room. The term refers to the fact that you use a web service to make entries or posts similar to blogging except you are limited to a small number of characters for each entry. At the time of this writing, by far, the most popular microblogging platform is Twitter.[1] In this section, I discuss the popular Twitter platform and its effect on social media marketing, including how businesses can use Twitter productively. In the following section, I'll discuss private microblogging networks and how businesses can use them productively.

If you already use Twitter, you know how addictive[2] it can be. Yet, there are many who have no interest or just don't get it. I have always maintained that as useful as Twitter can be, it's not for all businesses. Twitter can be an effective marketing communication tool, for those who embrace it. The idea behind Twitter is that you selectively follow people's

---

1   Twitter: http://www.twitter.com/
2   You're Addicted to Twitter if.... http://www.findandconvert.com/blog/2008/ youre-addicted-to-twitter-if-you/

updates, and people selectively follow yours. You write what you are cur-rently doing or thinking about in short posts limited to 140 characters. Admittedly, the idea sounds absurd at first, and it does take a little getting used to. But as many people will tell you, once you are following people and people are following you, it can become somewhat intoxicating. If this still sounds a little absurd, read on, looking beyond the platform and its quirky terminology to its potential in marketing communication and branding. I'll help you get there.

When you tweet (the verb for posting comments on Twitter), you are communicating a thought to your followers. It can be a random thought, or it can pertain to a specific topic. There are many people who shun Twitter, and there are many people who are addicted to it. In late 2008, HubSpot delivered the State of the Twittersphere Q4 2008 Report.[3] The report is full of interesting Twitter statistics, including the fact that new Twitter accounts opening daily approached ten thousand. At the time of this writing, in mid-2009, the total number of Twitter users is nearing ten million.

At the time of this writing, Twitter is a free service. There is much speculation about Twitter's monetization strategy because there are no advertisers. While Twitter's business model is not the main purpose of this chapter, it's worth mentioning because there is at least some risk that Twitter could cease to exist as a business, though its huge popularity would give it better odds of becoming an acquisition target than running the risk of folding up shop, as reported by some media. Still, even if Twit-ter disappeared, the microblogging platform appears to be here to stay, as evidenced by how each of the major social networking services now offer Twitter-like functions enabling you to post entries such as, "What's on your mind?" on Facebook, or "What are you working on now?" on LinkedIn. Due to Twitter's popularity and open API, it's easy to link to your Twitter profile from an RSS feed in your website or blog and display your most recent tweet. You can also link your most current tweet to your

---

3   State of the Twittersphere: http://blog.hubspot.com/blog/tabid/6307/
    bid/4439/State-of-the-Twittersphere-Q4-2008-Report.aspx

social networking profile. Still sound absurd? What is all the attraction with microblogging and Twitter? Be patient and read on....

Twitter allows for a stream of thoughts, comments, and links to flow throughout your day. Both individuals and businesses use Twitter as a social media communication tool. Let's pause right here. Digest this: Twitter is a communication tool. And since communication is at the heart of what marketing is, begin by embracing the fact that Twitter is another—and very contemporary, if different—form of marketing communication. Even if you choose not to use it, understand that it is a marketing communication platform.

Rather than outdated forms of marketing communication that can easily be filtered out by your target market, microblogging allows you to engage people in your target in a very multidirectional communication medium. People will follow you only if they want to follow you. So, if you do an effective job of selecting people to follow based on common interests and you are actively engaged in Twitter conversations, the effect on your brand and your business development effectiveness can be very exciting.

In Twitter, you only follow people you want to follow, and anyone can choose to follow you—unless you set up your profile as private, which then sends you a request to be followed. Twitter followers can use their PCs as well as their mobile devices to send and receive tweets.

You can use Twitter by going to the Twitter.com website and logging in (generally, once you sign on, you stay signed on from your computer). Once you are at Twitter, all the most recent tweets (entries by people you are following) are displayed in the sequence of most current to older. The stream of tweets flows throughout the day. You can scroll to read older posts. A picture or graphic representation of each person you follow is displayed next to their post. Many people upload a real photo image while others use cute or weird cartoon images instead. When a business hosts a Twitter profile, the photo is usually not a person but rather a logo or some other image representing the brand.

There are countless tools emerging to enhance the use of Twitter. If you use the popular Firefox web browser, TwitterFox allows you to see updates coming into your browser. Other tools such as TinyTwitter let you send tweets from your mobile device. TweetDeck is a popular freestanding application that runs on your computer and organizes your Twitter stream allowing you to set up groups of different people you follow. This is helpful as the list of people you follow grows. It sits in the background and signals you that there are Twitter notifications in the upper right corner of your screen. Your Twitter conversations are displayed in columns, including all public and private replies.

Twirl is another application that functions much like instant messaging. As tweets come in, they pop up in the lower right, and you can click to see or to hide them. TwitterBerry is the application used on the Blackberry mobile device. Tweetburner is a URL tracking tool that lets you track the popularity of the URLs you have posted in Twitter. Tweetburner is one of my favorite Twitter tools because you can see which URL links your followers visited. You can learn which topics are popular by the people following you. And, you can plan to offer similar content to them to keep your followers interested in you. When your Twitter following demonstrates interest in your content, you start to harness the power of Twitter in your Marketing 2.0 strategy. Your thought leadership reputation and brand equity are strengthened through good content sharing on Twitter. Tweetburner also helps you determine which followers you may want to engage further, either online or offline. But, as I've cautioned previously, use social media common sense when approaching people online. Explore their interests in your content. Don't spam them with your content. Remember that someone can un-follow you with just a click if you prove to be a pest.

The opportunities for businesses to use Twitter are plentiful. Individuals within your company can create a Twitter profile. They can post comments about things that are happening in your company or your industry as well as personal tidbits. They can search to find and follow people who share common interests by searching relevant keywords on Twitter's search platform. For example, I follow people whose profile includes keywords pertaining to social media marketing, Web 2.0, SEO, SEM, and Inbound marketing, Internet marketing or web marketing, as well as other related marketing topics. Your follower network can grow if you follow some basic principles. Your profile should be descriptive and interesting. Your profile should include a photo. Studio photos are not as popular as casual, environmental photos. Upload a background image in the settings area. The background image should communicate your personality or accomplishments with links to your social profiles, blog or website. Allow the background image to literally paint a picture of you or your brand if your Twitter profile is of your company. To grow your Twitter network you must actively post interesting thoughts and links to meaningful content every day—yes, every day. You should post several times throughout the day. You should also seek to follow people. Don't expect to get a lot of followers if you don't follow others. The opportunities for businesses to create brand awareness, thought leadership, and general networking using Twitter are terrific. It is truly a social networking phenomenon.

Twitter limits each entry or tweet to 140 characters. A new Twitter strategy should follow the social media strategy guidelines provided throughout this book. Post comments and thoughts that can be of interest to your followers. Admittedly, some people offer meaningless tweets notifying you they are at a Starbucks on the corner of Fifth and Elk. On the other hand, if you are going to an industry event, you should tell your followers you will be attending the event. Throughout the event, send tweets about it to help keep your followers informed. Include links to interesting content from the event.

Start out your Twitter career by sharing thoughts about issues and events taking place in your industry. Be sure to be genuine with your followers. Tell them what you really feel is happening. Make your posts interesting. If no one ever replies to your posts, you are probably not interesting enough or you are not engaging with your following by replying to their tweets. The 140-character limitation offers good incentive to provide links to other content such as blog posts or articles. By providing a link to content, you can promote your own content using Twitter as long as your community agrees your content is meaningful. If you spam or shamelessly promote your business, your followers will not appreciate it. Anyone can stop following another follower at anytime. A general rule of thumb I use is to include links to my blog posts as the exception, not the norm. The vast majority of my tweets are comments, observations, links to interesting articles from relevant news sources, and replies to other tweets. I want followers to see links to my content as an occasional occurrence and relevant. You should, too. Otherwise, you run the risk of being perceived as self-serving and even somewhat of a spammer.

When someone has a response to your Twitter posts, they can reply either publicly or privately. A public reply references your Twitter name along with the reply. For example, a reply to me would display as @berniebay (my Twitter name) followed by the reply. These public replies are displayed to anyone following me. More importantly, I will see all public @ replies using my Twitter name.

Private replies used the letter "D" to designate a direct reply. These replies are not visible to all my followers. Rather, a direct reply is only visible to me. You cannot send a direct reply to someone who is not following you. However, you can send a public reply for all your followers to see your reply.

Anyone can join a conversation on Twitter, which can result in good exposure on the conversation topic. The microblogging platform's use of short bursts of commentary tends to inspire conversations that can thrive and carry over into other forms of conversations, including offline conversations. I've seen people make requests for opinions with a link to a survey.

Many organizations are setting up Twitter profiles. The list includes both nonprofit and commercial organizations. For example, in my hometown, Tampa Bay ABC Action News and the Tampa Red Cross have Twitter profiles. They regularly tweet about current events and community needs. Other well-known businesses actively using their company names in Twitter are Dell, Apple, Comcast, HubSpot, and Jet Blue Airways, as well as the Los Angeles Fire Department and many, many others. At the time of this print, lists of prominent people and businesses with Twitter profiles are becoming readily available.[4]

---

4   List of prominent people and businesses using Twitter: http://blog.

A typical Twitter community is vibrant, energetic, and very conversational. The relationships formed in Twitter can carry offline. The businesses that benefit most from Twitter have more than one person regularly hosting a Twitter profile. Progressive Marketing 2.0 organizations have several people with active Twitter profiles creating and participating in conversations. If you think it's a time-waster, think again. By actively using Twitter, you can identify influential people in your market who have common interests and create potentially valuable relationships. Don't hesitate to take some of those relationships offline.

One company well known for its extensive use of Twitter is the online shoe seller Zappos. At the time of this writing, more than four hundred Zappos employees are on Twitter.[5] Zappos' commitment to outstanding customer service includes using Twitter as a marketing communication tool.

Twitter's growing popularity is amazing. But, there is a growing landscape of microblogging platforms in the enterprise beyond Twitter. Commercial microblogging tools have sprung up around the world. Here are just a few:

- http://www.yammer.com/

- http://www.socialcast.com/

- http://laconi.ca

- http://statushq.com/

- https://trillr.coremedia.com/

And IBM has a private Twitter-like network called BlueTwit. These microblogging tools allow companies to build Twitter-like communities within their corporate firewalls to facilitate private microblogging communities.

Twitter widgets are also available, enabling you to connect to a web-

---

fluentsimplicity.com/twitter-brand-index/

5   Zappos Employees on Twitter; http://twitter.zappos.com/employees

site or blog to display your most recent Twitter post. The ReTweet widget allows a blog post to be automatically posted to Twitter.

Another popular use for Twitter is the use of the hashtag symbol, which creates a Twitter stream or conversation stream around a specific topic. For example, a Twitter post which includes *#pubcon* was used by people who attended an industry conference called Pubcon. When a hashtag is used, anyone in the world can follow this conversation. For example, if you couldn't attend the Pubcon conference, you could follow the Twitter stream from those who attended. People comment on the speakers and include links to informative articles mentioned at the conference. Even those who attend the conference benefit because one can't be everywhere at a conference so you can catch something interesting at another session in the conference you didn't attend. I remember seeing comments from people in Europe who couldn't attend the Pubcon conference in Las Vegas. These comments are made in real time, and they remain on Twitter. So, you could visit a conversation that occurred in the past to catch conference insights.

The Twitter hashtag function is also used in another way known as a Twebinar—and no, I'm not kidding. Founded by popular social media strategist Chris Brogan,[6] a Twebinar is a webinar and Twitter mash-up where conversations take place on Twitter in real-time before, during, and after the webinar using the hashtag.

The Twebinar format uses the very same principle as described in the *#pubcon* example. It may sound a bit strange, but consider the opportunity for engaging people through comments and conversations during an event hosted or attended by your business such as an annual user conference. Simply give it a name such as *#ourconference* and promote this Twitter hashtag identifier to attendees. Encourage people to tweet actively during your event. This allows people to engage in comments during the event. Consider that most events offer very limited opportunity for conversations to occur in a format that can be captured in real time. There is no shortage of conversation or thoughts from event attendees. Using

---

6   Chris Brogan: http://www.chrisbrogan.com/

the Twitter hashtag function, people can actively engage in the event and share thoughts, insights, opinions, and generally enjoy the event at another level even if they are not actually attending the event. While this concept may take a little getting used to, once you attend one or two, you get the hang of it quickly and you can see the benefits.

People use Twitter streams to follow any event or topic. Some examples of topics that used and benefited from the Twitter stream using hashtags include:

- the terrorist attack in Mumbai, India, at *#mumbai*

- the 2009 Super Bowl at *#superbowl*

- the popular Consumer Electronics Show in Las Vegas at *#ces09*

Consider starting your own Twitter streams for popular topics or events in your industry. To see the most current popular Twitter streams using hashtags, visit http://search.twitter.com/search and you'll see "trending topics" listed on the right. However, these topics may have nothing to do with your industry. But, if you've never experienced this mash-up experience on Twitter, select one of the topics to visit the Twitter stream to observe it firsthand. You may get inspired to create a hashtag for an upcoming event or topic in your industry.

Some Twitter Do's and Don'ts

The Twitter platform should generally not be viewed as a broadcast medium or a megaphone, though in many respects that is exactly what it is. Exceptions include retail or hospitality Twitter accounts whose followers want to stay informed of special deals and offers. Even in these business-to-consumer settings, be careful not to use "shouting" methods in a Marketing 2.0 platform. Engage your community even when informing them of specials.

In a business-to-business environment, Twitter is more about making connections and brand building. When you click on someone's profile and you see they follow thousands of people but very few people follow them, that's a sure indication they use Twitter as a broadcast medium. Stay away from those people. They will spam you.

In order for a business to use Twitter productively in a social media strategy, it should ideally have several people with active Twitter accounts as well as a company-branded Twitter profile. The individuals should post a photo, and the brand should post an image, which is often a logo. The individuals should mix their Twitter conversations between company happenings and their personal interests. While too much information on personal interests is not advised (use discretion), it's a good idea to let people know something about you as a person. Links to photos or comments about your kid's soccer game are good examples of personal tidbits, especially during evening and weekend tweeting. Comments and replies to marketplace issues are strongly advised to prove your interest in engaging your community in relevant conversations.

If you're going to use Twitter, don't drop in once in a while and disappear. When I'm notified of a new follower, one factor I consider before I choose to follow them is how often they use Twitter. If they use it very infrequently, I don't follow the person. I look for Twitter posts in the past twelve to twenty-four hours. Active Tweeple are posting throughout the day, and often seven days a week. Use your own judgment on the frequency and just be selective that the people you follow are truly interested in using Twitter for active conversation, regardless of the frequency of their posts.

It's a good idea for a company Twitter profile to follow everyone who follows you. When a business Twitter account follows everyone following it, you send the message that you are interested in listening to your followers. A web page on your company site listing the people by name, displaying photos and their Twitter profile links is a great way to get your community engaged. Promote that web page to build your Twitter community.

Be selective about who you follow, generally limiting it to people who are consistent with your profile and interests and have a history of posting and replying to tweets, demonstrating they are active in conversations.

Generally, it's not a good idea for individuals to follow every person who follows you, unless each one is truly worth following. Be selective and avoid Twitter broadcasters with a two-to-one (or more) ratio of following compared to followers.

One good way to develop a following is to use the Twitter search feature and find people with common interests, then check out whom they are following. Click on them and decide who you're going to follow. Start by going to http://search.twitter.com, find people in your market, and follow them and the people they follow. This will give you visibility into their conversations and their followers' conversations, as well as provide opportunity for engaging in some of those conversations. But remember— it's up to you to get engaged in those conversations. It's a little like being at a social event. If you stand on the sidelines and don't get engaged in any conversations, you'll stay on the sidelines.

As your Twitter following grows, as will the number of people you are following, it's a good idea to select some of them as favorites. Twitter provides a favorites feature so you can track a subset of your followers. This is a good way to stay in touch with those certain people whose conversations are most interesting to you.

If you use Google Alerts, or one of the other social media monitoring services, you can track mentions of your name or your company according to your monitoring criteria. For example, if you track your company name in Google Alerts, it will send you email notices of Twitter posts with your company name. It's a good idea to also track your Twitter name, not just your company name, for example, *@yourtwittername*. This is an effective and free way to monitor any mention of your brand in Twitter. Google indexes Twitter names, too. So you can search people by name, and if they have a Twitter profile using their name, you'll find them.

Measuring Twitter Results (Twitter Metrics)

There are several ways you can measure the effect of using Twitter in your business. Here are a few, and this list will continue to grow as Twitter and microblogging continue to evolve.

The size of your following has a twofold metric value. Both the quantity of people who follow you and the influence of your Twitter following are important factors. I'm not a mathematician, but I remember studying permutations in college. Twitter has an exponential effect on reach in your target community. Tools are rapidly emerging to help you measure the reach and influence of your Twitter account. Some of these tools include Twinfluence[7] and Twitter Grader.

The more people that follow you, the more reach you have. However, it's somewhat dangerous to take that number at face value, but a review of your followers can reveal the consistency of the relevance to your community interests. In some businesses that have very active social media marketers, one factor considered when hiring a new candidate is the size of their Twitter following. I'm not joking.

Another metric for you to review is to select the *@replies* function in Twitter. This shows how engaged you are in your community. If you are not getting engaged in Twitter conversations, you are not receiving the full value from it.

One very useful metric to track closely is in your web analytics. Track the growth in referrals to your website from Twitter. As it grows, track the growth in your Twitter community and track the trend in your business development activities, including your sales. Depending on the length of lifecycle of interaction between prospects and new customers, you can likely draw some correlations between your Twitter activities and your growth in sales. It may be one of many referral sources and one of many aspects of your social media strategy. Whether or not you can draw a very solid correlation between Twitter and sales growth, if your Twitter community is vibrant and comprises influential people in your market, you can bet that you are getting a contribution from Twitter.

---

7   Twinfluence: http://twinfluence.com

Enterprise Twitter Uses

I will offer a few possible ways that businesses can use Twitter. I hope these ideas generate other ideas centered around the platform as a marketing communication tool, offering you the potential to leverage the collective wisdom of online communities.

Sales. A sales team can use Twitter as a private network to tap into the collective wisdom of all available sales resources. This can often be accomplished in real time when sitting in a prospective customer's conference room (or equivalent). Imagine being in a key sales presentation, needing instant access to a subject matter expert to get a question answered. Just send a tweet to your community and someone may respond in real time with just the answer you need. You could conceivably even conference the expert into your meeting in a matter of minutes. This scenario obsoletes the, "I'll get back to you," response and offers you a considerable competitive edge.

Product Marketing. Product marketing teams responsible for product development can build communities of people using your products or exhibiting the profile of potential product buyers. Engaging these communities in conversation about product direction, features, problems that need to be solved, and anything else pertaining to your product marketing strategy can be very cost-effective. You can post a link to a survey and get a lot of fast responses. People often enjoy giving you honest and candid input, feeling that they are contributing to product ideas and product improvements. This form of market research is potentially faster and costs less than conventional product marketing research. A blog can have a similar effect. Depending on the online communities you build in a blog or a microblog, the insights you gain may be very insightful and delivered very quickly.

Corporate Marketing. Corporate marketing plays a different role than product marketing. Even in smaller companies with smaller marketing staffs, the role of corporate marketing is generally branding, marketing communications, and lead-generation strategies. A Twitter profile can help you build a loyal online community, but it requires that you genuinely participate in the community. If you give more than you try to get, when you do offer insights, comments, or links to your content, they will be well-received. If you use Twitter wisely, you can inform your community of promotions, contests, product launches, and other marketing events and activities. There are three ways to approach Tweeple when using Twitter for corporate communication:

1. Individuals within your company can host a Twitter profile as openly representing your company.

2. Create a Twitter profile in the name of your company. In this approach, your Twitter account *is* your company brand. It's advisable that two people (or more) are given sole responsibility for maintaining your branded Twitter profile for purposes of consistency and sharing knowledge of the community and its history of online conversations.

3. You can have a third person be an advocate of your company brand. This approach is advisable only as a supplement to the first two.

All three approaches combined can be effective. Just remember to be genuine with your Twitter community by engaging it in meaningful conversations. Don't just sign on to send it links to your promotions, your ideas, your specials. If you limit your Twitter presence to promoting your company, you will get limited results, if any at all.

Customer Service. This is one of my favorite applications for microblogging. If your business has a robust customer service activity, invite your customers to follow you on Twitter. Proactively communicate things you're working on that demonstrate your commitment to customer satisfaction. This isn't about reporting bugs or problems you're working to resolve. Simply maintain an open dialogue with your customers on any relevant issues. Take JetBlue as an example:

Twitter Name: @JetBlue

Jet Blue Official Tweeter: Meet Morgan Johnston, manager of corporate communications with Jet Blue. Morgan's high-flying Twitter philosophy is to tweet as the community sees fit saying, "Our role on Twitter is driven by the requests of our followers. Twitter is a great way to talk to many, but even better for listening."

So why is JetBlue tweeting?: "Our goal would be to make ourselves available, help whenever possible, and to show that our brand is built by real people who care about our customers."[8]

Research. As in the approaches described above, engaging a community of people who offer potential for research and insights can be a low-cost and intimate way to gather market intelligence. Remember that your Twitter followers can be worldwide. Whether you're collecting research or conducting research, a Twitter community can provide a viable platform.

Branding. In social media marketing, branding opportunities are plentiful. Branding effectiveness is not limited to the corporate communications department. In fact, in smaller businesses, every employee can and should contribute to the brand in different ways. By allowing select individuals to set up Twitter accounts and building their community through engagement and good content, your company's brand can grow. Good content can go viral and Twitter can be an avenue to leverage. The JetBlue example provided earlier is as much about brand building as it is about customer service.

Thought Leadership. Individuals who have vision and the ability to express themselves can leverage Twitter. These individuals have an interesting way of posting thought provoking comments and insights, as well as links to articles full of good content. These are people we want to follow

---

8   Best Twitter Brands: http://mashable.com/2009/01/21/best-twitter-brands/

because they feed us good content. These thought leaders achieve branding value, too.

All industries have people who fit this characteristic. I call them "rock stars." These rock stars can emerge quickly. They don't need to be highly visible people in a high position of authority or with an impressive title. They just need to be really interesting and good at communicating on platforms such as Twitter. In my industry rock stars such as Chris Brogan,[9] Aaron Wall,[10] and Danny Sullivan[11] may not be household names with the general public. But, they have demonstrated thought leadership in online marketing strategies and they have created sizable followings. And as a result, they are very influential. Who is a potential future rock star on Twitter or in any social media platform in your business?

Microblogging Summary

Each of these examples follows the guidelines provided throughout this book, which center around engaging community in authentic and interesting conversations and building relationships. Be genuine. Give of yourself by sharing your expertise and content. Put your community first. Promote yourself and your brand modestly, and only in ways that serve your community. If you truly put your community first, you'll strengthen your brand and bridge the gap between you (the seller) and your buyer.

Microblogging, made popular worldwide by Twitter, is rapidly growing as a social communication platform allowing organizations to creatively communicate with an online community. These organizations extend their reach and brand by creating new conversations and relationships. Give it a try. Follow me on Twitter at http://twitter.com/berniebay.

---

9   Chris Brogan: http://twitter.com/chrisbrogan
10   Aaron Wall: http://twitter.com/aaronwall
11   Danny Sullivan: http://twitter.com/dannysullivan

Case Study: The 2008 Presidential Campaign—Was the Election Decided on Facebook and Twitter?

The following commentary is not politically motivated. Rather, it is a summary of the successful (and not-so-successful) web marketing strategies used by Barack Obama and John McCain during their presidential campaigns in 2008. Both Obama and McCain courted a voter who has proven apathetic in years past, at least when it comes to turning out to vote on election day. That voter is the younger generation. We know them as *millennials,* or Generation Y. This is a demographic that grew up on Facebook, owns an iPhone (regardless of income), and sends and receives text messages more than it makes phone calls or watches television. So it's no surprise that, unlike any other previous presidential campaigns, both the Obama and McCain campaigns used web marketing strategies.

On November 5, the day after Obama's election victory, his Twitter page posted this message: "We just made history. All of this happened because you gave your time, talent, and passion. All of this happened because of you. Thanks." Obama's Twitter following at the end of 2008 was 148,000 people. Obama is following 153,000 people on Twitter. McCain's Twitter following at the end of 2008 was about 5,000 and he was following about 5,800 people. McCain's last post on Twitter was on October 24, eleven days before the election, implying the campaign didn't consider Twitter an important enough medium of communication to keep it up to date. Even though we know the candidates aren't personally following their followers on Twitter, the symbolism is the point. Obama's campaign staff and volunteers were listening to the people's comments on Twitter in real time. Obama's 263 total updates (Twitter entries), compared to McCain's 25 total updates, are another sign of how important the social web was to Obama's campaign.

Obama's campaign also tapped into the 08 iPhone application to organize the phone numbers in the user's address book into a call list sorted by state in order to use the phone's GPS to locate the nearest Obama campaign office. This is another example of how the Obama campaign leveraged social technologies to engage his target audience.

Both Obama and McCain used Facebook to reach their target voters. Obama's Facebook page has 3.4 million supporters. McCain's Facebook page has about 600,000 supporters.

Obama understood how to reach millennials by engaging them where they spend time—on the social web. This audience doesn't want to be shouted at with messages. They want to be involved with each other and to be listened to. The Obama campaign staffers did a more effective job of engaging their online community. Everyone knows that Obama himself is not the one posting messages on Twitter and Facebook. But the persona of the candidate was posting. His staffers did a masterful job of conveying both a listening and an engaging spirit on the social web.

The marketing takeaway here is to know where your target audience spends time, go meet them there, and show them you care and want to engage them and listen to them.

PODCASTING

===================

Though it's beginning to grow in popularity, podcasting is one of the remaining areas in social media that is still underused. Because of this, much of its potential for marketing remains untapped. Let's begin this subject with a basic definition of a podcast from Wikipedia:

> "A podcast is a digital media file, or a related collection of such files, which is distributed over the Internet using syndication feeds for playback on portable media players and personal computers. Though podcasters' websites may also offer direct download or streaming of their content, a podcast is distinguished from other digital media formats by its ability to be syndicated, subscribed to, and downloaded automatically when new content is added, using an aggregator or feed reader capable of reading feed formats such as RSS or Atom."[1]

I encounter many people who just do not understand podcasting and its potential role in social media marketing. So let's dissect this definition. A podcast is a digital media file. Podcasts are digital format files created to be listened to, or watched, on a PC or portable media player such as an

---

1   Podcast definition: http://en.wikipedia.org/wiki/Podcast

iPhone, iPod, or another portable MP3 player. Podcasts are not watched on a television screen (although that could change when television delivers RSS-enabled content). Podcasts are distributed over the Internet. The only way you can get a podcast is from an Internet-based medium such as a website or web-based directory such as iTunes[2] or Podcast Pickle.[3] The iTunes directory provides access to podcasts you can download to an Apple iPhone or iPod. All other podcast directories are for downloading to non-Apple MP3 media players.

Podcasts can be consumed by your audience in one of three ways: 1) played on a computer by clicking a play button, 2) downloaded to a computer to listen to it offline at their leisure, and 3) subscribed to for downloading to their portable MP3 players for listening at their leisure. The third option is the most popular. This concept is one we are all very familiar with, and with good reason. It is the concept of time-shifted content consumption. In plain English, it's the same as recording a television show on your DVR or VCR, and watching it at your leisure. Now does this sound familiar?

When people subscribe to podcasts, they do so by clicking a subscription button in a website or directory made possible by an RSS feed. Each time they connect their portable MP3 device to synchronize it, the most current subscription podcast episodes are downloaded to their device.

Before we explore ways marketers can harness the podcasting medium, let's look at some ways the mainstream media are using podcasts. Many of the mainstream news services offer podcasts that can be downloaded from their websites. Visit mainstream news outlets online such as ABC, *BusinessWeek*, CBS, CNN, *Fortune*, Fox News, MSNBC, and the *Wall Street Journal*, and you'll see that you have the ability to subscribe to podcasts according to various topics of interest to you. And here's the best part of consuming podcast content: most podcasts are free.

A podcast is like a show. This is why each podcast is referred to as an episode. The vast majority of podcasts are audio, though video pod-

---

2   iTunes: www.itunes.com
3   Podcast Pickle: http://www.podcastpickle.com/

casts are also available. A video podcast is limited to being played on a device that can display video, such as an iPhone. Since the news outlets mentioned above are already experienced at producing content, making their content available in a podcast format has been a simple process for them. The mainstream news outlets view podcasting as a channel to keep you loyal to their brand and for you to tell others about your loyalty. I'm sure you've noticed there is a battle among major news providers to build and maintain loyalty. Delivery of podcast content is part of the battlefield tactics.

So who is listening to podcasts? At the time of this writing, the most recent research on podcast production and consumption presented by Edison Media Research[4] in April 2008 indicates that 18 percent of Americans have listened to at least one audio podcast. This figure equates to approximately 46 million Americans. The demographics of these people are attractive: most of these listeners are college-educated with a household income of $75,000 or more; 26 percent of them are active on MySpace; 15 percent are active on Facebook; and 5 percent are active on LinkedIn, which alone equals roughly 12 million people. These statistics are easily very conservative since we know podcasting is a growing medium and considering the date of this research.

Many auto manufacturers have started offering a built-in docking station for MP3 players. And many late-model car stereos offer an AUX-in jack that allows simple and low-cost connection between an iPod or MP3 player and your car stereo. As a marketer, do you understand what this means? Your target audience can listen to your content while driving to and from work. Whether or not they would do this is not what you should be thinking. People are listening to podcast content and wanting more of it. You should give people reasons to listen to your content in a podcast.

These statistics are broad and don't satisfy most marketers in relation to their specific market segment. Admittedly, podcast consumption

---

4   Edison Media Research: http://www.edisonresearch.com/home/
     archives/2008/04/the_podcast_con_1.php

within niche market segments is mostly unknown. However, one notable survey is the KnowledgeStorm/Universal McCann study in 2006, which surveyed 3,900 business and IT professionals.[5] This survey revealed "seventy two percent claimed that they have downloaded or listened to podcasts on technology topics on more than one occasion. Twenty-three percent do so frequently." The study also revealed that B2B technology buyers want to find podcasts delivering research content, such as white papers and analyst reports. Nearly 60 percent of respondents said that information on business or technology topics, currently delivered as white papers or analyst reports, would be more interesting as podcasts. Fifty-five percent of respondents would be more likely to consume white papers and analyst reports if they were delivered as podcasts.

But how can businesses harness the podcasting medium for marketing purposes, or make money by producing podcasts? Before I address these two questions, let's look at some possible podcasting strategies that might help guide us to answers regarding these two important questions.

• *Audience.* Who is your target audience? Begin with an understanding of your target audience and the topics of interest to them.

• *Content Strategy.* Review the content you currently have that meets the needs of your audience. Do you have white papers, case studies, FAQs, videos, newsletters, blog posts, tips, et cetera? Frequently, much of your existing content can be repurposed into a podcast format. If your content is in your head, that's okay, too, as long as it meets your audience needs.

• *Podcast Format.* Consider a format for your podcast show. Remember it is a show. Who will be the on-air personality or personalities? Will it be an interview style between two people or a monologue? Are the personalities you have in mind interesting enough to pull it off? To keep your audience's attention, you need

---

5 KnowledgeStorm/Universal McCann Survey: http://www.knowledgestorm.com

podcasters who will keep their attention. How long will your podcasts be? Most podcasts are generally not more than thirty minutes and often seven to fifteen minutes in length. It's better to segment topics to keep podcasts to a manageable time.

- *Podcast Frequency.* How often you will podcast? Similar to a blog, you should not start a podcast series and then stop. If you produce podcast content that is interesting and relevant to your audience, you will develop a loyal following. Don't disappoint them and damage your reputation by quitting after just a few podcasts. It may take three, five, or ten podcasts to develop a rhythm of podcasts.

- *Podcast Promotion.* Similar to a blog, your podcasts need promotion in order for them to produce marketing value. Podcasting is a form of social media marketing. Podcast content can be shared with your community as a link. Ask people to give you feedback on your podcasts, either by posting comments on your blog or by writing a review of your podcasts. Promote your podcasts through any other marketing communications in your business including emails to your permission list, news releases, company events, and of course on your website or blog.

- *Monetizing Podcasts.* Can you monetize podcasts? It's still a key question within the podcasting community, but I believe the answer is yes—with a few reservations. Within your podcasts, consider offering something to your audience. Ask them to visit a web page to receive something of value. Whether your goal is to gain more subscribers, because more subscribers increase awareness in your business for cross-selling opportunities, or your goal is to sell something directly, make them an offer. Still, your podcasts *must* have good content in order to make an offer that will yield results or you'll be received as a marketer rather than a provider of good content.

Let your content be your marketing in podcasts! If you truly offer your audience interesting and compelling content, you can ask them to visit a web page for a reason. Just make sure you have given them value before you ask them to do something.

So let's get back to the question of how you monetize your podcasts. The answer is different for every business—but the common denominator is truly good content. Start with good content and you can apply many of the common sense marketing strategies discussed throughout this book to build loyalty, differentiate yourself in your markets, and build relationships with your prospects and customers. It's the value of the relationships that eventually monetizes your podcasts or any other aspect of your social media marketing strategy. Tactics aimed at getting someone to give you their email address when you haven't built a relationship with that person simply don't work.

If monetizing your podcasting efforts is truly your goal, there are two well-known methods of accomplishing this. Since podcasts are really shows, one method is to recruit paid sponsors. This model is the age-old advertising model that has been with us since the dawn of television and radio. It works the same way in podcasting. If you can build a loyal audience on a topic or theme, you can sell advertisers on sponsoring your podcasts. Your sponsors receive air time commercials as well as possible brand recognition on your website or blog where your podcasts are located. Sponsorship fees are negotiated case by case. The factors used to determine rates range from the number of podcast subscribers you have and their demographics to whatever rate the advertiser is willing to pay.

The other monetization method for podcasting is offering fee-based premium content. This is harder to accomplish, given that it's imperative that you must provide compelling content that's of great interest to a niche audience willing to pay for it. This requires a huge commitment. However, if you do have content that's worthy of convincing your target audience to pay a fee to receive it, and you market it well, you can create good revenue streams from your premium content.

Marketing Your Podcasts

There are numerous ways to promote your podcasts. By now, the ideas discussed in previous chapters should jump to mind as ways to promote your podcasts. Podcasts are nothing more than content delivered in a different medium, and I've been discussing creative ways to promote content throughout this book. Remember to share your podcasts with your communities in social networks, blogs, Twitter, and other medium such as newsletters and your website. Always give people a reason to listen to your podcasts. Using teaser details that inspire people to tune in to your podcasts can be very effective.

Another effective way to promote your podcasts is by producing show notes, which are really nothing more than a text-based summary of your podcast's content. Publish your show notes on a web page or blog post. Your show notes should be a brief summary, not a verbatim translation of your podcasts. A text-based summary achieves two goals. It gives people insight into the podcast while creating interest in listening to it in order to hear the full version of the notes summary. Show notes also serve as search engine bait. Podcast content is audio, meaning search engines can't index it (at least at the time of this writing). By creating show notes, you create valuable content for search engines. This is especially true when creating show notes in a blog post using a permalink (unique URL) that includes keywords from the podcast. This way, your podcast show notes can be found in search engines, resulting in more potential traffic coming to your blog or website.

Podcast Summary

Whatever your podcast strategy, consider that podcast marketing is still unchartered territory for most marketers. Unless your competitors are early adopters, there is a good chance you can one-up them by producing good podcast content and marketing it effectively. Even if your competitors are already using podcasts in their marketing strategies, you can still look for ways to produce unique and valuable podcast content for your communities. Consider the power of reaching your target audience at their computers, on their iPhones, or in their cars while driving to and from work using the fast-growing medium of podcasts. Next you'll see how the Student Loan Network has used podcasting to help grow their market share.

Case Study: Christopher Penn and Podcasting at the Student Loan Network

Christopher Penn is the chief technology officer at the Student Loan Network.[6] The Student Loan Network has provided loans to U.S. college students since 1998. The company has helped approximately 25 million students and parents access more than $1 billion in federal and private student loans scholarships and consolidation funding for undergraduate, graduate, and continuing education. Its competitive advantage in the market is Christopher Penn.

Penn[7] is widely known in the social media community. His reputation is well-earned. Along with Chris Brogan,[8] another widely known social media strategist, he is the co-founder of Podcamp.[9] Penn has demonstrated practical implementation of new media marketing strategies to reach the student loan target audience. He is credited with researching and locating more than six hundred scholarships totaling more than $9 billion in free educational funding. To put this in perspective, consider that his employer is in the business of selling student loans. So why would he work so hard to offer free educational funding insights? The answer is because he is a visionary. He understands the value of community outreach and the effect it has on marketing. He embodies all the social media strategies discussed in Marketing 2.0. The information he reveals to his community is credited back to the Student Loan Network. Whether

---

6 The Student Loan Network: http://www.studentloannetwork.com/
7 Christopher Penn: http://www.christopherpenn.com
8 Chris Brogan: http://www.chrisbrogan.com/
9 Podcamp Boston: http://podcampboston.org/

through a direct referral or from a link on the web, the company receives inbound inquiries and leads for loans at an ever-growing pace.

Penn introduced podcasting to the Student Loan Network in 2005, long before it was popular. He originally started recording training material on his MacBook. Then, in June 2005, he uploaded a podcast to iTunes in order to make it accessible to anyone with an iPod. The rest is history.

Penn's marketing idea began with, and remains focused on, sharing advice, counsel, and ideas for students and their parents about ways to finance college educations. He started podcasting weekly. As the ideas kept flowing and the interviews with people in and around the student loan industry kept growing, his podcasts grew to daily episodes. Each episode has anywhere from five to thirty thousand listeners, depending on the popularity of the topic.

The novelty of Penn's financial aid podcasts has not gone unnoticed. He has been profiled in *BusinessWeek*, the *Wall Street Journal*, CNN, and *U.S. News & World Report*, as well as in many other local media coverage. He is also a frequent speaker at conferences across the country.

Penn speaks modestly about his accomplishments. He likes to discuss the relative simplicity of using podcasts as a marketing communication tool. One gets the impression he doesn't even want to admit it's a marketing tool. He records each podcast with incredible passion for a quality interview with guests that offer valuable insight into financial aid secrets for the college bound.

When asked about the Student Loan Network's marketing strategy, he describes it as being focused on content. The medium of the content delivery is multifaceted. Of course, his daily podcast is a big part of the strategy. But the Student Loan Network also uses permission-based email marketing, organic SEO, and good old-fashioned customer service. Penn is not a podcast geek. He clearly understands how all the marketing ingredients work together to drive results. He also encourages employees to blog to create more content so it doesn't all fall on one person's shoulders. The Student Loan Network has about twelve blogs on different topics. They try to engage customers wherever they are in ways they want to be engaged on topics of interest pertaining to student financial topics.

This marketing strategy has built very strong awareness with colleges and high schools. One reason for the high awareness is due to all the great content produced that is given away for *free*. In addition to the daily podcast, which gives away great free advice, Penn has written an ebook, *Scholarship Search Secrets*.[10] This ebook is a free download. No online form is required to download the ebook, which is a wise way to distribute great content. The branding of this ebook is credited directly to the Student Loan Network. It is a very popular guide for finding scholarships.

I asked Penn to share some lessons for those just getting started with a social media strategy. Here are his main points of advice:

- It takes time to get up and running. Plan, execute, and be patient.

- Executive buy-in is a must even though the returns will take some time to realize.

- You must be having conversations with customers at various levels of the company.

- You must be willing to give up some control to employees to have online conversations.

- You must be willing to experiment. Penn went to an event in Toronto where the Student Loan Network can't even conduct business. At this event, he was referred to *Business Week* and got the interview, which resulted in substantial exposure.

- Allow room for magic to happen. Don't put too much of a box around what you're doing. Let it flow and see where it goes.

Penn has a well-earned reputation in two industries. In the social media industry, he is recognized for his visionary work at the Student Loan

---

10   Scholarship Search Secrets: http://www.studentscholarshipsearch.com/scholarship-search-ebook.pdf

Network. And within the financial aid market, he is likewise recognized as a pioneer.

You can find Christopher Penn at these locations on the web:

- http://www.financialaidpodcast.com/

- http://www.marketingovercoffee.com/

- http://www.christopherspenn.com/

- http://twitter.com/cspenn

VIDEO AND PHOTOS

Throughout this book, I have been preaching the importance of producing content and sharing it with your community in order to create brand, buzz, loyalty, traffic, and sales value. Most of the references to content have been focused on text-based content (except the previous chapter on podcasting). The social media platforms for text-based content have been centered mostly around blogs, social networks, and microblogging.

Let's now turn our attention to a very popular form of content which many marketers overlook—video and still photos. I have given considerable thought to the reason why many marketers don't tap into the marketing power of video and photos. After all, unless you've been living in a cave, you have surely noticed the explosive growth and popularity of video sites and photo sites such as YouTube and Flickr.

If you're reading this book, my guess is that you've no doubt watched videos on YouTube. In fact, you can consume a brief summary of this book in a video format.[1] And you've probably seen still photos on websites or blogs, or on a social media platform such as Flickr, Photobucket, or Shutterfly. Pictures—whether moving or still—are always of interest to people, and their use can be a powerful addition to your marketing strat-

---

1   http://www.finadandconvert.com/video

egies. Let's begin this chapter by looking at video. You'll find that many of the reasons for using video in your social media strategy also apply to still photos.

Let's face it, the most prevalent reason online video has become so popular is because when video content goes viral, many people see it and the exposure is very valuable (assuming the video content is positive). But how can the average marketer in a small or medium-size niche business create viral video? Do you have to produce a blockbuster video to get noticed? Do you need a big budget?

Wikipedia Definition of Viral Video[2]

"A viral video is a video clip that gains widespread popularity through the process of Internet sharing, typically through email or IM messages, blogs and other media sharing websites. Viral videos are often humorous in nature and include televised comedy sketches such as *Saturday Night Live's* Lazy Sunday and amateur video clips like *Star Wars* Kid, the Numa Numa song, The Dancing Cadet, The Evolution of Dance and Web only productions such as I Got a Crush ... on Obama or even [Without Warning] (by Wired Comedy on YouTube). Some 'eyewitness' events have also been caught on video and have gone viral, including the Battle at Kruger."

As the Wikipedia definition above points out, a viral video gains "widespread" popularity through the process of Internet sharing. However, most marketers in small and medium businesses are marketing in a niche. You probably don't need 10 percent of every household in North America to see your video to gain valuable exposure for your products and services.

YouTube made the financial news in a big way when Google paid an astounding $1.65 billion to acquire the company. YouTube remains a platform that has not proved extremely valuable to Google, at least from a financial point of view. However, from a branding perspective, YouTube has been a home run for Google. YouTube may not be recognized as be-

---

2   http://en.wikipedia.org/wiki/Viral_video

ing the best at distributing online video, but it has certainly become the most popular. At the time of this writing, estimates are that more than 100 million videos have been uploaded to YouTube. However you shouldn't feel like you have to compete with 100 million videos.

In short, there are two ways any marketer can harness the marketing power of YouTube. The first way is an approach many marketers don't even consider. You can aggregate video content (produced by others) that is relevant to your niche. That's right. Without ever producing a single video, you can promote video content produced by others. Of course, you can produce your own video content. But even if you never produce a single video of your own, aggregating videos produced by others in your niche can be a great method for sharing them with your community. This approach allows you to tap into the marketing reach and viral benefits of online video.

Create a YouTube Channel. When you sign up for a free YouTube account, you can create a channel and brand it with your company name and logo. You can create a profile of your channel that reinforces your brand and the purpose of the channel. Your YouTube channel URL looks something like this: http://www.youtube.com/yourname. Your YouTube channel gives you the ability to display videos that you organize and present to your audience, whether those videos belong to you or not. This is the same concept I've been advocating throughout this book, which is to *share* good content with your community. By providing a single location for relevant content from one URL, you are providing your community valuable video content on topics of interest to them. The video content you aggregate in your channel doesn't need to be strictly focused on your topic. As you discover entertaining or inspiring videos that have significance to your community, you can aggregate them into your channel, sharing them with your community. For example, search in YouTube on the phrase *shift happens* and you'll find an informative video that is very thought-provoking and meaningful for any business owner.

One of the greatest features of a private video channel is that people can subscribe to your channel. As you update the video content in your channel, your subscribers receive it. You'll be building a loyal community that both trusts you and relies on you as a source of quality video content in your particular niche.

When you create your YouTube channel, you'll have a choice of one of four account types from which to select:

- *Director,* for those producing their own videos

- *Musician,* for those planning to promote music videos

- *Comedian,* for those planning to promote comedy videos

- *Guru,* for anyone possessing expertise in a particular field

In most cases, the appropriate account for a niche business is *guru.* This allows you to focus on your subject matter expertise and reduces the competition. You avoid getting lost among the 100 million videos, especially since people can search in the channel guide by topic.

Unless you are producing video for a very large demographic audience, the channel section of YouTube is the best place to market your videos as a guru. You can brand your channel using your colors and logo. You can assemble your video collection, so to speak, according to your niche topic. People can subscribe to your video channel, and YouTube provides sharing features allowing you to send links to others so you can promote your video content. And remember—you do not need to produce any of your own video to use channels.

You may be wondering how you can benefit from video content if you don't produce your own? When you are a subject matter expert, one of the most effective ways of using social media is to promote your subject matter expertise by sharing meaningful content with your community (have I mentioned this before?). Depending on your niche topic, there may be others who have produced video content that you can use. Even if they are competitive sources, consider using some of them. Once video content is available on YouTube, it is available for anyone to view and share. Your focus should be to organize and share any relevant video content within your community. Of course, if you produce your own video content, that helps contribute to your guru status, but it is not necessary. Often, assuming a leadership position and providing good content to your community earns you guru status within this context. If you are the only one in your niche organizing relevant video content for your audience, you will certainly benefit from that.

Consider the news media outlets as an analogy. CNN doesn't create news; it brings it to you. And often it reports the same news as Fox, CBS, NBC, and ABC. Think like a content publisher and provide video content to your community with your value-add, whether it's your video content or not.

Creating Your Own Video. If you are interested in creating your own video content, here are some guidelines. First, don't attempt to create a video that will go viral. The truth is that it's impossible to predict which videos will be popular, regardless of their topics. Focus your efforts on the following best practices:

- *Keep your video short.* The general rule of thumb is to produce videos that are under five minutes, and even as short as one minute. YouTube video viewing is not the same as television viewing. People come in and out of YouTube, often several times during their workday. When someone sends a link with your video during work hours, the person wants to view it very quickly, generally in five minutes or less.

- *Use humor, satire, emotion, or some element of great interest in your video to capture attention quickly.* You must capture the audience's attention in the first ten seconds of the video. Talking about a dry subject while standing on a cliff is different and potentially attention-getting. Using humor is always effective, but don't be offensive in your humor. If you have enough content for a long video, chop it up into short segments under five minutes each. This allows people to watch them in segments, makes it easier for people to watch a particular segment over and over, and makes it easier for people to share those short segments with others by forwarding a link to it.

- *Don't hold back your expertise.* Remember, social media is all about sharing content with your community. Tell people what you know. Be direct with your video content. Let your subject matter expertise shine through.

- *Don't be boring.* This is hard for some of us because we don't all have a personality comparable to Jay Leno's. So how do we spice up our video if we are boring? Consider adding music or another personality to spice it up. Adding another personality to complement yours or contrast yours can really break up the monotony of a boring personality. An effective approach is to use another person to deliver your content. However, if you are going to use professional actors, you run the risk of killing the authenticity of your brand. One of the greatest appeals of Internet video is its authenticity. When you create a Hollywood production with actors, you lose that. That said, if you create a professional video that entertains or touches emotional buttons, you can achieve good marketing results.

- *At the end of your video, leave the audience thinking about something that reinforces your brand.* It's generally not a good idea to have a direct selling call to action that sounds like an infomercial, unless that's your purpose. Instead, ask people to visit a website, or give them a word or phrase that ties directly to your message. Here is an example. When HubSpot created a successful video in December 2008, which happened to go viral, all it suggested at the end was doing a Google search on the phrase *inbound marketing.* The HubSpot name was never mentioned during the video. See the HubSpot case study for more on this.

- *Humanize your video using skits or parodies with actors (amateur or professional) to get your point across.* This is a very popular approach to communicating complex or seemingly mundane topics. For example, I once acted in a video where I played the part of a physician arguing with the chief of hospital administration. My character was the surgeon responsible for more surgical procedures than any other surgeon in this hospital, meaning that my character was a big revenue contributor to the hospital. However, the hospital had been experiencing increasing costs for supplies, for physician preference items in particular, and the hospital's bottom line had turned to red ink. So my character was asked to use different surgical instruments that cost less. As the video unfolds, it's clear that my character was irritated by the request and somewhat argumentative with the hospital administrator. He didn't care one bit about red ink. All my character cared about is ensuring that his surgical procedures resulted in positive patient outcomes. The heated exchange between the surgeon and the hospital administrator was clearly tense and the point was clear. The hospital was losing money but my character was in control because of his revenue contribution. At the end of the short confrontation, the surgeon stormed out and the administrator was left with no answers to his unprofitable nightmare. After the surgeon left the scene, the hospital administrator stood up from behind his desk to leave his office as if to go blow off some steam. When he stood up and the camera panned his body, it was revealed that he was wearing shorts below his waist, though above his waist, he wore a business suit as shown during the meeting with the surgeon in his office. This revelation added an element of unexpected humor to an otherwise tense and serious video. This particular video was produced for a conference attended by health care executives, focused on the business of health care. The video helped illustrate the realistic business challenges our hospital systems face and added an element of humor. Can you imagine how boring it would have been to create a short video interview between a hospital administrator and a surgeon? Instead, the conference attendees saw a video that made them laugh while illustrating the contentious topic of physician preference items driving up costs in health care. As an aside, if you're interested in seeing it, you can find this video on YouTube by searching for *Bernie Borges.*

The video described in the previous paragraph was shot on a very low budget. The hospital administrator and the surgeon were the only two characters, and neither of us got paid for acting in it. The only expense to the client was the professional videographer who shot and edited the video, which ran about a thousand dollars. Many marketers don't even hire a videographer; they do it themselves and often produce stellar results. Chances are you have many employees with acting potential who will jump at the opportunity to star in a YouTube video. They can get compensated by being able to send their friends and family a link to the video on YouTube. If the video goes viral in any way, they will get exposure in front of a global audience.

Promoting Your Video Content. There are several ways to promote your video content, whether it's content you've produced, or content you've aggregated into your channel. As discussed throughout this book, you should let your community know about your content by sharing it with them in other social platforms, such as a blog and social networking sites. Submit your video to social bookmarking sites as well as to your network on LinkedIn, Facebook, Twitter, and wherever else you hang out on the social web. If you produce your own video, submit it to TubeMogul[3] for distribution to other video channels. Ask your friends to write reviews about your video and give it a thumb's up—assuming it's deserving—on social sites that use this feature. Give your inner circle of friends a heads-up on the video. Recruit your biggest fans to help you promote it by asking them to blog about it and forward the video link throughout their networks. These tactics can get your promotional efforts off to a running start. One word of caution, though: make sure your video is a good one.

---

3   TubeMogul: http://www.tubemogul.com/

Asking your greatest fans to promote a bad video is sure to backfire on you.

Distribute your video to other blogs and websites that discuss topics relevant to the video's content. Visit all your groups in your social networking sites and share it—just be sure to give them a reason to want to watch it. Make it beneficial to them, not self-serving to you. Remember, you want them to enjoy your content. If they enjoy it, they may forward it to others.

If your video is really worthwhile and you consider it worthy of a news release, by all means announce it to the world. Write a news release using the SEO features available at press release distribution sites, such as BusinessWire, PR Web, PRWire, and Vocus. Make sure your keywords are well-linked back to your website or blog from the press release. Promote the value of your video content to your audience through the news release.

Don't forget to tell your customers about your video. Send it to them and ask them for their feedback. It's a good way to open up dialogue with customers in ways you may not get a chance to do on a day-to-day basis. Ask them to forward your video to their friends if they like it. Consider running a contest with your customers. Ask them to submit ideas for a future video. The winner (you decide) may actually get to participate in the video (if he or she wants to).

Don't forget to use the tools available on YouTube and most video content sharing sites. The most common available tools to use are tags and descriptions. Tags are keywords that you assign to your videos, allowing them to be indexed by both YouTube and Google and other search engines. When selecting your tags, take some time to think carefully about the keywords you use. Research similar content (text or video) and see what keywords were used to tag that content. And don't forget it to give it a short description, which is what users will read when it shows up in a search engine listing.

Put some thought into the title you give your video. Titles help sell a video. The title should be unique and catchy enough to arouse people's curiosity and inspire them to open up your video.

The thumbnail image you choose is what people will see when your video is displayed as a still image. This still image also plays into the curiosity factor of your video, so choose your thumbnail image carefully.

YouTube provides two very useful features that allow anyone to embed a video on any web page or blog post. Each YouTube video has a unique URL and Embed window that allows anyone to forward a link to your video or to embed the code that will play your video on a web page or blog. Allowing marketers to promote their video content is YouTube's way of promoting its platform. Share your video content using these tools and maximize your exposure.

YouTube also allows you to make playlists, which are lists of videos with clips from each one. This allows your audience to sample clips from your playlist and watch the ones that interest them. If you do a good job of producing your own videos, as well as aggregating video content, you'll win many fans by creating playlists of content from your channel.

Invite people to subscribe to your video channel. This is similar to subscribing to a blog, enabling your audience to keep current on your video content in their favorite RSS reader.

Lastly, while YouTube is the most popular video-sharing site, it is not the only one. You should submit your video to as many sharing sites as possible. You'll need to register with each one first. Here is a partial list of other video sharing sites: DailyMotion, Google Video, LiveLeak, Metacafe, Veoh, Yahoo Video, and VideoSift. And as mentioned previously, TubeMogul can distribute your video to all of the above. For a complete list, visit the entry in Wikipedia under the heading video sharing sites.[4]

Create Your Own Internet TV Show. This chapter has thus far been focused on using YouTube to aggregate content or to upload your own video content to share with your community. Another approach to consider is to create your own Internet TV show. Admittedly, this requires more effort and commitment. But if you have a business with a lot of useful content

---

4   Video sharing sites: http://en.wikipedia.org/wiki/List_of_video_sharing_
     websites

to share and a sizable community with whom to share it, this is a viable consideration. You'll need to have in-house personalities to produce a weekly TV show. The required video gear is very reasonably priced, and the Internet platform is readily available.

You'll need to purchase video equipment such as a digital camcorder camera, microphones, sound equipment, sound mixer, and lighting. Expect to spend between one thousand and three thousand dollars. You don't need to spend more. Use video-encoding software to create your video for live streaming. Some examples are AJA Video, Apple Quicktime, and Dolby Digital. They make the video-streaming software necessary to provide video feeds for an Internet TV station. Install the video-streaming software on your computer and start programming the device. Choose a video-streaming supplier such as Adstream, Aspera, or DGFastChannel. The streaming supplier feeds your Internet TV station and supplies you with hours of service, which ensures your shows are available to viewers. The video-streaming supplier provides multiple servers to host your streaming videos. Furthermore, you will not have to worry about bandwidth should your viewership increases. Choose a video format for your show; options include Windows Media Player, Quicktime, and Flash. These players will allow most people to view your Internet TV station from their computers with ease. Build a website or blog to host your TV station. You can also upload your videos on video hosting sites such as YouTube or other RSS enabled sites. Make sure people have the option of subscribing to your Internet TV show so they can watch it anytime they want. Once you've built your studio, you can start producing your TV programs based on the types of audience you are targeting. Attract an audience to your Internet TV show by using all the social media marketing principles discussed in this book. You may also want to attract advertisers to help monetize your video content.

As you can see, creating your own Internet TV show is a bigger commitment of both people and time. This is not probably something you'll want to do right away. However, if you decide you have enough content as well as a potential audience, and you're willing to allocate the resources and commit to the strategy, you may just reap some big marketing rewards. In the HubSpot case study, you'll learn how they are using Internet TV to create marketing value.

Beyond YouTube: From Viral Buzz to Branded Video Content

Most of this chapter has been dedicated to harnessing the YouTube plat-form and tactics for building general buzz for branding value. Social media sharing sites are great for building audience, generating awareness for your content, and establishing an online identity for your brand. These are all part of an effective video marketing plan. But as *pro-sumer* video content creators become more and more popular, they begin realizing they're missing out on other potentially significant revenue streams.[5]

Depending on the goals of your video marketing strategy—something you should determine early in the process—the type of tools required to support those goals can vary. In most cases, it comes down to control. How much control over content, audience, user experience, brand, and revenue model is required to make your video strategy successful? This is unique to each publisher. Some are only looking for brand exposure and leads. Others are willing to invest more in the development of premium (fee-based) content, while still others strive to build audience in order to sell ad space around the content.

The reality of YouTube and other social media sharing sites is that it's not really your tube; it's their tube. These communities provide sharing features, a built-in audience, digital media storage, and delivery, all for free. In return, users supply the content that drives the value of the net-work but forfeit the ability to generate revenue (or at least limit it to what the network allows) and maintain tight control over content. The network provider (in this case, YouTube) strives to monetize the network audience through its own monetization strategy.

What is needed to take full control over your content, audience, brand, and monetization options is an Internet TV platform that offers

---

5   This section was contributed by Shaun Pope, of EndavoMedia.

all the features of a social media sharing site but puts you in the driver's seat. Instead of your video site being a YouTube channel or a collection of embedded YouTube videos on your website, these platforms deliver turnkey methodologies for storing, managing, delivering, and monetizing your own branded online video destination.

Companies like Brightcove, Endavo Media, Ooyala, PermissionTV, the Platform, and Vidego are all evolving digital asset management (DAM) technology with the goal of putting these powerful tools into the hands of individual content creators, many of whom are small to medium-size business marketers. This phenomenon is similar to the effect that blogging platforms such as TypePad and WordPress have had on text-based content publishers. A similar type of explosion with video content is very likely over the next few years. I fully expect to see businesses of all sizes producing branded video content as a major communication vehicle for their target communities.

Modules for video asset management and Meta data definition, customization of the players, built-in sharing features, membership and subscription management, content syndication, and scalable video delivery are essential elements of a full-featured Internet TV platform. The business drivers for these tools are access to new revenue streams and more control over your specific video content strategy.

Each Internet TV platform provider has its strengths, so understanding what your goals are from the beginning helps you select the one best suited to help you accomplish your goals. Pricing varies, however, with most providers offering starter plans that include many of the capabilities listed above, as well as a base amount of storage and delivery, for between four thousand and six thousand dollars annually. This is far less than what it would cost to build your own video player and administration console. In the long term, you also benefit from new features and functions as the provider enhances the platform.

Your business should consider some form of video as an important element of your Marketing 2.0 strategy. Whether you use the free approach from popular video sharing sites, or you invest in building a branded video platform, the possibilities to communicate and engage your communities are astounding. From a popularity standpoint, the momentum driving video, coupled with its ability to be indexed by search engines, makes this medium too important to ignore, regardless of the size of your business.

Case Study: Indium Corp. and Viral Videos

In addition to Indium's blog strategy discussed earlier, Indium also produces videos to communicate product and company information. Some of the videos are direct and to the point about a product, while others are humorous and entertaining. No matter which style is used, many of these videos go viral, and if a company's video reaches that stage, it's a good thing.

Indium has embraced video as an essential piece of its social marketing plan. One reason for that is that Rick Short has a humorous side to him that is clearly evident in the videos he produces. He has produced nearly a dozen videos, all of which have an element of humor and all of which have gone viral in their market segments. The feedback from their community on these videos has been very positive. When Short walks through the halls of an industry event, even in other countries, he is often recognized for his appearances in these videos. Even the music and audio from these videos have reached a level of penetration in their target market that is beyond any expectations.

Indium's marketing strategy uses these videos in four ways:

• They are played at trade shows.

• They are played during speaking engagements.

• They are uploaded to YouTube.

• They appear on the company's website.

The point is that the videos show a human side to the company and expresses its desire for interaction with its community. Incidentally, Indium also recognizes their community is not limited to the buyers of their products. Consultants, suppliers, and anyone else involved in their niche industry are also welcomed as members of its community.

Photos

Now let's turn our attention to content in the form of still photos. Similar to YouTube, Flickr is not the only photo-sharing site on the web, but it is the most popular. Therefore, I'll devote this section to a discussion on how marketers can use Flickr (or any other photo-sharing site) in their social media marketing plans. As a niche marketer, you want to maximize awareness of your company, your expertise, and your value proposition. So how can still photos contribute to your social media marketing plan and assist you in achieving these goals? To answer this, we must examine Flickr, as an example of a photo-sharing site with social qualities. Incidentally, other popular social photo sharing sites include PhotoBucket, Shutterfly, Kodak Easy Share, Memeo Share, Picasa, and Snapfish.[6] Pick the photo sharing site you like best.

Let's get one thing straight about Flickr from the get-go: it is a social networking site. Flickr uses photos as the primary mode or theme for social networking. You can upload photos, organize them, find friends, manage your contacts, and share photos with anyone in your circle or community. You can also create or join groups, just as you do in any of the other social networks. While this may sound very consumer-oriented and not applicable to niche businesses, think again. There are many ways niche marketers can use Flickr to express themselves and share the resulting content with their community.

Consider that photographs are more common than video, and with good reason. Many of us have a camera built into our cell phones. Many of us have access to digital cameras and use them frequently to photograph a variety of activities. If you are a niche marketer who has not previously

---

6   List of social photo sharing websites: http://en.wikipedia.org/wiki/List_of_
     photo_sharing_websites

considered photographing activities and events, start thinking about it today. Here are some obvious—and some not-so-obvious—ways to share photos with your community and promote your brand using a social media platform like Flickr.

At every company or industry event, as well as local community events and social gatherings like the holidays or company celebrations, make sure someone is taking pictures. Make sure the photos are genuine and spontaneous. You don't want anything even remotely resembling a staged photo. When you upload your pictures to Flickr, personalize these photos with comments and tag them with relevant keywords. Then, share these photos with your community. Don't do this as a one-time thing; keep a camera handy and take photos often. Show your community that your business comprises real people. Let them see their personalities and their human side. You'd be surprised how powerful it is for your community to gain insight into the human side of your organization.

In addition to taking photos at events, take photos of everyday life at your business. Show your staff hard at work in meetings, at their desk, on a break and yes, even having some fun. One of the phenomena associated with social media is that we get to see people as real people, regardless of what they do to make a living. The lines between our work persona and our outside-of-work persona are blurring. Sharing photos is a great way to leverage this melding of work and life.

In this chapter, we discussed the power of using video and still photos in social media marketing. These are often two of the most overlooked aspects of social media marketing. The tools at our disposal in social media such as YouTube and Flickr really make it easy for us to leverage video and photos as content. Embedding links to your video and photos in as many social media platforms as possible including in your blog, Facebook, Twitter, YouTube, private video channel, and even email can help spread your content, build loyal community, and reach measurable goals. And, you guessed it, video and photos can help you bridge the gap between you (the seller) and your buyers.

Marketing Operations 2.0

Developing a social media strategy involves risks and benefits. In this chapter, we'll discuss the importance of processes in running a marketing department when implementing a Marketing 2.0 strategy. The process is known as *marketing operations* (MO).

MO is a relatively new discipline that can be defined as a comprehensive, end-to-end operational discipline that leverages processes, technology, guidance, and metrics to run the marketing function as a profit/value center, growth driver, change catalyst, and fully accountable business. MO reinforces marketing strategy and execution with a scalable and sustainable infrastructure. MO seeks to nurture a collaborative, well-aligned ecosystem, both within and outside the marketing department, to drive achievement of strategic objectives.

One way to think of MO is as job security for the chief marketing officer. The following are the key ingredients required to become a Marketing 2.0 organization using MO principles.

Converting Insight into Value

Many companies are guilty of underinvesting in their marketing intelligence. Even those organizations that invest heavily may lack confidence in the integrity of the data or data source. Knowledge gaps are prevalent, as insight tends to stay in the field. Disagreement over how to interpret a *fact* is the norm. Often, because executives don't hold one another accountable to explain the assumptions underlying their thinking processes, the modus operandi is *gut feel and seat-of-the-pants decision-making.* Power and authority, not necessarily the best business case, tend to rule the day.

MO uses tools such as gap analysis, win-loss analysis, competitive and industry benchmarking, surveys, and customer advisory boards to document key lessons, anticipate market/customer shifts, benchmark against best practices, better understand where customers are in the buying cycle and create customer-driven solutions. MO leverages Web 2.0 technologies by harnessing the collective input of online communities.

Accelerating the Sales Process

Marketing is typically vested with generating sales leads, but often has been viewed as guilty of providing sales with unqualified leads. As a result, according to a study conducted by Sirius Decisions,[1] only 20 percent of the leads from lead-generation programs are followed up by sales, 70 percent of which are disqualified. Shockingly, within twenty-four months, 80 percent of those *disqualified* leads buy anyway—from the company, or worse, a competitor.

MO helps marketing understand how to take ownership of low-touch prospects who are deemed not ready to buy today through lead-scoring methodologies and automated permission-based lead nurturing systems and processes, enabling sales to focus on high-touch, ready-to-buy prospects. It can also help develop a pipeline of qualified customer references that supports both sales and marketing requirements and ensures that these references are a renewable resource. In short, MO can help the marketing-sales brotherhood become a true partnership, rather than an

---

1   Sirius Decisions: http://www.siriusdecisions.com/live/home/document.php?dA
     =LeadScoringAPhasedApproach

antagonistic relationship. This is crucial to a Marketing 2.0 strategy that requires some experimentation before positive returns materialize.

Scaling the Marketing Function for Growth

As companies grow, they tend to become increasingly complex and correspondingly inefficient. This tends to lead to poor resource optimization, siloed thinking, duplication of efforts, ineffective knowledge transfer, and a variety of other dysfunctions.

MO tackles this challenge by conducting regular health checks to determine investment leverage areas, uncovering inefficiencies, and defining a prescriptive roadmap for change. MO maps out key marketing processes and best practices and defines key selection criteria for marketing automation investments. It recommends change in the marketing department to overcome employee ambivalence, confusion, resistance, and passive-aggressive behavior that can be unintentionally or consciously transferred to customers, partners, press, analysts, and other target audiences. When you implement Marketing 2.0 strategies, recognize that any of these characteristics may rear their ugly heads at any time. Through MO processes, the marketing department can help the company grow in line with the rest of the company in a healthy manner.

Delivering the Strategic Agenda

Marketing has a significant opportunity to play a more influential role in the business. In order to do so, it needs to align its priorities with the strategic agenda.

New Marketing 2.0 strategies have great potential to create new achievements through methodologies such as messaging alignment; building shared purpose and vision; marketing governance aimed at helping the organization live the brand; and education and socialization to achieve buy-in for new marketing initiatives. MO can raise the stature of marketing from a perceived cost center and a resource drain to a valued strategic partner.

Optimizing Customer Profitability

Thanks to the level playing field the new Internet provides, customers are more sophisticated. It's continually more expensive to entice new customers in the midst of exponential advertising venues. Companies that retain high-value customers have great advantages in cost reduction, market share, price premium and profitability compared to those companies focusing resources on customer acquisition alone.

The social web can play a vital role in some of the MO approaches used to optimize customer profitability, including calculating customer lifetime value; capturing the voice of the customer through advisory boards, user groups, blogs, surveys, complaints, and other forums; mobilizing customer-facing resources to meet customer expectations; and refocusing resources to winning back at-risk customers. By giving customers the ability to engage directly with subject matter experts in your business, you optimize this MO best practice.

Demonstrating Measurable Return on Marketing

Most executives view demonstrating marketing's value and return on marketing as the Holy Grail for MO. Over the past decade in particular, company executives have been demanding, with growing intensity, clarity in the return on investment related to marketing budgets. This has put marketing in the defensive position of having to prove its value to the organization, to quantitatively select marketing projects with the highest expected return, and to prove the necessity of funding its marketing strategies and staffing levels.

Social media marketing strategies are inherently risky and require nontraditional measurement strategies, making this principle even more challenging. Therefore, MO is vested with overcoming this challenge through strategies such as defining metrics; linking CEO-level goals to marketing level goals that cascade through the organization; identifying and tracking leading and lagging indicators through dashboards and balanced scorecards; tracking and managing individual and team performance; and fine-tuning forecasting with predictive modeling. By putting operational focus on the measurement process, MO enables marketing to be more accountable and in better control of its charter, its resources – and ultimately – its destiny.

The Impact of Marketing Operations in 2.0 Organizations

Though still in its relative infancy, marketing operations has made its mark on the corporate world. As companies embark on Marketing 2.0 strategies at a faster rate, MO best practices should continue to grow. For example, MO is spawning the following:

- A new breed of professionals whose sole purpose is to improve efficiency and effectiveness of their companies' marketing departments.

- The injection of left-brain thinking into the typically right-brained marketing function.

- A budding marriage between marketing and IT, as well as other interdependent stakeholders.

- A predisposition toward deploying marketing automation solutions to address such challenges as optimizing scarce resources, capturing ROI insight, and sharing knowledge among all the stakeholders.

Organizations that embrace MO are being viewed as profit centers (not cost centers) and fully accountable businesses. Marketing executives with the foresight to build a marketing operations function in their organizations are blessed with an operational partner, similar to the COO/ CEO relationship.

MO provides directors and managers with an invaluable resource to help them get the most out of their marketing programs, make course corrections, and learn from their experience. Even the most inexperienced professionals gain by being part of a learning-oriented environment where they develop fundamental skills to operate effectively, stay accountable, and benefit from marketing operations-driven improvement programs.

Marketing operations provides the internal transportation system and supporting infrastructure to ensure that new social media strategies are implemented successfully for all stakeholders who will watch closely and measure their success.

This chapter was contributed by Gary Katz, CEO of Marketing Operations Partners.[2]

---

2   Marketing Operations Partners: http://www.marketingoperationspartners.com/

Case Studies—SMBs Succeeding with Social Media

Thank you for reading this far. This section is likely to interest you because we will visit with companies and individuals who are using social media marketing in very diverse and interesting ways. Those I've written about all have one thing in common. Wherever they are in the process of implementing their social media strategies, it is a work in progress. Since social media is still young, each of the companies discussed in this section is learning as it goes. In some cases, they have considerable understanding and expertise in their social media strategies while others are experimenting and making mistakes. In fact, even those with expertise make mistakes. Social media is new territory, and mistakes are inevitable. However, the rewards are so meaningful that even the mistakes can be rewarding, even if they amount to nothing more than learning experiences. As you know, my sentiment is that the biggest mistake you can make is choosing *not* to experiment with social media marketing strategies. I refer to it as *social media abstinence*.

I will give you the same disclaimer I provided in the introduction. Some of the companies in this section are companies with whom I have a business relationship. I assure you that the sole purpose of writing about the companies and individuals in this section is to share with you—my valued reader—a viable example of how each is using social media, relationships notwithstanding.

Finally, I've attempted to assemble a list of case studies comprising companies and organizations whose names are not of household brand recognition since the target reader for this book is the small and medium-size business that probably doesn't enjoy household name brand recognition, either. There is one exception. I've included a case study of a pilot project at NASA, which studies the productivity of social networks inside an organization.

There are two case studies embedded in previous chapters. I wrote about Indium Corp. led by Rick Short's vision and passion for customer engagement on the social web. Visit this great Marketing 2.0 example in the blogging chapter. Likewise, I wrote about Attorney 2.0 Brent Britton in the Personal Branding chapter. If you skipped to the case study section, be sure to visit these chapters to read these two inspiring examples of Marketing 2.0 mind-sets in action.

And now, on to the case studies.

HubSpot: Internet Marketing Company Selling Internet Marketing

HubSpot[3] is a Cambridge, Massachusetts-based Internet marketing company. It doesn't provide Internet marketing services similar to my Find and Convert Internet marketing agency. Instead, it provides a web-based software platform that marketers (including agencies like mine) can use to optimize, manage, and track the results of their Internet marketing campaigns. HubSpot is a young company, in business for just over two years as of this writing. To market its software, guess what strategy it has employed? If you guessed Internet marketing, you are correct! They refer to it as Inbound Marketing. In short, it eats its own dog food.

---

3   HubSpot: http://blog.hubspot.com/Default.aspx

There are many smart people at HubSpot. They work hard and have a lot of fun doing it. Mike Volpe, vice president of marketing (as well as the author of this book's foreword), leads its marketing strategies. Mike and his (really smart) colleagues devote their entire marketing strategy to dreaming up ways they can build their community, feed them truly amazing content, and engage them in interesting and fun ways. They believe the key to successful online marketing is to produce tools and content that will be useful to their community, and then use every possible technology to publish and promote it. Here is how they do it.

Blogging. The HubSpot blog is updated daily with an interesting post about something relevant in Internet marketing. The blog identifies topics, divvying up the responsibility of writing a blog post, and also seeks guest blog posts from people working in the industry, like me. Unlike a lot of company blogs, the HubSpot blog rarely mentions its products or services directly. The blog is more of a resource for marketers and business owners. This neutral viewpoint has helped build the audience of the blog to more than ten thousand subscribers, as well as a top 10K ranking on Technorati.

Forum. Its forum is a closed network for HubSpot customers. It's a typical forum where customers post comments and ask questions about anything related to the HubSpot platform or Internet marketing. The community in the HubSpot forum is vibrant and engaged, with posts happening at all hours of the day.

Twitter. HubSpot does as good a job of using Twitter for business as any organization I've seen. There are more than a dozen people at HubSpot who have active Twitter profiles (http://www.hubspot.com/twitter/), and they do a great job of engaging their relevant communities. The cofounders talk about start-up strategy, the marketers talk about marketing, and the developers talk about software. Additionally, they maintain a branded Twitter profile in the name of HubSpot. Individuals actively post comments ranging from thoughts about their daily events and activities pertaining to Internet marketing to updates on personal tidbits. For example, I've learned that Ellie Mirman (Twitter name *@ellieeille*) is not a morning person. As you know, Twitter users commonly blend work and personal personae very effectively, and the HubSpotters are no exception. The branded Twitter profile regularly comments on HubSpot's activities, events, and links to new blog posts.

Webinars. HubSpot conducts free webinars on popular Internet marketing topics such as how to use Twitter and Facebook for business or optimizing landing pages. Anyone can attend these webinars. After holding webinars for a year, they are now attracting more than five thousand sign-ups for each webinar. And when a new webinar is announced, usually fifty-plus people promote it to their friends on Twitter, and a dozen or more bloggers write about it to suggest that their audiences register. This is a true testimony to the influence of this community.

Video. HubSpot conducts a weekly Internet video called *HubSpot TV*, featuring a format similar to that of CNN's *Larry King Live*, except it doesn't always have outside guests. Mike Volpe and his co-host, Karen Rubin, conduct a live video streaming show each Friday at 4 PM U.S. EASTERN. If you're in Cambridge, you can also attend it live at their office. The show is RSS-enabled, so if you can't watch it live, you can subscribe to it through the blog or through iTunes, and watch or listen to it at your convenience online or on your iPod. HubSpot TV is entertaining and educational, two qualities that are very important for successful social video marketing. In addition to HubSpot TV, HubSpot has a YouTube channel with dozens of videos that include interviews with marketing experts, marketing tips and tricks, and some funny and entertaining marketing videos. HubSpot embeds these videos in its blog and use them as part of its presence in social media.

In December 2008, HubSpot released a video[4] that went viral. It's a parody on the ineffectiveness of outbound marketing contrasted by the

---

4   Inbound Marketing video: http://www.youtube.com/watch?v=4-IGe5MnBlY

effectiveness of inbound marketing. The video doesn't directly market HubSpot. In fact, it never mentions the HubSpot name. At the end of the video, the closing shot features the phrase *inbound marketing* being typed into a Google search. That's the call to action. As you might guess, HubSpot ranks at the top of results when this phrase is Googled. The HubSpot team did a remarkable job of hyping the video for weeks before its release, building anticipation among its thousands of followers. At the end of the first day of the video release, it ranked number one on YouTube for the single word *marketing*. This video is a good example of viral marketing because it uses humor and creativity. No professional actors were used. It was shot with a standard video camera. It doesn't feature any fancy Hollywood production attributes or special effects, yet it's still very entertaining and effective in conveying its message. HubSpot is quick to point out it had previously created several other videos that did not go viral. This one did. I liked it so much, I wrote a blog post about it titled, "Top Five Reasons the HubSpot Viral Video Rocks!"[5]

Flickr. HubSpotters regularly take pictures at events and post them to their Flickr account as well as their personal Facebook profiles. This is just another way for HubSpot to show its human side and engage with its community. The photos are not all business-related. HubSpot also posts photos of events like the bowling party celebrating HubSpot's second birthday.

Events. HubSpot attends industry events and conferences. It exhibits at some of them, speaks at some of them, and just shows up at others. This allows the company to carry online relationships offline as well as build new relationships, spreading its name around the industry. While events can be expensive, HubSpot thinks the ability to take online relationships into the physical world is worth the added cost. Events are really the only traditional brand-building activity HubSpot uses in its marketing strategy.

---

5   Top Five Reasons the HubSpot Video Rocks! http://www.findandconvert.com/ blog/2008/top-5-reasons-why-the-hubspot-viral-video-rocks/

Interactive Tools. HubSpot has four popular web-based interactive tools that attract links and builds awareness: *Web Site Grader* allows anyone to submit his or her website and receive a free report that grades the Internet marketing effectiveness of the website. To date, more than five hundred thousand websites have been graded. *Twitter Grader* allows anyone to submit his or her Twitter name and get graded on the influence of his or her Twitter account, and more than four hundred thousand Twitter profiles have been graded. Facebook Grader measures the reach and influence of your Facebook profile. *Press Release Grader* automatically analyzes news releases for relevant search engine optimization and Internet marketing factors and provides tips on how to improve them. All of these tools spread virally and also help to attract organic links. For example, Web Site Grader alone has more than forty thousand inbound links.

SEO. Using all of the above plus media relations activities, HubSpot has been able to achieve high search engine rankings for quality keywords relevant to its business. As a result, HubSpot regularly receives leads for its Internet marketing software from its search engine traffic. Over the past twelve months, HubSpot has tripled its SEO traffic from Google.

Sales force. HubSpot has an inside sales team, but unlike other inside sales teams where marketing gives them a list of companies to cold-call, this sales team makes *no* cold-calls. All it does is follow up on the all the leads that result from people downloading content from HubSpot. This has a number of advantages. First, the people the sales reps are calling are a lot more responsive because they have had some experience with HubSpot beforehand through the blog, a webinar, or an interactive tool. Second, it is a lot easier to recruit and hire high-quality sales reps when you can tell them they don't have to make cold-calls and they will be provided with a nearly endless flow of qualified leads.

Results. HubSpot is growing very rapidly. Founded in 2006, it has grown its web traffic to hundreds of thousands of monthly visitors, been featured in top industry blogs like TechCrunch, attracted $17 million in investment monies, generated thousands of leads per month, and has more than one thousand active customers. What is even more remarkable about all this is that, because of the inbound marketing strategy, its cost per lead is below five dollars, where most software companies pay an average of ten to twenty times that amount on a per-lead basis.

The HubSpot case study is exceptional for some other reasons as well. First, it is truly innovative and proactive with its social media marketing strategies. Of course, it is in the Internet marketing business, so we expect it to implement these strategies. But it's testimony to the fact that when a business devotes as much staffing, intellectual capital, and energy to social media marketing as HubSpot does, the results can be truly impressive. I urge you to avoid thinking that HubSpot's success using social media is because it is in the Internet marketing business. It is successful because the company gets it, and it dedicates its entire staff to using social media. Brian Halligan, HubSpot's CEO, has his performance reviewed by the company's investors and it is measured against bottom line metrics, just as any other CEO's would be. Brian's investors are very pleased with the pace of growth enjoyed by HubSpot. But then, who wouldn't be?

Blendtec: Viral Video Fuels Explosive Growth for Utah Blender Manufacturer

I attended the 2008 PubCon[6] Conference in Las Vegas. On day two, the keynote speaker was George Wright, the director of marketing and sales at Blendtec.[7] He told the story of how Blendtec has used viral video marketing to exponentially grow its sales over the previous two years. This is truly a textbook case study on viral marketing using the social web.

Blendtec is a relatively small Utah-based manufacturer of commercial high-performance blending products sold primarily to restaurants. It also has a retail product called the Total Blender, which uses the same technology as its commercial products.

---

6   Pubcon: http://www.pubcon.com
7   Blendtec: http://www.blendtec.com

When George Wright joined the company about three years ago, he quickly figured out the company's marketing challenge. Blendtec had great commercial blender products that extended into the consumer market, but there was no brand recognition for its consumer product. As Wright said during his keynote presentation, "Great products plus a weak brand equals weak sales."

Wright approached his boss, CEO Tom Dickson, and proposed doing a brand-building campaign to create awareness for the Total Blender. Dickson agreed with Wright's recommendation—but there was one catch. Blendtec didn't have a budget for a brand-building campaign. Dickson gave Wright a fifty-dollar budget. Not per month—just fifty dollars. Wright got creative—there really wasn't any other option—and turned lemons into lemonade ... but not in the blender.

Using his small budget, he bought the following: registration rights to the URL www.willitblend.com, a lab coat, and a McDonald's Happy Meal. Right now, you're probably thinking that George Wright had lost his mind. Brilliance can seem that way to the people not experiencing the aha! moment that accompanies it.

One day, inspired by a walk through the warehouse, Wright came upon a winning idea that would eventually solve the branding problem. During his trek, Wright saw a pile of sawdust on the floor and heard the sound of grinding wood. When he looked further into it, he learned the engineers were running two-by-four-foot chunks of wood through the blenders to test the durability of their cutting blades and the motors powering their blenders. That's when the light bulb went on!

He came up with the idea to build a website called WillitBlend.com. The strategy was to provide videos that answer the question, "Will it blend?" On the website, Tom Dickson, without the benefit of a script, answers that question by putting odd objects into the company's consumer product, the Total Blender. He wears a lab coat and sports protective eyewear. He blends a variety of things—golf balls, marbles, and that Happy Meal.

One of the most popular videos shows Dickson blending an iPhone. In this video, the camera zooms in for a slow motion shot that captures the destruction of the iPhone. In a few seconds, it is blended into black dust! Given the popularity of the iPhone, this video has been viewed by millions, and shared globally via the web. The exposure for Blendtec has been nothing short of amazing.

Did this strategy work? You bet!

Here are some of the results:

- The Total Blender retail sales grew 700 percent in two years.

- The videos have more than 5 million views on YouTube and more than 7 million views on its website.

- It has received national media coverage that is equivalent to millions of dollars in advertising.

- The brand strength of the consumer product has increased pull through sales in its commercial products.

- The SEO value from the videos drives a lot more traffic to its website.

Additionally, Blendtec auctioned the blended iPhone on eBay. It sold for about one thousand dollars. Those proceeds were donated to a children's hospital. That's awesome!

I guess Wright has been given a little more budget because the company has produced more than seventy videos for the Willitblend website. Blendtec's viral video strategy is nothing short of brilliant. Wright has this to say about the company's success: "Using viral video, even a small company can have a big presence."

He has set these guidelines for Blendtec's video strategy:

- *It must be entertaining.* Each video must be worth watching and have the potential of being shared with a friend.

- *It must meet the corporate objectives.* Blendtec's objective from day one was to build brand awareness. National media coverage for its viral video strategy has included interviews on CNN,

NBC, CBS, Fox, The Food Network, Discovery Channel, History Channel, and others. All this media attention has helped build brand awareness for Blendtec at a very low budget compared to what it would cost to advertise on these national media outlets.

- *The manufacturer is the sole sponsor.* Blendtec produced all the videos with no third-party endorsements, an approach that fuels its credibility. The fact the videos are not Hollywood quality, yet not low-quality either also adds to the credibility of the video content.

- *It must use real people.* Tom Dickson, Blendtec's CEO, stars in all the videos, wearing his lab coat while explaining what he plans to blend. He is a little cheesy, too, but it works in his favor in a viral video. It's the overall content that makes the video appealing.

- *It must be interactive.* Allow people to add comments to each video, being sure to respond to comments as a way of engaging with people who had enough interest to post comments. Allow the word-of-mouth factor to fuel itself through interactivity with the community. Invite suggestions for future videos from the community.

Wright told the PubCon audience that one of the greatest risks in using social media is the reluctance of companies to try it. He believes that avoiding experimenting with the social web is a greater risk than experimenting with it and failing. Using in-house creativity and a willingness to experiment with the social web, the Willitblend website and YouTube strategy pays great dividends for Blendtec.

Using LinkedIn Groups to Spread the Word at Genoo

Kim Albee is founder and president of Genoo, LLC, an online lead generation tool for B2B marketers. The software as a service (SaaS) launched into public beta in June 2008. The start-up is using social media to help spread the word about its product offering.

Albee hosts a blog site called http://www.salesxmarketing.com, in which she actively posts on lead generation topics. The blog site traffic is growing and starting to produce good brand exposure for Genoo.

Albee's most successful results in social media have come from LinkedIn. In fact, I met her through our interaction on LinkedIn. I submitted a question on LinkedIn to the B2B Online Marketing Group, using the platform's Answers feature. My question was a request for introductions to small businesses using social media marketing successfully that might serve as interesting case studies for this book. Albee responded, and introduced me to her company. What intrigued me was that she is the founder of the B2B Online Marketing Group at LinkedIn. She is also the publisher of the B2B Online Marketing Pros website, http://www. b2bonlinemarketingpros.com. Naturally, Albee is using her company's own toolset for this website. The site aggregates subjects of interest for B2B online marketers and also has relevant links pointing to Genoo, her company. The B2B Online Marketing Group was started in March 2008, and at the time of this writing, has more than seven hundred members. The three online destinations—the blog, the B2B Online Marketing Pros website, and the LinkedIn group—all complement her company's product offering and website.

Let's look more closely at the LinkedIn group. Albee is leveraging the targeted audience on LinkedIn, which comprises primarily business professionals. The group's primary purpose is to provide a community for B2B marketers to receive valuable information by sharing experiences and links to interesting articles and success stories. Since the group is sponsored by Genoo, Albee's company receives exposure from this LinkedIn group.

The LinkedIn group also sends out a monthly newsletter that contains updates to the group's content, as well as new topics from people producing content relevant to B2B online marketing. The monthly emails have a 35 percent open rate and a 20 percent click-through rate, which is pretty darn good.

Genoo has received a few customers from active participation on LinkedIn. Most importantly, it's expanded its network of marketers, producing brand awareness. Albee is building relationships with marketers, which builds trust, credibility, and word-of-mouth advertising for her company. The marketers and bloggers she reaches help to spread the word and participate in conversations about online marketing, all of which has a positive effect on her brand building.

As Albee says, "I believe that social media marketing is a long-tail endeavor. What we're doing is a great example of something that is growing and providing a great venue for B2B online marketers. It's also a great vehicle to get the word out about Genoo, along with other great content, products, and services for B2B online marketers."

Genoo is a young company, so these efforts are a work in progress. I believe that Albee's dedication to using social media content through the LinkedIn group will help her company continue to gain exposure and she will prosper from this strategy.

Residential Real Estate Sales Triple Using Social Media

Chris Griffith understands the meaning of the term *long tail*. Griffith is a residential real estate agent with Keller Williams in Bonita Springs, Florida. She helps sellers and buyers in southwest Florida, focusing on the communities of Bonita Springs, Estero, Naples, and Ft. Myers. Although Florida was one of the hardest-hit states in residential real estate sales during the 2008 economic downturn, Griffith is capturing a healthy share of the available market. This is mostly due to her all-out efforts in using the social web to bring opportunities to her front door. Griffith is truly using every conceivable Internet marketing strategy.

If you do a Google search for one of her favorite long-tail keyword phrases, *Bonita Springs Realtor,* you'll find Griffith in the top five search results. In fact, you'll find her listed twice, once with her website, www.bonitaspringsagent.com, and again with her blog, www.lifeinbonitasprings.com. Way to go!

Even in a weak economy, people looking to buy or sell real estate in her long-tail section of Florida can find Griffith, and they do. Frequently, people find her through the content she provides about Bonita Springs either on her website, on her blog, or even on Flickr. Griffith frequently takes pictures of places of interest in Bonita Springs, including restaurants and golf courses. She uploads her pictures to Flickr, tags them with keywords pertaining to Bonita Springs, and also connects these photos to her blog and website.

Griffith has come to understand a simple concept. Because her marketing strategy is 100 percent web-based (she uses no print ads), all this exposure is free! Griffith also has scoured the Internet and listed herself with any social networks where other Realtors can be found. With a focused eye on her long-tail strategy, she has left no stone unturned on the social web.

The Naples News, a local print publication, has noticed Griffith's prowess for great local content and has provided her with an editorial column: http://www.naplesnews.com/staff/chris-griffith/. There you'll find Griffith's articles on relevant topics including bank financing tips and other tips on buying and selling real estate. Each of her stories offers great advice. Her marketing value from this column is derived through being recognized as a trusted source for the content.

Griffith is also an active Twitter user. She seeks out local people on Twitter and follows them to see what they're talking about. She also searches for people on Twitter based on keywords related to her local real estate interests. She follows relevant Twitter streams such *#NAR2008*. By following this Twitter stream, she learned of a speaking engagement by a well-known social media advocate in real estate. She quickly drove to the event, enjoying both the content and the networking value of the event.

Griffith's long-tail strategy has resulted in her being known as Ms. Bonita Springs. By focusing on providing great content about Bonita Springs, including topics about lifestyle, education, transportation, economy, things to do, et cetera, Griffith has set herself apart from all other Realtors in her locale. She comments that her clients often say, "We knew we had the right agent when we read something of interest on her blog."

Griffith's clients say they feel they already know her when they start to work with her just based on what they learned about her content online.

Griffith says her sales performance in 2008 is three times better than in 2007 despite a weak real estate economy. She claims all of her sales except one came from a referral from one of her web profiles or her online content.

Below is Griffith's auto signature on email. Take note of how she lists *all* of her online content connections. This is such a simple, yet often overlooked, tactic. She doesn't overlook these details. She gets it! Her results prove it.

Chris Griffith, Realtor˚
CRS, GRI, ABR, CNHS, SRES, ePro
Keller Williams Elite Realty
24851 S. Tamiami Trail
Bonita Springs, FL 34134

Specializing in the SW Florida Real Estate Market.
239-273-7430 Direct
239-949-8339 Fax

Websites:
http.//www.LifeInBonitaSprings.com
http://www.BonitaSpringsAgent.com
http://www.EsteroFloridaRealEstate.com
http://www.naplesnews.com/staff/chris-griffith/
Naples Daily News & Bonita Banner Column:
http://LifeInBonitaSprings.WordPress.com—Mobile Blog
http://twitter.com/twitterzilla

BatchBlue: Building Strategic Customer Relationships on the Web

BatchBlue Software is a young start-up company located in the New England area. The three co-founders share a common passion for providing customer relationship management (CRM) software on the web for business professionals looking to achieve work-life balance. From day one, a core value of the company is being extremely customer-focused. Two of the three founders previously worked at Amazon, where they learned the art and science of doing anything to make the customer happy.

At the time of this writing, the company has eight people. The employees work virtually in order to allow themselves the work-life balance they seek, although they have an office where they hold staff meetings. Most of them have young children. Working virtually and being connected through the web allows them the freedom to develop their product, market it, and support it without long commutes and the accompanying stress on family life.

At the heart of BatchBlue Software's product, called BatchBook, is a CRM software product that lives up to the vision of being easy to learn and easy to use. The founders believe that other CRM software products have a steep learning curve that inhibits small business people from getting up and running quickly, which also prevents them from becoming productive or receiving true value from the product. BatchBook delivers on conventional CRM features such as managing contacts and communications but goes beyond conventional contact management by integrating the social aspect of relationships such as tracking communications on Twitter, following contact's latest blog posts and even viewing pictures from photo-sharing sites like Flickr. BatchBook's easy interface allows each user to customize their database in the way that makes the most sense for each business.

BatchBlue Software has been incorporating customer input from day one. The founders started close to home in their closely knit Rhode Island technology community to get feedback and momentum. They launched their alpha version in the spring of 2007. They launched their beta version in September 2007 at the annual Demo event in San Diego, where they were invited to showcase BatchBook. The Demo[8] event is an invitation-only venue for new and emerging technology companies. Participating at Demo was a major milestone for BatchBook in that it allowed the company to make important connections both within the tech industry and with journalists. It also put it on the international radar sooner than would have normally been possible.

They launched the commercial version of BatchBook in February 2008. Their marketing strategy can be summed up as being extremely customer-focused and fully engaged. BatchBlue Software presents itself as people first, and a company second. It has personified the purpose of CRM, which is relationship management. Everything about BatchBlue has a human voice to it, starting with their website and blog and including their company Twitter account, error messaging and monthly newsletters.

Since social media is all about conversations and relationship-building on the web, BatchBlue is naturally leveraging several of the tools and technologies that are built for that. They are passionate about listening to their customers, resulting in new features being added to their product, which have been well received by their customers and community.

Their blog, which is found prominently on their website at http://www.batchblue.com/, is focused on helping their community understand how to get maximum value from the BatchBook product. I really like this example of a product-centric blog because it is a proof statement that a blog can be product-centric without being a shameless promotional vehicle. Just browse the blog and you'll find useful posts about topics such as:

- Managing your contacts and your social network

- Tracking communications and to-dos

- Customizing your data with *super tags*

- Importing contacts and data

---

8   Demo Event: http://www.demo.com/

- Sending email and to-dos to BatchBook

- Sending email newsletters from BatchBook

All blog posts are supplemented with video tutorials or digital photos to help the reader easily understand the tips. Other blog posts include best practices such as how to connect with your customers and how "real world" customers are using their product.

Everyone in this small company contributes to the blog. All comments from the community get a response from the company. The Batch-Book blog is a true testimony to the value of giving your community good content to get the most value from a product. Clearly, the word-of-mouth result from such great content continues to add wind to BatchBlue Software's sails.

It was at SXSW in March 2008 where BatchBook's designer Adam Darowski recommended to Michelle Riggen-Ransom, BatchBlue Software's co-founder and marketing director, that she get on Twitter. Riggen-Ransom initially resisted the idea because for the uninitiated, Twitter can seem unproductive at best and weird at worst. She decided to give it a go but struggled with the decision of whether to have a company Twitter profile or a personal Twitter profile. The BatchBlue team decided on a BatchBlue Twitter persona that is staffed by three people, allowing multiple perspectives. They send links to relevant blog posts. They've experimented with small promotions on Twitter such as, "Take the first ever Twitter usability test in 140 seconds or less."

At one point, BatchBlue was planning to make changes to their home page, so they wanted to get input from their Twitter following. They provided a link to a survey asking about impressions of the home page content. The survey feedback gave the company direction for home page revisions. At the time of this writing, BatchBlue Software has more than 2,000 Twitter followers. The number of followers isn't as important as the potential those followers represent to provide continual updates and links to good content, maintain loyalty, and spread goodwill. The occasional survey feedback potential is pretty cool, too.

Twitter has become BatchBlue Software's number one tool for making connections with influential people. Now, all BatchBlue staffers also have active personal profiles on Twitter. Communications Director Riggen-Ransom likes to tell the story of how marketing guru Guy Kawasaki once asked for volunteers to edit one of his books. This offered her the opportunity to connect with him and gain exposure to him. He subsequently sent her an autographed copy of his new book. The BatchBlue team has been actively connecting with other influential people on the social web. This exposure is invaluable from a business perspective and often hard for a young start-up company to come by.

BatchBlue has also started a weekly discussion on Twitter called SB-Buzz, where small business owners can talk for two hours on issues related to technology, social media and business. This format has been very successful. In three months it has over 3,600 followers, with a rotating mix of participants and guest moderators each week focusing on a select topic.

Riggen-Ransom and her team regularly monitor the quantifiable metrics from the social web but don't use it as the only gauge to measure success. BatchBlue really is focused on building relationships, which in the long run is building its business. Some of the metrics they do track include:

1. Google paid and organic searches (mostly organic)

2. Blog reviews

3. Twitter traffic and relationships started

4. Page views

5. Click-through and bounce rates

Another part of BatchBlue's content marketing strategy is publishing blue papers—a takeoff on white papers. The papers, available on its website, offer tips and advice on topics such as establishing a virtual office, guidelines for small businesses using CRM, and CRM best practices.

BatchBlue Software's social media marketing strategy has no hard-

and-fast rules. BatchBlue experiments with things that are customer-focused and seem interesting, and it notes what works and what doesn't. When something works well, BatchBlue does more of it. For example, it created a glossary of terms and saw people embrace it, so it continued to build it out.

BatchBlue also has a Facebook profile, but it's not as active in that space. It does occasionally post videos and send messages out to its fans on Facebook and has been slowly acquiring new fans using these methods.

One social media space that BatchBlue is actively participating in is Flickr. It often posts photos of staff, corporate events, and employees' family members. It uses its Flickr account in part as a digital scrapbook of the company, which it posts on its website and on the blog. It helps to humanize the company and convey the personality of the people, which is very important to the corporate culture. BatchBlue also has posted design and logo choices and encouraged folks to vote, taking advantage of the participatory nature of the site.

BatchBlue is also starting to experiment with video. It recently shot a video of how real estate agents are using social media and uploaded it to YouTube, where it got picked up in several real estate blogs.

BatchBlue Software recognizes that a person's network is a huge asset, especially in a down economy. If you find yourself out of a job or in a new job, you want to take your network with you. Staying connected to your network is very important because it belongs to you. BatchBlue Software makes it easy to manage as well as transport your network through a simple export/import process.

BatchBlue Software is currently in the process of customizing Batch-Book for some vertical industries. For instance, feedback from the real estate community has been encouraging, as has the continued growth of real estate agents signing up for their online BatchBook software. This led BatchBlue to develop a real estate-specific version of BatchBook, customized with fields that would be of interest to that group.

Other recent BatchBook additions are versions for designers and marketing and PR professionals. The decisions for what versions are created are heavily influenced through the feedback BatchBlue collects from people on Twitter and their blog. They also rely on industry advisory boards that they've put together based on people's interest in being part of the BatchBook development process. The social web is where Batch-Blue Software builds relationships and collects valuable customer input for product direction.

BatchBlue Software will likely continue to roll out niche versions of its software. They will keep building strategic relationships in niche markets by leveraging the people who stay closely knit to them on the web. If BatchBlue Software is in the relationship-building business, then the social web has become the engine that powers their success.

WOMbeat! Word of Mouth for Local Businesses

WOMbeat![9] is a start-up company whose entire business model is based on word of mouth. The company's tag line is, *"Word of Mouth ... Only Better!"* Launched in the summer of 2008, WOMbeat! provides a platform for its user community to share personal opinions in order to find trustworthy recommendations about all sorts of local consumer businesses such as dentists, plumbers, nannies, car mechanics, and restaurants. The service is in beta launch in my local metropolitan area of Tampa Bay. The plan in 2009 is to expand nationwide and beyond, based on community growth and acceptance.

The premise of WOMbeat! is based on the power of word-of-mouth referrals by consumers and the power of the social web. This is a potent combination. How many times have you asked a friend to recommend a local business so you can avoid making a costly mistake? We depend on word-of-mouth referrals to find local service providers such as lawn maintenance companies, carpet cleaners, and pet sitters. We've all had or heard horror stories about selecting a service provider blindly from the Yellow Pages or online equivalent with no personal referral. WOMbeat! allows a local community to recommend and vote on local busi-

---

9   WOMbeat! http://www.wombeat.com

nesses, similar to the way social content sharing sites vote on content with thumbs-up or thumbs-down plus comments.

The service is free to consumers. Local businesses can list on the site for free as well, which allows the user community to share its opinions regarding those businesses in the form of recommendations to other users. Optionally, business owners can choose to pay for premium services that help them grow their businesses by getting them more actively involved and even incentivizing more word-of-mouth referrals. Given the power behind customer referrals, businesses can reap tremendous value with even a free listing. Thus, business owners cannot treat WOMbeat! as just another place to advertise. Its reputation is on the line.

The social aspect of WOMbeat! is prevalent throughout the site. Even though WOMbeat! serves as a directory of local businesses with local recommendations, the idea is to provide consumers with the most credible recommendations from other consumers they actually know and trust. Alternatively, consumers turn to recommendations of friends of friends and so on.

Marc Mandt and Linda Olson are co-founders. Mandt characterizes WOMbeat! as Yellow Pages meets LinkedIn. I like this characterization because the community can truly network with a purpose. For example, if I really like my chiropractor (which I do) I want to tell others about her. I wouldn't think of sending an unsolicited email to my friends recommending my chiropractor. Now, WOMbeat! provides a social website where I can share my support for my chiropractor. Similarly, if I had a bad experience with a local merchant, I can share that, too.

For business owners, WOMbeat! can help turn their happy customers into their online marketing team by both incentivizing more word-of-mouth referrals and making it easy for them to do that. Thus, WOMbeat! gives the consumer a voice and control but also provides a benefit to both the online community and the great businesses that deserve it the most. Once a local business is listed on WOMbeat!, it can also receive reporting on the reviews from consumers, as well as the number of referrals it has received, thus measuring the value of word of mouth

WOMbeat!'s marketing strategy is—you guessed it—entirely word of mouth, but it is not solely relying on traditional word of mouth. WOM-beat! actively participates in a variety of online communities, integrating them with each other and some offline communities to spread the word.

One key element of WOMbeat!'s strategy is its corporate blog for company news and developments. It also maintains complementary blogs aimed at educating small business owners and the local community about WOM and other relevant topics, all with links back to the corporate blog and the company website.

Of course, WOMbeat! has found great success using a variety of so-cial media tools, including Facebook, MySpace, Twitter, LinkedIn, and even YouTube, to stay top of mind with its current fans. It often links fans back to its company website or one of the corporate blogs. It also uses these cost-effective tools to attract new users and build its community by growing its base of friends or fans on each of these sites.

WOMbeat! even uses offline elements in its overall marketing strat-egy. For example, both Olson and Mandt are very active members of a sev-eral local networking organizations and chambers, including WOMMA (Word of Mouth Marketing Association), SWOM (Society for Word of Mouth), and the Tampa Bay Technology Forum (TBTF), where they build valuable relationships that help attract new users and build loyalty for the website. Yet, they pull these offline relationships into their online communities through email marketing campaigns and invitations from one or more of their social media profiles.

WOMbeat! plans to add other social media elements to the mix, in-cluding podcast recordings to help educate the user community or busi-ness owners about WOMbeat!

WOMbeat! is still beta testing its business model in Tampa Bay. Just as brands are determined by consumers, so too will consumers deter-mine if WOMbeat! has a viable business model. One challenge it needs to overcome is the propensity for many small business owners to ignore the social web. Many of them have not yet bought into the power of the social web, displaying an "I don't have time to spend on the web" mentality. Just ask your plumber or mechanic how much time he spends on the web. However, there are many forward-thinking business owners embracing

WOMbeat! as an important tool for collecting candid consumer feedback that they might not otherwise have access to. Additionally, it can be an effective means for tapping into the friends of their best customers to help grow their businesses.

In the long run, WOMbeat!'s success will be determined by the acceptance of the consumer. If you and I turn to WOMbeat! to find our next refrigerator repairperson, the local merchants will eventually wake up and understand the importance of word of mouth on the web. Perhaps when they reach that point, they'll take a few minutes to list their business on WOMbeat! and find ways to get their customers to recommend them on the site. Or maybe they'll ask their teenage kids to list their business on WOMbeat! That would be a start.

WOMbeat! is yet another example of how the power has shifted to the consumer. With a minimal monetary investment, WOMbeat! has enjoyed fantastic user and fan base growth due to its integrated viral marketing strategies, consistently doubling in size about every two months. I'm hopeful that WOMbeat! will someday make its brand known as the online destination to find local businesses.

Camino Argentinean Steakhouse: Sizzling on the Web

Camino Argentinean Steakhouse is a small traditional steakhouse restaurant—with Argentinean influence—in Northampton, Massachusetts. Its size and a weak economy don't allow for much expenditure on traditional print advertising. Considering that people have cut back on eating out anyway, partners Joseph Gionfriddo and Justin Levy don't even see much logic in casting a wide net in hopes of catching the few who are eating out. Gionfriddo is the head chef and concentrates on giving patrons an amazing meal. Levy applies his marketing and business development talents to the restaurant, focusing his marketing energy on Internet-based advertising and social media. His efforts create awareness and buzz about the restaurant. He'd rather let those who are eating out in the Northampton area find his restaurant.

The restaurant has two websites. The main restaurant website is www.

caminitosteakhouse.com, and they also run a blog at http://primecutsblog.com.

The blog is a prime cuts blog, functioning as a source on cooking, grilling, cooking techniques, and product reviews for prime cut lovers. They don't treat it as a company blog, instead applying their expertise in the restaurant industry to fuel the conversation and build authority. They also created *Prime Cuts TV* on YouTube, Viddler, Vimeo, Blip.tv, and Seesmic, where they post weekly videos describing some of the techniques and how-to's of cooking. They use Tubemogul to distribute these videos to all of the major video players. They also created a customized Viddler player where they also publish their episodes. Visit either the restaurant's website or the blog, and you'll see Gionfriddo talking about what makes his restaurant so special, or demonstrating how to pan sear a salmon or steak. Before you ever eat at Camino Argentinean Steakhouse, you'll get to know him from his videos on the website.

For all restaurant-related news such as the new wine and beer menu, wine dinners, and partnerships, Levy sends an Internet-based news release and also posts it on the website, enhancing the restaurant's SEO benefits. He also sends all of these news releases to local organizations and chambers to be posted on their websites.

Levy maintains ten Google Alerts to help him monitor what people are saying about the restaurant, as well as what is being said about other Argentinean steakhouses in the area and across the country. These help him stay up to date on any changes to menus, new ideas to consider, good or bad reviews about the restaurant, or news on similar restaurants located locally and nationwide. These also help him to find new sites to sign up for, to list the restaurant on, or to network on with the restaurant community. Levy also uses RSS feeds to find news on the restaurant industry through Google Blog Search.

The restaurant sends a monthly opt-in digital newsletter to announce special events, special menus, and more. Levy has signed up for all restaurant service industry websites, and he either claims his restaurant listing or creates a new one.

He is also active on Yelp!, where he provides a link to his website to encourage users to leave reviews. He analyzes Google Analytics reports on a weekly basis (and sometimes daily) to keep tabs on where the website traffic is coming from, judge ROI on certain campaigns, and make decisions about what sections of the website to enhance or update.

Levy maintains a MySpace page as a way of reaching college-age residents; there are several colleges in the area, including Smith, Mount Holyoke, and UMass-Amherst. Levy also uses MySpace to post bulletins, blog posts, and other events to attract the college crowd. He has an Upcoming page where he posts new events.

Both Levy and Gionfriddo are on Facebook, and they have listed the restaurant, as well as the website and blog site. All new posts feed into both MySpace and Facebook accounts. They recently created a Camino page on Facebook where Levy is uploading all videos, photos, and events.

Levy is active on Twitter, Facebook, and FriendFeed, as well as commenting on other blogs. Whenever there is a new blog post, it is sent to all Twitter and Facebook followers, which then posts it to FriendFeed.

He also uses LinkedIn and has the restaurant listed there. He plans to explore ways to use LinkedIn Answers as another way to network. He has a Flickr account and has posted pictures of the restaurant and plans to upload a lot more.

Camino Argentinean Steakhouse is a local business. I asked Levy how he measures results of his efforts when the reach of the social web is far beyond the local community. He closely monitors SEO results in Google for several desirable keywords. The website has attracted more than five thousand links. Restaurant sales are growing about 20 percent month over month, and it is up 25 percent year-to-date. And this is in the face of a weak economy in which some restaurants around the steakhouse are in decline; others have even closed shop.

The most difficult part of writing this story is that when I watch the videos on the restaurant website and blog, I know this is a restaurant I would thoroughly enjoy. But since I live in Florida, I can't enjoy it. That's a bummer. But the next time someone tells me he or she is traveling to the New England area, I will tell them about a restaurant they must visit.

I will also email them links to the restaurant website, the blog, and the Facebook page.

These partners know where their customers are on the web. They go meet them there and attract them to their restaurant.

Cause Marketing: Raising $10,000 in 48 Hours on Twitter

In 2007, Stacey Monk traveled through Africa with her friend, Sanjay Patel. During this trip, she met an extraordinary person who changed her life. Mama Lucy, as she is known, sold chickens to raise money to start a primary school in Tanzania, believing that education was the key to transforming a country gripped by poverty. Now, hundreds of children from local villages attend her school. Her school charges a small tuition to provide a good education as well as to subsidize attendance by orphans and the poorest children in the area. Monk was so moved by Mama Lucy's dedication that she and Patel founded a 501(c)(3) nonprofit in 2007 called Epic Change[10] to ensure Mama Lucy and changemakers like her across the globe could get access to capital in order to grow and expand their successful community improvement efforts.

A former management consultant, Monk has worked with Deloitte Consulting, Genentech, and Santa Clara County. Her experience helping others create and lead organizational change was ready to be applied to a new cause that is transforming lives.

Epic Change uses a unique funding model. Donations are raised from private donors, primarily using social media. Funds are provided to a particular cause as an interest-free loan. Then, Epic Change collaborates with partners and the cause leaders to arrange income-producing projects that will facilitate loan repayment. Examples of such projects include children's performances and making candles, stationery, and greeting cards. When the loan is repaid, funds are recycled to provide loans to other causes. What an awesome model!

Cause marketing is nothing new. But Epic Change's cause market-

---

10   Epic Change: http://www.epicchange.org/

ing strategy is different. It's a zero-dollar marketing strategy. Imagine a marketing plan with no budget! Epic Change does it entirely through relationships built on the web.

Epic Change is using most of the popular social web tools and technologies discussed in this book to build awareness and relationships. Here's the list: LinkedIn, Facebook, Flickr, YouTube, MySpace, Twitter, and blogging. Monk maintains an active profile in each of these social web platforms and blogs frequently about cause-related activities. In Facebook, she has a personal profile, a cause page, and a fan page. In YouTube, she tells the Epic Change story through video. In Flickr, she posts photos of the kids whose lives are transformed through education. She also maintains a personal Twitter profile (*@staceymonk*) and a Twitter profile for Epic Change (*@epicchange*).

I learned of Epic Change through Twitter during the Thanksgiving holiday 2008. I was most impressed with its Twitter fund-raising effort, which was branded Tweetsgiving. A Tweetsgiving website[11] was set up to track the fund-raising. Tweetsgiving set out to raise ten thousand dollars during the forty-eight hours preceding Thanksgiving. The results: Epic Change exceeded the goal! Here's how it happened.

Earlier in 2008, Monk was following Sam Lawrence, CMO of Jive Software, on Twitter. So she knew about him and his blog, www.Gobigalways.com. One day, Lawrence tweeted that he didn't feel like blogging that day so Monk offered (through Twitter) to blog for him, knowing that he has a big audience. He accepted her offer. So she wrote a blog post about "going big," which gave her a lot of exposure, created many new Twitter followers, and drove more traffic to the Epic Change blog. This is her inspiring and watershed blog post: http://gobigalways.com/guest-post-stacey-monk-goes-big/.

Previous to writing this blog post, Monk was fairly new to Twitter. Like most Twitter newbies, the light bulb didn't go on until her following grew, and she experienced the power of reach and community. Monk got hooked on Twitter, and many doors opened from her new social con-

---

11 Tweetsgiving: http://tweetsgiving.org

nections as her Twitter following more than doubled soon after this blog post.

One of her new social connections, a volunteer named Avi Kaplan, wrote a blog post titled, "Thank You Stacey Monk of Epic Change," recognizing Monk's giving heart and influence on him. She was very moved and inspired by the blog post. She wondered if people on Twitter could get inspired to donate to her cause. She came up with the idea of Tweetsgiving. Just six days before Thanksgiving, she approached a designer to design the logo and assembled a team to develop the website. In total, seven people contributed several components of Tweetsgiving. She launched the campaign on Twitter on the Tuesday before Thanksgiving for forty-eight hours to raise ten thousand dollars to build a classroom in Tanzania. From the beginning of the event, the buzz started to grow. Several influential social media people tweeted about it, including the King of Twitter, Chris Brogan.[12] The exposure Brogan gave Tweetsgiving really helped to grow the buzz, and the donations started coming in. It became like a telethon—rather, a tweetathon—with regular updates throughout the entire forty-eight hours. It was one of the top 10 Twitter topics during this time period. It's worth noting that every part of this event was organic. Remember, this was zero-dollar marketing.

This social media campaign was successful for the reasons given in this blog post: http://epicchange.org/blog/2008/12/05/why-tweetsgiving-worked-imho/.

The monetary goal was clearly stated and attainable. But it wasn't just a monetary goal. The objective was to build a classroom for children in Tanzania. These tangible and specific goals help to make the cause very understandable and credible. A donation of ten dollars would purchase one of a thousand bricks necessary to build a new classroom. This is a low threshold amount. The average donation was $30.92.

The campaign was successful for these reasons:

---

12   Chris Brogan: http://www.chrisbrogan.com

Ease of online donations. There was an element of fun. Visiting the Tweet-sgiving website gave a sense of this being a vibrant, fun event. One con-tributor tweeted during the campaign, "I'm thankful that I can make a difference at the click of a button."

The cause was easy to embrace. Stories and pictures of Mama Lucy and the children who attended the school humanized the cause and tugged at the heartstrings.

Multiple sources of donations. While most donations came from Twitter followers, the tweets caused bloggers to write about Tweetsgiving, which broadened the reach on the web.

Expansion of Monk's network. Ninety-eight percent of the donors were first-time donors to Epic Change.

Flattery. Those who donated one hundred dollars or more were placed on a "Top Turkey" list. Those who wanted to see their name on a list were motivated to donate the minimum of a C-note.

Willingness to innovate and take some risk. This type of campaign had not been done previously. Monk and her friends were blazing a new trail, go-ing big.

It was Thanksgiving, and people were in the mood to give. A graphi-cal widget was designed that allowed website visitors to check the status of the donations throughout the forty-eight hours.

The Tweetsgiving campaign was a huge success for Epic Change. It exceeded its monetary goal required to build a classroom in Tanzania. Monk's social media strategy to promote her cause marketing with zero dollars is very impressive and it works. Mostly, what's impressive is her willingness to reach new heights using the social web to have a positive affect on the world. She is also quick to acknowledge the hard work and passion of her loyal volunteers (Avi Kaplan, Matt Blasi, Vincent Hunt, Sarah Evans, and Carrie and Dave Kerpen).

At the time of this writing, more than seventy thousand dollars have been raised, four classrooms have been built, more than three hundred children are in Mama Lucy's school, and there are more than two hundred bloggers who have blogged about Epic Change. These bloggers, along with the connections Monk has made through LinkedIn, Facebook, YouTube, and Flickr, create traffic to their website, which fuels growth in awareness and donations.

It's safe to say that marketing on the social web is not just very possible, but it can also make a difference in lives around the world.

To connect with Monk, find her on LinkedIn at http://www.linkedin.com/in/staceymonk or Twitter at *@staceymonk*.

Even Bankers Hang Out on the Social Web: De Novo Strategy

De Novo Strategy is a consultancy firm in a niche industry. It helps banks get started, acquire other banks, or implement growth strategies. Wendell Brock, founder and CEO, was invited by his good friend Andrew Anson to attend a webinar sponsored by HubSpot about social media marketing in business. Before attending this webinar, Brock's impression of social media was that it mostly pertained to Internet dating or kids talking about their favorite music artist online. He truly had no idea of the opportunity to help grow his business. As he says, "Wow, were my eyes ever opened from this webinar!" In 2008, he learned new ways to develop his business and engage his target audience on the Internet through social media.

Shortly after his introduction to social media marketing ideas, Brock revamped his website to include social media elements. The most significant addition to his website was a blog appropriately named BankNotes.[13] Brock is quick to point out that he is not a marketer. His background is in financial services. As an entrepreneur, he understands the importance of marketing, but it's not his forte. His new blog has helped alleviate some of

---

13 De Novo Strategy: BankNotes blog: http://www.denovostrategy.com/ BankNotesBlog/

his marketing concerns. Anson helped him to understand the power of social media marketing in relation to his business.

Previous to implementing the blog on its website, De Novo Strategy had very few site visitors. In fact, Brock didn't even track his website traffic. As he says, "I think my traffic count was somewhere just above zero, limited to the people I invited to the website." He decided to implement some of the ideas he learned from the HubSpot webinar, trusted advice he received from Anson and launched his new website in mid 2008. Brock started to write a blog post about once or twice a week. His posts are about industry issues and events of interest to banking professionals, such as bank acquisitions.

He didn't see an immediate increase in website traffic. However, after just a few months, his traffic went from zero (other than friends and clients) to about a hundred visits, then three hundred, eventually reaching a thousand new visitors per month. He is now tracking his website traffic and observes that about 10 percent are repeat visitors and 2.5 percent are turning into new sales leads.

In addition to the leads De Novo Strategy gets from its website, the blog has had another positive effect on Brock's strategy. He says, "The blog has caused me to implement a new discipline to my marketing strategy by committing to writing a blog article at least once per week. This keeps me engaged in my website and inspires me to continuously strive to make it better." He admits it is sometimes difficult when his workload gets heavy and there are many demands on his time. But he has seen the results from his blog strategy, which is all the motivation he needs to make his blog writing a priority. And since he is by his own admission not a marketing genius, he gets to apply his banking industry expertise to his blog and reap a marketing benefit. So this is not a painful action item.

Brock has also learned the importance of engaging in other social media sites. He seeks out other relevant blogs where he can post comments and get feedback on various business ideas. He appreciates the ability to engage with people on the social web on relevant topics and draw them into conversations. He is convinced these conversations are very valuable to his business.

Wendell Brock is bridging the gap between him (the seller) and his buyers on the social web in ways he never anticipated.

Internal Social Networks Prove Productive at NASA

NASA embarked on an experiment to use social networks internally for collaboration and improved communication. Inspired by a presentation given by Tim Young, CEO of Socialcast[14] at the KM World conference in 2007, a pilot was established called NASAsphere.[15] Tim's presentation spoke of internal productivity gains available through his software as a service (SaaS) application which allows employees to post status messages, ask and answer questions, share documents and generally collaborate across disparate locations.

NASAsphere is an online social network that enables employees to move across physical boundaries established by disparate locations of centers, to move across traditional communication boundaries established by organizations, and to move outside personal networks, in order to share and foster collective intelligence for the betterment of conducting NASA business. Eighty- seven people responded to an inquiry to join the pilot.

The social network was used by NASA employees in these general ways:[16]

- Sharing a day in the life of a NASA scientist.

- Asking where to find critical information and data to support NASA tasks.

- Presenting and vetting ideas to NASA's collective intelligence.

---

14   Socialcast: http://www.socialcast.com/

15   NASAsphere published results: http://www.reuters.com/article/pressRelease/idUS177105+25-Feb-2009+BW20090225

16   http://www.slideshare.net/cmerryman/piloting-social-networking-insidenasa-presentation

- Enhancing the employee directory with interests, expertise and contact information.

By the end of the pilot, at least person from every NASA center participated. The results of the pilot are compelling:

- NASAsphere participants invited 398 of their colleagues from around NASA, with 55% acceptance rate.

- Within the 60-day span of the pilot, the NASAsphere community grew from 78 activated accounts to 295.

- Communications truly crossed geographic centers. When employees posed questions, 93% of the answers came from users at remote locations. By the end of the pilot, at least one person from every NASA center had participated in the NASAsphere community.

- A survey of NASAsphere users found that 52% recommended the platform be implemented for contractors and civilians, in addition to employees.

- In the same survey, 45% of users said they expected they would contribute to the NASAsphere platform weekly.

- Not surprisingly, the report recommends a broader implementation of the Socialcast solution.

The general take-away from this case study example is that the social networking tools at our disposal offer powerful communication and collaboration potential. Relationship building among internal staffers as demonstrated in NASAsphere is not just possible, but very productive. These principles transcend from external marketing to internal application of social media.

It's All About Content and Relationships

Marketing 2.0 is as much a mind-set as anything else. While this book discusses the use of social media technologies in development of a marketing strategy, I am well aware that each business is unique. There are industry drivers that affect your strategy decisions. Many industries require a sales force calling on companies Monday through Friday, setting appointments, making presentations, delivering proposals, and following up in an attempt to close deals. The Marketing 2.0 mind-set in industries that employ a sales force may use some traditional marketing tactics effectively. In some industries, the target market is very defined. It's black and white. You may have a list of the entire universe of companies qualified to buy your product or service.

You can still employ a Marketing 2.0 mind-set when you know exactly whom you are selling to through a sales force. I hope this book has inspired you to think like a publisher and engage your target buyer in conversations. Feed them great content. Differentiate your company from your competitors through creative use of today's and tomorrow's tools and technologies that facilitate content marketing and relationship-building. Great relationships can start online long before contact with your business is established. Great relationships lead to sales (or your company's equivalent).

If you take nothing else away from this book, know that your buyers want to be engaged differently than they have been in the past. Shouting at your buyers just doesn't work anymore. Buyers can filter out your shouting. You can reach them through your content and through social connections. You should strive to be a trusted source to your buyers.

The technology enablers are just that—enablers. Marketing 2.0 requires that you build or aggregate good content and demonstrate interest in engaging your buyers in authentic conversation. Doing so will open doors for sales activities that deliver financial returns. Not doing so will close the doors to sales activities, or at least make it so cost-prohibitive that your sales results will suffer. If you're getting away with a shouting marketing strategy, just wait and see. It won't last long.

This book was never meant to discuss technology. My hope is you've been inspired to go where your customers are on the web and hang out with them, friend them, follow them, invite them to friend and follow you, and build new and stronger relationships. By now, if all this social media stuff is still weird to you, consider how social media abstinence may put you at risk of losing market share, your job, or both.

What if your customers don't spend time on the web? There are industries where the target audience is not very web-savvy. If your business markets to a demographic that is proven not to spend time on the web, you are in the minority. That said, you can still employ a Marketing 2.0 mind-set by offering them great content in a media format they will accept. Just don't shout at them. Use the principles we've discussed here: inform, educate, entertain, enlighten, be a trusted source. Whether or not you reach your target customers on the web, the Marketing 2.0 principles apply across all contemporary marketing practices.

RESOURCES

This section offers several resources to help you learn more about social media strategies from a growing list of experts. This list is not exhaustive, but I'm confident you'll find great insights and information. I offer a comment on the books I've read. If there is no comment, I didn't read it, but the reputation of the book and authors(s) qualifies it for the list. You should research any of these resources to make your own decision before you buy or consume their content. The online resources provided are constantly evolving. The following resources are broken into three categories: books, blogs, and lists. I list them in the order of influence they have had on me.

Books

Title: Get Content. Get Customers: How to Use Content Marketing to Deliver Relevant, Valuable and Compelling Information that Turns Prospects into Buyers
Authors: Joe Pulizzi and Newt Barrett
Foreword: Paul Gillin, author of *The New Influencers: A Marketer's Guide to the New Social Media*
Publisher: Voyager Media, Inc.

Comment: This book was very influential in my inspiration to write my book. Pulizzi and Barrett explain in clear terms the importance of marketing through good content.

Title: *The New Rules of Marketing and PR: How to Use News Releases, Blogs Podcasting, Viral Marketing & Online Media to Reach Buyers Directly*
Author: David Meerman Scott
Foreword: Robert Scoble, co-author of *Naked Conversations*
Publisher: John Wiley & Sons, Inc.
Comment: Scott does a great job of explaining the changing paradigm of marketing and how to use contemporary platforms to market and conduct public relations strategies with good examples of large and small companies as well as nonprofits using them effectively. It's an easy and credible read.

Title: *World Wide Rave: Creating Triggers that Get Millions of People to Spread Your Ideas and Share Your Stories*
Author: David Meerman Scott
Publisher: John Wiley & Sons, Inc.
Comment: Scott follows his best-selling *New Rules of Marketing and PR* book with another one chock-full of real stories from real people around the world using Marketing 2.0 principles to get others raving about their content. This book is a must-read!

Title: *Groundswell: Winning in a World Transformed by Social Technologies*
Authors: Charlene Li and Josh Bernoff of Forrester Research
Publisher: Harvard Business Press
Comment: Groundswell is a national best seller and considered by many a must-read on the subject of social media. Li and Bernoff interviewed many large brands to offer credible insights and metrics. Most stories are about large companies. Smaller companies may ask, "Can I do this?"

Title: *Secrets of Social Media Marketing: How to Use Online Conversations and Customer Communities to Turbo-Charge Your Business!*
Author: Paul Gillin
Foreword: Larry Weber, founder of The Weber Group and W2Group
Publisher: Quill Driver Books
Comment: Gillin offers marketers hands-on tips that educate them on how to extend their brands, generate leads, and engage customer communities using an array of online tools.

Title: *The Long Tail: Why the Future of Business is Selling Less of More*
Author: Chris Anderson
Publisher: Hyperion
Comment: *The Long Tail* is must-read book for all business executives. It is not about social media. It is about a paradigm shift known as the "economics of abundance." The Internet has changed the way businesses target and reach customers. This book can change the way a business thinks, possibly reinventing itself to compete in new ways not previously understood. To say *The Long Tail* is thought-provoking is a gross understatement.

Title: *Blog Marketing: The Revolutionary New Way to Increase Sales, Build Your Brand and Get Exceptional Results*
Author: Jeremy Wright
Foreword: Dave Taylor, Publisher, *The Intuitive Life Business Blog*
Publisher: McGraw-Hill
Comment: If corporate blogging is of interest to you, Wright's book is a deep dive into the topic. The emphasis is on how large brands such as Sun Microsystems and Disney have used blogging productively. The best practices and examples provided can be applied to any corporate blogger, no matter its size.

Title: *Meatball Sundae: Is Your Marketing out of Sync?*
Author: Seth Godin
Publisher: Portfolio

Comment: Seth Godin is a prolific best-selling author on marketing. *Meatball Sundae* takes a somewhat humorous view of marketing, offering fourteen trends in marketing you can't ignore. The title of his book suggests that if your marketing message is a meatball and you dive into the new tools on the Internet (add ice cream and whipped cream), your sundae will taste terrible. Godin points out that the answer is not in the tools. Your meatballs must become ice cream.

Title: *The 4 Hour Workweek: Escape the 9–5, Live Anywhere, and Join the New Rich*
Author: Timothy Ferriss
Publisher: Crown Publishers
Comment: This book is not about marketing or social media. I offer this to supplement all the social media marketing books and blogs you read. This book has changed the way I think in business. I haven't cut my hours, but I have applied principles from this book to help me manage better and enjoy life more. It's thought provoking, entertaining, and downright life-changing. I now ignore many problems, and they get fixed without my involvement or the related stress.

Title: *Naked Conversations: How Blogs are Changing the Way Businesses Talk with Customers*
Authors: Robert Scoble and Shel Israel
Foreword: Tom Peters, best-selling author on management and sought-after speaker.
Publisher: Wiley

Title: *Radically Transparent: Monitoring and Managing Reputations Online*
Authors: Andy Beal and Dr. Judy Strauss
Foreword: Robert Scoble, co-author, *Naked Conversations*
Publisher: Sybex/Wiley

Forthcoming books: The following books were not yet published at the print time of this book. The credibility of the authors and the topics of these books warrant my recommendation. I plan to read each of them.

Title: *Trust Agents*
Authors: Chris Brogan and Julien Smith
Publisher: Wiley (August publication date)
Description: "If You Build It, They Won't Come. What happened to the early days? You built a baseball stadium, a store, a web app, and people flocked to it ... now what? We are suspicious of marketing. We don't trust strangers as willingly. Buzz is suspect. It can be bought. Instead, consumers and business people alike are looking towards trust. We want our friends to tell us it's good. We want someone we know to say we should look into it. Marketing spend might start at awareness, but in the Trust Economy, communities are king, and ROI stands for Return on Influence."

Title: *Twitterville*
Author: Shel Israel
Publisher: Portfolio (September publication date)
Comment: Shel Isreal's work on *Twitterville* is well-known to the thousands who follow him on Twitter. His book is sure to provide valuable insights into businesses using Twitter in their social media strategy.

Title: Inbound Marketing
Author: Brian Halligan & Dharmesh Shah
Publisher: Wiley (October publication date)
Comment: Halligan and Shah are the co-founders of HubSpot. It's only fitting they have written a book on Inbound marketing. The subtitle is "Get Found Using Google, Social Media and Blogs." I expect this book to be in total alignment with everything in Marketing 2.0.

Blogs

Title: Community and Social Media
Web address: http://www.chrisbrogan.com/
Blogger name: Chris Brogan
Comment: Brogan is the top dog in social media evangelism. If you only
 want to follow one person in social media, it has to be Chris Bro-
 gan.

Title: HubSpot's Inbound Marketing Blog
Web address: http://blog.hubspot.com/
Blogger name: Various HubSpot employees
Comment: The HubSpot blog is an excellent compilation of many tal-
 ented marketing minds that offer trends and measurable tips for
 marketers to drive inbound marketing results.

Title: Online Marketing Blog
Web address: http://www.toprankblog.com/
Blogger name: Lee Odden

Title: WEBINKNOW: Online Thought Leadership & Viral Marketing
 Strategies
Web address: http://www.webinknow.com/
Blogger name: David Meerman Scott, author of *The New Rules of Market-
 ing and PR*

Title: Join the Content Marketing Revolution
Web address: http://blog.junta42.com/content_marketing_blog/
Blogger name: Joe Pulizzi, co-author of *Get Content. Get Marketing.*

Title: Marketing Pilgrim
Web address: http://www.marketingpilgrim.com/
Blogger name: Andy Beal

Title: Newspaper Death Watch
Web address: http://www.newspaperdeathwatch.com/
Blogger name: Paul Gillin

Title: Conversational Media Marketing
Web address: http://www.conversationalmediamarketing.com/
Blogger name: Paul Chaney

Title: Global Neighborhoods: Following Social Media Wherever It Leads
Web address: http://redcouch.typepad.com/weblog/
Blogger name: Shel Isreal

Title: Web Strategy by Jeremiah
Web address: http://www.web-strategist.com/blog/
Blogger name: Jeremiah Owyang

Title: Inbound Marketing Strategies, SEO, Social Media Marketing, Pod-
    casting
Web address: http://www.findandconvert.com/blog/
Blogger name: Bernie Borges
Comment: This is my blog. I blog about marketing trends and best prac-
    tices on the Web for SMB marketers.

Lists

Several social media consultants have compiled lists that make research easier and faster. Note: the Web addresses listed below may someday change by the author of the list.

Title: Social Brand Index for Twitter
Web address: http://www.socialbrandindex.com/twitter
Source: Unknown

Comment: If you want to find out if a business is on Twitter, go here. If
  you want to add your business to this list, submit it here.

Title: 20 Free ebooks on Social Media
Source: Chris Brogan
Web address: http://www.chrisbrogan.com/20-free-ebooks-about-social-
  media/

Title: Junta42 Top Blogs
Source: Junta42
Web   address: http://www.junta42.com/top_42_content_marketing_
  blogs/

Title: Social Media Monitoring Tools
Source: Nathan Gilliat, Principal, Social Target, LLC
Web   address: http://net-savvy.com/executive/tools/monitoring-social-
  media-before-you-have-a-bud.html

Title: Best Books on Social Media
Source: Lee Odden
Web   address: http://www.toprankblog.com/2008/11/best-books-on-so-
  cial-media/

Title: Best Podcasts on Social Media
Source: Lee Odden
Web   address: http://www.toprankblog.com/2008/12/best-social-media-
  podcasts/
Comment: A list of the top podcasts on social media in 2008. Sixteen
  podcasts were identified and voted on by social media communities. My podcast finished in third place.

Podcasts:

Podcaster: Susan Bratton
Web address: http://personallifemedia.com/podcasts/232-dishymix
Comment: Susan Bratton interviews accomplished business leaders in the field of digital media, advertising, and social media.

Title: Buzz Marketing for Technology
Podcaster: Paul Dunay
Web address: http://buzzmarketingfortech.blogspot.com/
Comment: Paul Dunay interviews innovators in social media with a focus on business-to-business marketing.

Title: Marketing Voices: Weekly Perspectives on Social Media Marketing
Podcaster: Jennifer Jones
Web address: http://www.podtech.net/home/category/marketing-voices
Comment: Jennifer Jones interviews innovators in social media.

Title: HubSpotTV
Podcasters: Karen Rubin and Mike Volpe
Web address: http://www.hubspot.tv/
Comment: HubSpotTV is a live video stream that airs every Friday at 4 PM U.S. EASTERN. Anyone can subscribe through iTunes and watch or listen at his or her leisure.

Title: Marketing Over Coffee
Podcasters: John Wall and Christopher Penn
Web address: http://www.marketingovercoffee.com/

Title: Six Pixels of Separation
Podcaster: Mitch Joel
Web address: http://www.twistimage.com/blog/podcast/

Title: Duct Tape Marketing
Podcaster: John Jantsch
Web address: http://www.ducttapemarketing.com/podcast.php

Title: Inbound Marketing Strategies
Podcaster: Bernie Borges
Web address: http://www.findandconvert.com/blog/podcasts/
Comment: This is my podcast. I podcast about marketing trends and best
practices on the web for SMB marketers.

BERNIE BORGES LIVE AT YOUR EVENT

ernie Borges got his initial inspiration for *Marketing 2.0* from his
speaking engagements and interaction with clients through his Internet marketing agency, Find and Convert. Borges
is available for keynote presentations and
full-day seminars. He is a frequent speaker
at trade shows, conferences, and company
events.

Borges's speaking style is high energy,
engaging, and entertaining. He doesn't use
a typical PowerPoint style presentation to get his message across. His
highly interactive, thought-provoking, and engaging presentations leave
audiences inspired. Borges will challenge you while motivating you to
reach new levels of performance with Marketing 2.0 strategies that are
actionable.

Visit   http://www.findandconvert.com/social-media-speaking-en-
gagements.html/ for more information or call 1-888-660-1981.

LaVergne, TN USA
29 October 2009
162297LV00003B/67/P